Clear - People
white

WHAT COUNTRY HAVE I?

Herbert J. Storing EDITOR

WHAT COUNTRY HAVE I?

ST. MARTIN'S PRESS   NEW YORK

Political Writings by Black Americans

AFFILIATED PUBLISHERS: Macmillan & Company, Limited, London—also at Bombay,
Calcutta, Madras and Melbourne; The Macmillan Company of Canada, Limited, Toronto.

Preface

This book contains a selection of the best political writings of black Americans. The aim has been to select those writings that explore most deeply and widely, and in fairly brief compass, the American polity and the blacks' place in it—or out of it. A wide range of opinions and many well-known men are represented here, but the emphasis is on quality, not quantity. Writings were chosen for their fundamental interest as serious political thought, a rigorous standard which, with only one or two exceptions, has been strictly applied. This book differs in that respect from most collections of black writings, which are appearing in growing number. Of course a large body of substantial political writing by black Americans had to be omitted for reasons of space, and several books could be made from it. What is presented here, however, can fairly be described as the core of black American political thought.

The writers in this book often disagree with one another, sometimes vehemently and profoundly; and in that disagreement can be the beginning of understanding. For these men are distinguished by their capacity to give coherent, deep-rooted, well thought-out *reasons* for their positions. They invite the reader to join them in arguing, thinking, reasoning about some of the most important questions that men face—questions of justice, of rule, of morality. Disagreement and controversy are of course disturbing, and many people respond by merely reiterating their prejudices. Such people will not be touched by a book like this; their fears are too great and their crusts too thick. But to one who can open himself to new (and old) ideas, who can entertain strange suggestions, who can follow a line of reasoning, the black writers in this book provide a challenge and an opportunity.

Each selection stands alone and states with reasonable completeness the writer's views. In order to reduce the scope for editorial partiality and to allow each writer to give his full argument, the pieces are, wherever feasible, printed in full; and the few abridgments are clearly indicated. It should be emphasized that the aim is to direct attention to the thought, the teaching of these men, not to the historical circumstances within which they wrote. Many of them wrote years ago, but they all speak *today.* They are treated as serious political thinkers and not as "representative" blacks or as interesting objects of sociological or historical analysis. Thus the general introduction and the brief introductions to each section direct attention to the arguments, and the suggested additional readings are not secondary sources but other works of black political thought. Generally speaking, more is to be gained by reading the best black political thinkers themselves than by reading about them.

The need for black Americans to recover and study their history and traditions is today a commonplace. This book is intended, among other things, to facilitate that recovery through the exploration of black political writing. But that writing is not the exclusive possession or concern of blacks, and it would be less significant, for blacks and for whites, if it were. These writers ascend through distinctively black problems and aspirations to a level of universal human concern. They stand out in the black tradition precisely because, remaining black, they speak, in ways that count, to men.

W. E. B. Du Bois, in a well-known passage, described the Negro as "a sort of seventh son, born with a veil, and gifted with second-sight in this American world. . . ." "One ever feels his two-ness,—an American, a Negro; two souls, two thoughts, two unreconciled strivings; two warring ideals in one dark body, whose dogged strength alone keeps it from being torn asunder."[1] No one perhaps has surpassed Du Bois's sensitive portrait of life within the Veil, and no one has been more concerned with the integrity and dignity of black identity, tradition, and principles. But Du Bois knew that all men live within their veils of prejudice, convention, and particularity, just as, at the same time, all thoughtful men reach out for the world beyond.

I sit with Shakespeare and he winces not. Across the color line I move arm in arm with Balzac and Dumas, where smiling men and welcoming women glide in gilded halls. From out the caves of evening that swing between the strong-limbed earth and the tracery of the stars, I summon Aristotle and Aurelius and what soul I will, and they come all graciously with no scorn nor condescension. So, wed with Truth, I dwell above the Veil.[2]

The black political thinkers represented in this book belong, first, to black Americans who will cherish them as fathers, brothers, friends, and leaders. They belong, next, to all Americans, for they stand among the noteworthy makers and critics of the American regime. They belong, finally, to those who seek to understand men and their relations with one another. They are teachers of all who aspire to wed with Truth and dwell above the Veil.

Contents

WHAT COUNTRY HAVE I?

Introduction

When young Frederick Douglass, speaking before the American Anti-Slavery Society in 1847, asked, "What Country Have I?",[3] he put a question that circumstances compel every black American to ask. And when Douglass affirmed that he had no love for America and that, indeed, he had no country, he gave an answer that every thoughtful black in America has had to consider. This was not Douglass' final answer, as it has not been the final answer of most blacks in America; but the *question* does not thereby lose its potency. This question is the glass through which the black American sees "his" country. It is a glass that can distort. Anger, frustration, hopelessness, confusion, excessive inwardness often result from the black's situation; and they can lead to blindness and an utter incapacity to see the country in anything like its true shape. But the glass of the black's peculiar situation can also provide a clean, sharp view of America, exposing its innermost and fundamental principles and tendencies, which are largely ignored or vaguely seen through half-closed eye by the majority of white Americans, whose circumstances do not compel them really to look at their country and to wonder about it. This does not mean that the black is necessarily revolutionary—most blacks are not; but it does mean that he takes seriously the possibility of revolution, or rejection, or separation. He thus shares the perspective of the serious revolutionary. He appeals, at least in thought, from the imperfect world of convention and tradition (very imperfect, indeed, from his point of view) to the world of nature and truth. In important respects, then, black Americans are like a revolutionary or, more interestingly perhaps, a founding generation. That is, they are in the difficult but potentially glorious position of not being able to take for granted given political arrangements and values, of having seriously to canvass alternatives, to think through their implications, and to make a deliberate choice. To understand the American polity, one could hardly do better than to study, along with the work and thought of the Founders, the best writings of the blacks who are at once its friends, enemies, citizens, and aliens.

Although never dominant, there have always been articulate blacks who deny that America is their country. They insist that there is a fundamental incompatibility between America and the blacks who find themselves physically within, but in all significant respects alien to, this polity. "No, I'm not an American," Malcolm X protested, "I'm one of the 22 million black people who are victims of Americanism." (See page 149.)

This view takes a number of forms. Some men argue that American society (or, more generally, Western society) is fundamentally and intrinsically corrupt, quite apart from any race problems. This was the view, for example, of the later Du Bois. "We tax ourselves into poverty and crime so as to make the rich richer and the poor poorer and more evil. We know the cause of this: it is to permit our rich business interests to stop socialism and to prevent the ideals of communism from ever triumphing on earth. The aim is impossible. Socialism progresses and will progress."[4] The criticism, if not the conviction of historical inevitability, continues to find expression in some radical black thought. "Societies and countries based on the profit motive will never insure a new humanism or eliminate poverty and racism."[5] Because the black is excluded from the society, he remains relatively uncorrupted by it and thus better able to see its true character; but the corruption does not, fundamentally, have anything to do with him. Capitalistic exploitation—or any evil of similar kind—may be exacerbated or given its specific form by racial conditions; but it exists and has its cause independently of racial conditions.

A more common argument points to America's views of and actions toward the black man as the essential flaw in American society. A version of this argument, rather common among early black separatists, is that America is not bad intrinsically, but that it is bad for blacks. Much more common today is the view that white racism has eaten into the soul and psyche of America, harming not only (indeed, not mainly) the black but also the white, and corrupting the country perhaps beyond any possibility of reform. "America is mad with white racism," Eldridge Cleaver contends. "Whom the gods would destroy, they first make mad. Perhaps America has been mad far too long to make any talk of sanity relevant now."[6]

A third view of the incompatibility between the black and America is concerned less with the deficiencies of America and more with the needs of blacks. The argument here is that the black man has certain needs, certain opportunities, certain duties to bring himself to full manhood, and that he cannot do this successfully, or he can do it only with great difficulty, in the United States. It requires independence from the advanced, powerful, overwhelming, unfriendly white community and the establishment of a black nation. The building and managing of political communities is the highest business of man; it is the activity in which the highest development of human potential takes place. And unless a people finds or makes for itself opportunities to engage in that high business, on its own account and not just as laborers in someone else's garden, that people will suffer in its very character and competence as men. "Nationalism is a prerequisite for statehood," Floyd McKissick has written, "and membership in a state is imperative if a man is to have self-respect, if he is to command the respect of other men."[7] LeRoi Jones also had something like this in mind when he wrote, "The Black Man will always be frustrated until he has a land (A Land!) of his own. All the thought processes and emotional orientation of 'national liberation movements'—from slave uprisings onward—have always given motion to a Black National (and Cultural) Consciousness."[8]

The bulk of recent discussion among those who reject America has turned on the more immediate question, what is to be done? The prescriptions range from advice to leave the country to programs to destroy it or to engineer some more or less radical revolution (which are also forms of "leaving"). If none of these is possible, some way may have to be found of living among enemies, or living in the midst of an evil society. It is not surprising, when one considers the implications of these suggestions, that discussions about means so often degenerate into blind striking out, with little or no attempt to show any relation between means adopted and ends desired. Yet there is some reason even here. Just as no thoughtful black, however cool his reason and moderate his conclusions, can entirely discard the possibility that his country is at war with him, so he cannot entirely discard the possibility that under some circumstances the most rational and noble course may be, after all, naked defiance of an inhuman, oppressive society, even at the price of certain annihilation.

Most black Americans have decided that, for all its defects and injustice, America is their country. The black abolitionists like Frederick Douglass fought the American Colonization Society and all efforts to rid the country of its black population hardly less vigorously than they fought slavery; and typically they regarded these as but two sides of the same coin. We are here, Douglass affirmed repeatedly, and here we intend to stay. With all her faults, America is a better home and school for her black step-children, as Douglass called them, than any African or South American wilderness. The American principles of equality and individual liberty are, indeed, often violated or ignored in their application to the black, who has been closed out from the rights and opportunities that he ought to enjoy. The problem basically is to hold America to her own principles, so that the black can share American liberty and civilization.

This has, of course, been the basis of the twentieth century civil rights movement, which has attempted to protect individuals from racially-inspired injustices, such as job discrimination, or legal inhibitions on voting, or inferior education. The civil rights movement has not, generally speaking, been very philosophical. Partly this is because the battles of political and constitutional principle seemed to have been fought and won in an earlier day. Partly it is because, in its individualistic ends and its legal, conventional means, the civil rights movement accepted without reservation basic American political principles. The job seemed to be to keep up the pressure and to secure implementation of the civil rights program. The civil rights movement also accepted the widespread indifference among contemporary American political leaders and thinkers about what individuals *do* with their rights and opportunities, standing in this respect in striking contrast to the older fighters for civil rights, such as Frederick Douglass.

The recent civil rights movement shares with the older one the ultimate aim of assimilation. The focus, politically, legally, socially, and in every other conceivable way, is on the individual human beings, the color of their skin being fundamentally irrelevant. These were the views of the old CORE, described so charmingly by James Farmer, where a young white female worker failed to identify an attacker as black, for fear of somehow betraying the principle that race differences should not be "noticed."[9] Assimilation or racial amalgamation seems to provide the final step that completes the whole civil rights program. Whether because amalgamation is seen as the only way, finally, to destroy race prejudice, or because it seems demanded in principle by the brother-

hood of all men, or because it seems to follow from the radical individualism of civil rights, "integration" as a goal has meant men living together
without consciousness of color differences, which leads to, if it does not
require, the elimination of those differences by racial amalgamation.

In the last few years the movement for civil rights and integration
has come under criticism with respect to its commitment to legal and
nonviolent means, its assimilationist ends, and even its individualistic
philosophy. Questions that were considered closed in the heyday of
NAACP legal action for civil rights have been reopened. There is again a
good deal of agitation of basic theoretical issues, and while the result is
often merely confusing, it can be highly illuminating. Separatism and
other radical positions are again being taken seriously by thoughtful and
responsible blacks. More common, however, are renewals of the old
quest of the black American for a position that is neither assimilationist
nor separatist and neither individualistic nor racist, but that attempts to
unite these elements in theory and in practical programs. Although quite
different from what has recently been thought of as "integration," this
new (or new-old) line of thinking is nevertheless integrationist in the
proper sense of the word. While the civil rights movement often assumed
or looked forward to racial *amalgamation* or homogenization, the more
recent thinking is in the direction of integration in the more precise sense
of making a whole out of parts that are and remain distinct.

The recent movement towards Black Power is, by and large, integrationist in this sense, although it begins with a kind of separation. It begins
with calls to blacks to "collect ourselves," but to do so in preparation for
entering the broader community. The principle of "collecting ourselves"
concerns both means and ends. On the level of means, Stokely Carmichael and Charles Hamilton, for example, argue that those who say that
blacks ought to engage in coalition politics are putting the cart before the
horse—or trying to pull the cart without any horse. The first requirement
of coalition politics is to collect oneself, to collect one's power. The rule
of the game is that if you go in with nothing, you come out with nothing;
and that is the way the blacks have played it in the past.[10]

The more fundamental, philosophical ground of Black Power is to be
found in the same principle of "collecting ourselves," but here in the
sense of black self-understanding. The argument is that blacks need to
collect themselves psychologically, morally, and socially, as well as in
power terms; only then will they have a real basis for conducting their
own lives and participating in the broader American community. Thus
there has been a resurgence among blacks of interest in and commitment
to black institutions and standards and black ways of thinking and acting.
In the opinion of the advocates of Black Power, the practical result of the

amalgamationist view, for all its individualism, was to teach that the Negro future lies in being white, whereas the practical result of Black Power is to teach pride in being black. Thus Carmichael and Hamilton say, "The racial and cultural personality of the black community must be preserved and that community must win its freedom while preserving its cultural integrity. Integrity includes a pride—in the sense of self-acceptance, not chauvinism—in being black, in the historical attainments and contributions of black people. No person can be healthy, complete, and mature if he must deny a part of himself; this is what 'integration' has required thus far. This is the essential difference between integration as it is currently practiced and the concept of Black Power." (See page 181.) As Carmichael and Hamilton make clear, black cultural integrity is to be the basis not for leaving the American community but for significant participation in it.

This concern for cultural integrity obviously points to the need to understand and to give expression to the identity, the worth, the way of life associated with being black. To the exploration of these questions much of the best thought of American blacks has been and will no doubt continue to be directed, for the subject is far from having been exhausted.

One possible source for an understanding of the significance of being black is Africa. But except for some separatists and missionaries (who saw the black American as the model for Africa, rather than the other way around), Africa has seldom been more than a peripheral concern of American blacks. Africa has seemed to be capable of enriching but not of defining the identity of black Americans. Similar considerations apply to attempts to ground black identity in Islam. As James Baldwin said, "the Negro has been formed by this nation, for better or for worse, and does not belong to any other—not to Africa, and certainly not to Islam."[11]

A second possible source of black self-understanding is "black culture," a distinctive and valuable style of life developed by blacks in America. While many of the writers included here are concerned with black culture, in one form or another, a full exploration of it would lead to other writings and other authors, especially in literature and the arts.[12] The problem is to articulate exactly what black culture is (and, more basically, what "culture" in general is) and to show that it has sufficient substance and viability to serve as the basis for a people's self-conscious development. A simple but difficult question is whether the distinctive values of an oppressed people will not inevitably die with the removal of the oppression. W. E. B. Du Bois, for example, described the black men as "the sole oasis of simple faith and reverence in a dusty desert of dollars and smartness." (See page 91.) Yet Du Bois fought to secure for the black man an opportunity to function on equal terms in American society. There is an obvious question whether the simple faith and reverence with which the black responded to exclusion will or can be retained when the justice he demands is done him. Will he too not chase the dollar when he has a full opportunity to do so?

Another less obviously political version of the same problem arises out of the growing tendency to describe "black culture" as a distinctive experience or behavior and to resist any demand to explain it or talk about it. It is what it is. "The uniqueness of black culture can be explained," Julius Lester says, "in that it is a culture whose emphasis is on the nonverbal, i.e. the nonconceptual. The lives of blacks are rooted in the concrete daily experience. . . . In black culture it is the experience that counts, not what is said. . . ."[13] Yet culture seems to require at least some agency of transmission and interpretation, if it is to be more than a series of random responses to chance stimuli. Some of those concerned with black culture look to the nonverbal or largely nonverbal arts to perform this function in a way that does not fall into the white trap of verbalizing and conceptualizing. This view would have to be seriously considered in any full exploration of black revival. Lester's own work strongly suggests, however, the principal difficulty, which is that some "verbalizing" seems to be necessary, both to transmit the culture or experience, from man to man and generation to generation, and to make sense of it, to understand it. Can we know the lash of slavery, for example, for what it is—not merely as one bit of unpleasant experience but as something unjust and inhuman—without fundamental reliance on words and concepts?

A third source of black identity (and the most fruitful one) is the political and moral history of the black in America. The search here is for a higher harmony arising out of the antagonism between being black and being American. The broad answer—given in a variety of ways by black writers of differing views—is that the black has been placed in the position of being uniquely fitted to call America to be her true or best self. Thus when W. E. B. Du Bois wrote in 1903 that "there are to-day no truer exponents of the pure human spirit of the Declaration of Independence than the American Negroes," (See page 91.) he was suggesting that what distinguishes the black American from the rest of the country is also what ties him to the country: his unique appreciation of the principles on which the country is based.

There is today a renewed understanding that in the history of slavery, oppression, and degradation of the black American there is much for him to be proud of. The assimilationists regarded that history as something to be put aside or lived down, which is another way of saying that being a Negro is degrading and has to be sloughed off in order to move into the mainstream and find one's liberty as an individual. On the contrary, it is now again argued, there is something ennobling in this tradition, which contains the materials of the self-understanding and dignity of black Americans. This is a tradition of fortitude, patience, dignity, and independence under extreme adversity, a tradition of persistent striving for freedom and civilization. It does not need to be ignored or discarded; nor, it should be added, does it need to be inflated or fictionalized. There is merit enough in the truth. "To accept one's past—one's history—is not the same thing as drowning in it; it is learning how to use it. An invented past can never be used; it cracks and crumbles under the pressures of life like clay in a season of drought."[14]

Properly understood, this tradition reveals the basis of the black American's own integrity and self-understanding and also the basis of his relation to America. Almost all of the non-assimilationist, non-separatist writers have pursued this line of thought, but none more profoundly than Booker T. Washington. (Remember that we are not here discussing Washington's program but his philosophy.) Washington thought that the American black had gone through a school that had, paradoxically, taught him about freedom and civilization while holding him in slavery and degradation. It had taught him, Washington thought, something about the meaning and value of freedom and independence and self-respect; and these lessons were to be not only the basis of the black's rise but his gift to America. The American black learned that the kind of respect that counts is self-respect, not the fickle opinions of others. He learned that real freedom rests on a foundation of reason and order. He learned that the useful arts are respectable in themselves and are the beginning of the liberal arts. In all these ways, Washington thought, the black was put in the way of acquiring an understanding of freedom and self-respect that his former white masters were themselves sadly in need of. Here is a basis of black pride that is distinct from, yet harmonious with, the American whole.

In one of the most profound passages in Washington's writings, he reflects on a white man whose proud boast of never doing menial labor amounted to a confession of utter poverty with respect to the real purpose of education, "the making of men useful, honest, and liberal."

Here is a citizen in the midst of our republic, clothed in a white skin, with all the technical signs of education, but who is as little fitted for the highest purpose of life as any creature found in Central Africa. My friends, can we make our education reach down far enough to touch and help this man? Can we so control science, art, and literature as to make them to such an extent a means rather than an end; that the lowest and most unfortunate of God's creatures shall be lifted up, ennobled and glorified; shall be a freeman instead of a slave of narrow sympathies and wrong customs? (See pages 71–72.)

The problem, this representative of the recently freed blacks suggested, was to find a way of reaching down far enough to touch this white "slave of narrow sympathies and wrong customs." This is the source of Washington's gentle concern for whites, often mistaken for pandering or weakness. It was the concern of the strong for the weak, the superior for the inferior, the teacher for the pupil.

The characteristic and perhaps most noble posture of the black American has been that of the friendly, though badly mauled, critic, calling America to live up to her own principles. Several versions of this profound and ironical theme—the oppressed and degraded black as the conscience of America, the teacher of America, the source of needed values and principles—will be found in this volume. According to this view, the problems could not be solved by separation, even if that were feasible, because the blacks and whites are in a relation of mutual dependence. Each would be worse off without the other. Writing of "Our Spiritual Strivings," W. E. B. Du Bois held up "the ideal of fostering and developing the traits and talents of the Negro, not in opposition to or contempt for other races, but rather in large conformity to the greater ideals of the American Republic, in order that some day on American soil two world-races may give to each other those characteristics both so sadly lack." (See page 91.)

America is our country, blacks as diverse as Washington, Du Bois, King, Baldwin, and even Malcolm X and Cleaver, have thought, not only because blacks value and demand the rights and opportunities of American liberty and civilization, not only because the history of black and white in America has bound them together inextricably, but above all because America has a void that none can fill so well as America's black victims, citizens, friends, teachers. This is one of the deepest themes of black American political thought, and no serious consideration of American government and political theory can fail to give it a prominent place.

Like most other American political thought, black American political thought is not "closet philosophy." The viewpoint is usually not that of the scholar or the philosopher but of the statesman or the adviser to statesmen. The statesman, however, is carried beyond immediate practical issues by a need to understand the deeper ground on which they rest. Thus the writers here deal not only with problems of black Americans and of the United States but with many of the perennial questions of political life. These broader themes are often lost sight of or distorted in the clamor of everyday political contention; and it will take a deliberate effort for most readers to suspend judgment on the immediate issues long enough to follow the reflections of these writers on the broader implications. Four themes are especially important and worth watching for and thinking about.

First, there is the question of the extent of an individual's responsibility for what he is. Although there is still a considerable tendency in some circles to dismiss any criticism of or prescription for the behavior of blacks with the claim that the "fault" lies elsewhere, one of the consequences of the upsurge of black militancy is a renewed unwillingness by blacks to accept the implication of this easy explanation: that blacks are the mere product of white action and have no genuine independence of action or thought and therefore no independent responsibility. "What others did was their responsibility," James Baldwin wrote, reflecting on his early years in the church, "for which they would answer when the judgment trumpet sounded. But what *I* did was *my* responsibility, and I would have to answer, too—unless, of course, there was also in Heaven a special dispensation for the benighted black, who was not to be judged in the same way as other human beings, or angels."[15] This is a question of individual morality, but it is also a political question of the first order. One of the major concerns of the best black writers has been to explore the relation between the inner and external obstacles to black advancement and independence, and to human fulfillment in general. One of the great questions of emigration, for example, was whether separation or integration would be the better condition under which blacks could develop those inner resources of character and independence that had been weakened by slavery but that were necessary to any meaningful progress. How does a leader, any leader, teach his people the duty of independent, manly use of such opportunities as are available without encouraging them to be satisfied with narrow and demeaning circumstances? How does he move his people to fight to remove unjust external obstacles without teaching them to think of themselves as being merely the product of such external forces? How far is it true, or in what sense is it true, that each man is finally responsible for himself, and what are the political implications of an answer to this question?

Second, there is the question of prejudice. Situated as he is, the black writer can scarcely avoid some reflection on the nature of prejudice in general and on its political function—and malfunctioning. Is prejudice the basic problem, as is so often said? If so, is that because prejudice causes objective injustice and harm to blacks? Or because it stands in the way of seeing men as individuals? Or because it is psychologically harmful to the holder? Each of these answers has different implications. There is the further question of how far prejudice has some foundation in reason. James Baldwin somewhere confessed a prejudice against doormen, but the sound and rational basis of this pre-judgment is easy to understand and accept, even though it no doubt led often to injustice to particular doormen. How far is something like this true of prejudice generally? Can the victim of prejudice destroy or weaken it, as Frederick

Douglass suggested, by acting so as to remove the basis in truth, thus making slanderers of his vilifiers? Can racial prejudice be overcome through the neutrality of the market, as Washington thought? Can it be destroyed by law? Or is there some deeper cause of prejudice, unreachable by any rational appeal? Further, there is the crucial question whether race prejudice is one species among many or a unique kind of prejudice. Does the depth and virulence of race prejudice require, as a political matter, the elimination of the race difference, either by separation or by assimilation? Finally, there is the question whether all political organizations or human associations depend on prejudice. Does race or group pride imply, at least in practice, race or group prejudice? Perhaps it is necessary to refine the issue, regarding both race prejudice and prejudice in general, by distinguishing between prejudice that is more or less in touch with some rational foundation, more or less conducive to beneficial group cohesion, more or less harmful to outside persons and groups.

Third, there is the ancient question of the relation between the political whole and its parts. Is government the tool and protector of the individual, and society an aggregate of homogeneous or undifferentiated individuals? This has been the view of many black American thinkers, as it has generally been the view of white American political thinkers. There has, however, also been a different line of argument, perhaps most fully and thoughtfully presented in Du Bois' early essay on "The Conservation of the Races," but explored also by Washington, Baldwin, and Carmichael, and currently undergoing a marked revival. The "new integration," in contrast to the old or assimilationist integration, rests on or points to a theoretical view that a polity is a unity of distinct and purposive social parts—*e pluribus unum*—and that an individual is part of a series of increasingly larger groups, including family, community, race, and country. The utterly homogeneous nation, in this view, is weak and sterile. "What a tiresome place America would be if freedom meant we all had to think alike or be the same color or wear that same gray flannel suit!"[16] These various social groups extend, define, and give significance to the individual; and they are in turn bound together in a diverse, mutually supporting and enriching whole. Social and political thought ought to aim to help men find their way into broader and higher levels of significance. The aim should be, however, not to abandon the narrower, particular associations but rather, by sustaining their integrity and exploring their implications, to enrich and elevate the whole community. The immediate thrust of this line of argument is in the direction of restoring and strengthening black cultural integrity as part of a broader association. Carried to its fullest extent, the argument suggests some basic questions, as Du Bois saw, about the accepted foundations of American government and politics and even about the accepted foundations of politics in the modern world.

Finally, there is the question of the relation between law and right. The black American, more than most others, suffers from imperfect and unjust laws. He is less likely to adopt the simple view that the law is right because it is the law. His circumstances make law-abidingness a larger question for him than it usually is for most other people. He is more likely to admit the legitimacy, under some circumstances, of disobedience to law. At the same time, however, the black American, as one of a disadvantaged and even hated minority, has a disproportionately great dependence on the protection of law. "Even poor whites do not have to rely on the law for protection as do Black People."[17] A victim of imperfect law, the black is nevertheless a prime beneficiary of law. What should he do? The situation of the black is only an extreme version of the situation that confronts every man who benefits from the law while suffering from its imperfections. Some argue for blind obedience to preserve the benefits. Others, on principle or in despair, argue for utter rejection to eliminate the imperfections. But most have seen that any viable solution must somehow combine the claims both of a stable legal system and of transcendent justice. Martin Luther King, Jr. is, of course, well known for his treatment of this theme, and his "Letter from Birmingham Jail" is a major political document of recent times. But the theme is treated by many black political thinkers. In this respect, as in so many others, they bring the unique experience and perspective of the black American to bear on the fundamental political questions that have always concerned thoughtful men.

Augustus Washington

Throughout the history of black American political thought, an articulate and able minority has advocated some form of emigration or separation. Marcus Garvey's Back to Africa Movement and the more recent demands of the Nation of Islam for a portion of the United States (a proposal also entertained by Augustus Washington) are well known. But perhaps the most thoughtful consideration was given to this question during the decade before the Civil War. The letter printed here, although written, as the writer says, by "a mere private business man," provides a good brief account of the reflections of black Americans who seriously turned to emigration. As was usual among such men, Augustus Washington saw the black man in the United States as suffering both from the direct harm of slavery and discrimination and from the moral debasement and frustration of his inferior position in American society. "He who would not rather live anywhere on

earth in freedom than in this country in social and political degradation, has not attained half the dignity of his manhood." The
writer was not anti-American; and like most of the early colonizationists he admired American political principles, which were
utterly incompatible with the institution of slavery. Indeed, he
thought that American injustice to blacks would, ironically, be the
instrument for planting American principles of liberty on African
soil. This latter is an important subsidiary theme of Washington's
statement. Although the main emphasis is on the needs of the
American blacks for separation, that separation is elevated and
given an added significance by the great work they had to perform: the redemption of the people of Africa.

Additional Readings: The most substantial full-length discussion of emigration by a black writer before the Civil War—and
perhaps at any time—is Martin Delany's *The Condition, Elevation,*

African Colonization—
By a Man of Color

To the Editors of The Tribune:

As the infant Republic of Liberia is now attracting the attention of the
enlightened nations, and the press of both England and America, I may
hope that a communication in regard to that country, and the Afric-
Americans in this, may not be deemed a subject intrusive nor foreign to
the public interest. And I am encouraged by the just and liberal course
you have taken in favor of the proposed line of Steamers to the Western
Coast of Africa, and also the boldness with which you have lately urged
the propriety and interest of some of the colored people, emigrating from
our crowded cities to less populous parts of this country, as the great
West, or to Africa or any other place where they may secure an equality
of rights and liberty, with a mind unfettered and space to rise. Besides, as
your paper is generally read by the progressive and more liberal portion

From the *New York Daily Tribune*, July 9 and 10, 1851.

Emigration and Destiny of the Colored People of the United States, published in Philadelphia in 1852, a major portion of which is printed, along with other emigrationist writings of importance, in Howard Brotz's *Negro Social and Political Thought.* An interesting collection of letters from Negroes to the American Colonization Society is printed in Carter G. Woodson's *The Mind of the Negro as Reflected in Letters Written During the Crisis 1800– 1860.* The basic writings of Marcus Garvey will be found in Amy Jacques-Garvey (ed.), *Philosophy and Opinions of Marcus Garvey.* Louis E. Lomax's *When the Word is Given* contains several speeches by Malcolm X made before his break with the Muslims, explaining the Muslim position and demands for a separate state. See also Robert S. Browne's "The Case for Black Separatism," a recent essay arising out of the 1967 Newark Conference on Black Power and published in *Ramparts,* December, 1967.

of white Americans and some of the most intelligent of the colored, I may also hope to be confirmed in my present sentiments and measures or driven to new and better convictions. I do not wish to be thought extravagant, when I affirm what I believe to be true, that I have seen no act in your public career as an editor, statesman and philanthropist, more noble and praiseworthy than that of turning your pen and influence to African Colonization and civilization, after finding that you could not secure for the black man in America those inalienable rights to which he with other oppressed nations, is entitled and for which you have heretofore labored. Though the colored people may not appreciate your kind efforts, and those of many other good and true men who pursue your course, we trust you will not on account of present opposition be weary in well doing. Though dark the day, and fearful as is the tide, oppression is rolling over us, we are certain that it is but the presage of a more glorious morrow. We do not despair. We thank God that notwithstanding all the powerful combinations to crush us to the earth, as long as the bible with its religion endures, there will ever be a large number of the American people whose prayers, sympathies and influence will defend us here, and assist and encourage our brethren who have sought, or may in future seek liberty on a foreign shore. If these no other reward awaits, the time is not distant when they shall receive at least the thanks and benedictions of a grateful people, "redeemed, regenerated and disenthralled by the genius of universal emancipation." Ever since the annexation of Texas and the success and triumph of American arms on the plains of Mexico I have been looking in vain for some home for Afric-Americans more congenial to their feelings and prejudice than Liberia. The Canadas, the West Indies, Mexico, British Guiana and other parts of South America have all been brought under review. And yet I have been unable to get rid of a conviction, long since entertained and often expressed, that if the colored people of this country ever find a home on earth for the developement of their manhood and intellect, it will first be in Liberia or some other parts of Africa. A continent larger than North America is lying waste for want of the hand of science and industry. A land whose bowels are filled with mineral and agricultural wealth, and on whose bosom reposes in exuberance and wild extravagance all the fruits and productions of a tropical clime. The providence of God will not permit a land so rich in all the elements of wealth and greatness to remain much longer without civilized inhabitants. Every one who has traced the history of missions in Africa and watched the progress of that little Republic of Afric-Americans on the western coast, must be convinced that the colored men are more peculiarly adapted and must eventually be the means of civilizing, redeeming and saving that continent if ever that is done at all. Encouraged and supported by American benevolence and philanthropy, I know no people better suited to this great work—none whose duty more it is. Our servile and degraded condition in this country, the history of the past, and the light that is pouring in upon me from every source fully convinces me that this is our true, our highest and happiest destiny, and the sooner we commence this glorious work the sooner will 'light spring up in darkness and the wilderness and the solitary place be glad, and the deserts rejoice and blossom as the rose.'

I am aware that nothing except the Fugitive Slave Law can be more startling to the free colored citizens of the Northern States, than the fact that any man among them whom they have regarded as intelligent and sound in faith should declare his convictions and influence in favor of African Colonization. But the novelty of the thing does not prove it false, nor that he who dare reject a bad education and break loose from long established prejudices may not have the most conclusive reasons for such a course.

I am aware, too, of the solemn responsibility of my present position. It must result in some good or great evil. I maintain that clinging to long cherished prejudices and fostering hopes that can never be realized, the leaders of the colored people in this country have failed to discharge a great and important duty to their race. Seeing this, though a mere private business man, with a trembling pen I come forward alone, joining with friend and foe in moving the wheel of a great enterprise, which though unpopular with those it designs to benefit, must result eventually in the redemption and enfranchisement of the African race.

With the conviction of a purpose so noble, and an end so beneficient, I cannot notice the misrepresentations, slander and anathemas, which I must for a while endure, even from those whose approbation and good will I would gladly retain. It was no difficult task to have seen, that unless they could force emancipation, and then the perfect social and political equality of the races, human nature, human pride and passions would not allow the Americans to acknowledge the equality and inalienable rights of those who had been their slaves. One or the other must be dominant. For this reason, seven years ago, while a student, I advocated the plan of a separate state for colored Americans—not as a choice, but as a necessity, believing it would be better for our manhood and intellect to be freemen by ourselves than political slaves with our oppressors. I enlisted at once the aid of a few colored young men, of superior talent and ability; and we were earnestly taking measures to negotiate for a tract of land in Mexico, when the war and its consequences blasted our hopes, and drove us from our purpose. About five years ago I told my excellent friend, Geo. L. Seymour of Liberia (who, after a residence of some years there, had returned to this city to take out his family) that I knew only one way to develop the faculties of our people in this country, and that by their entire separation from oppression and its influences; and that if I was compelled to abandon my plan of a separate State in America, I would devote my voice, my pen, my heart and soul to the cause of Liberia. I have since written to him that he has my heart in Africa now, and in two or three years, if we live, I will shake hands with him on the banks of the St. John.

Ever since a lad of fifteen, it has been my constant study to learn how I might best contribute to elevate the social and political position of the oppressed and unfortunate people with whom I am identified; and while I have endeavored, in my humble way, to plead the cause of three millions of my enslaved countrymen, I have, at the same time, thought it no inconsistency to plead also for the hundred and fifty millions of the native sons of Africa. But every word uttered in her behalf subjects us to the imputation of being a Colonizationist, and covers us with the odium our people attach to such a name; as if something unjust and wicked was naturally associated with the term, when in fact that odium, if such I may call it for the sake of argument, can exist only with those who have forgotten the history of Plymouth Rock and Jamestown, or who are determined not to know the truth, in spite of facts and the evidence of the most enlightened reasons. What is Colonization? For the benefit of those who treat it with contempt, and think that no good can come out of it, I may merely remark that the thirteen original States, previous to the Declaration of Independence, were called the Colonies of Great Britain, the inhabitants colonists. The companies and individuals in England that assisted in planting these Colonies, were called Colonizationists. These colonists came from the land of their birth, and forsook their homes, their firesides, their former altars and the graves of their fathers, to seek civil and religious liberty among the wild beasts and Indians on a foreign, bleak and desolate shore. Oppressed at home, they emigrated to Holland, and after remaining there twelve years, returned to England, and found not the hope of rest until they came to America. That very persecution and oppression of the mother country planted in America the purest civil and religious institutions the world had ever seen. And now this powerful Republic, by her oppression and injustice to one class of this people, will plant in Africa a religion and morality more pure, and liberty more universal, than it has yet been the lot of any people to enjoy. I never have been of that class who repudiate everything American.— While I shall never make any compromise with Slavery, nor feel indifferent to its blighting, withering effects on the human intellect and human happiness, I cannot be so blind as not to see and believe that in spite of all its corrupting influences on national character, there is yet piety, virtue, philanthropy and disinterested benevolence among the American people; and when by the progress of free thought and the full development of her free institutions, our country shall have removed from her national escutcheon that plague-spot of the nation, she will do more than all others in sending the light of liberty and everlasting love into every portion of the habitable globe. In our enthusiam and devotion to any great benevolent cause, we are generally unwilling to make the best use of men as we find them, until we have wasted our energies in accomplishing nothing, or a calmer reflection convinces us of our error. It is well for those to whom this reflection comes not too late. We have been an unfortunate people. For 400 years the avarice, fraud and oppression of Europeans and their descendents have been preying upon the children of Africa and her descendents in America. Says my eloquent correspondent, in writing upon this subject: "I know this was the soil on which I was born; but I have nothing to glorify this as my country. I have no pride of ancestry to point back to. Our forefathers did not come here as did the Pilgrim fathers, in search of a place where they could enjoy civil and religious liberty. No; they were cowardly enough to allow themselves to be brought manacled and fettered as slaves, rather than die on their native shores resisting their oppressors." In the language of Dr. Todd, "If the marks of humanity are not blotted out from this race of miserable men, it is not because oppression has not been sufficiently legalized, and avarice been allowed to pursue its victims till the grave became a sweet asylum."

During the past thirty years two influential and respectable associations have arisen in our behalf, each claiming to be the most benevolent, and each seemingly opposed to the intentions and purposes of the other.

The American Colonization Society on the one hand proposed to benefit us by the indirect means of planting a Colony on the western coast of Africa, as an Asylum for the free colored people and manumitted slaves of the United States; and by this means also to send the blessings of civilization and religion to the benighted sons of that continent. The principal obstacle in the way of their success has been that the free colored people, as a body, everywhere, have denounced the whole scheme as wicked and mischievous, and resolved not to leave this country; while those who have gone to that Colony, from a state of Slavery, as the condition of freedom, have been least able to contribute to the knowledge and greatness of a new country, and impart civilization and the arts and sciences to its heathen inhabitants. This Society was one of the few that are popular in their very beginning. But that which made it most popular with the American public furnished the cause of the opposition of the colored people. They erected a platform so broad that the worst enemies of the race could stand upon it with the same grace and undistinguished from the honest and true philanthropist. It could at the same time appeal for support to the piety and benevolence of the North, and to the prejudices and sordid interest of the South. I state this simply as a fact, not for the purpose of finding fault. It is always easier to show one plan faulty than to produce a better one.

Notwithstanding the different and adverse motives that have prompted the friends of Colonization, they certainly have labored perseveringly and unitedly for the accomplishment of one great purpose. And in spite of all our former distrust we must give them the credit at least of producing as yet the only great practical scheme for the amelioration of the condition of the free colored man, and the manumitted slave. They did not profess nor promise to do more. Instead of engaging in clamorous agitations about principles and measures, they turned what men and means they had to the best purpose, and engaged industriously in founding and nurturing a Colony for the free colored people, where they have an opportunity of demonstrating their equality with the white race, by seizing upon, combining and developing all the elements of national greatness, by which they are surrounded. Thus far the end is good—we need not stop now to scan their motives.

The Abolitionists, on the other hand, proposed by moral means the immediate emancipation of the slave, and the elevation of the free colored people in the land of their birth. And this they did at a time which tried men's souls. Theirs was a platform on which none dared stand who were not willing to indure scorn, reproach, disgrace, lynch law and even death for the sake of oppressed Americans. At first, interest, reputation, office nor profit, but the reverse, were the reward of an Abolitionist. Now that Anti-Slavery has become popular with many of the American people, it assumes another name, and is converted into political capital. Even Free Soilism was not so much designed to make room for our liberties, as to preserve unimpaired the liberties of the whites. The Abolitionists have not yet accomplished anything which we can see to be so definite and practical. Yet they have divested themselves of personal prejudices, aroused the nation to a sense of its injustice and wrongs toward the colored people, encouraged them in improving and obtaining education here, broken down many arbitrary and proscriptive usages in their treatment, and convinced this nation and England that they are a people capable of moral, social and political elevation, and entitled to equal rights with any other community. Both of these benevolent societies might perhaps have accomplished more good, if they had wasted less ammunition in firing at each other. While one has formerly declared a moral and intellectual inferiority of our race, with an incapacity ever to enjoy the rights and prerogatives of freemen in the land of our birth, the other has declared that hatred to the race and the love of Slavery were the only motives that prompted the Colonizationists to action. In taking a liberal and more comprehensive view of the whole matter, we believe that whatever may have been the faults, inconsistencies and seeming opposition of either, both have been instrumental in doing much good in their own way; and under the guidance of an all-wise Providence, the labors, devotion and sacrifices of both will work together for good, and tend toward a grander and more sublime result than either association at present contemplates.

For our own part, under the existing state of things, we cannot see why any hostility should exist between those who are true Abolitionists and that class of Colonizationists, who are such from just and benevolent motives. Nor can we see a reason why a man of pure and enlarged philanthropy may not be in favor of both, unless his devotion to one should cause him to neglect the other. Extremes in any case are always wrong. It is rare to find that all the members of any association, untrammelled by interest, act solely from high moral principle and disinterested benevolence. The history of the world, civil, sacred and profane, shows that some men have, in all ages, espoused popular and benevolent causes, more or less influenced by prejudice or selfishness. Human nature, with its imperfections, remains the same.

Ever since the adoption of the Constitution, the Government and people of this country, as a body, have pursued but one policy toward our race. In every contest between the great political parties we have been the losers. But this result it is reasonable to expect in a Republic whose Constitution guarantees protection alike to our peculiar and our free institutions—thus securing the rights and liberties of one class at the expense of the liberties of another. Besides this, Texas and all the States that have since come into the Union have surrounded us with political embarrassments. Every State that has lately revised or altered her Constitution has been more liberal in extending rights to the white and less so to the colored man. In view of these facts, I assume as a fixed principle that it is impossible for us to develop our moral and intellectual capacities as a distinct people, under our present social and political disabilities; and judging by the past and present state of things, there is no reason to hope that we can do it in this country in future.

Let us look a moment at some of the consequences of this social and political distinction on the entire mass. They are shut out from all the offices of profit and honor, and from the most honorable and lucrative pursuits of industry, and confined as a class to the most menial and servile positions in society. And what is worse than all, they are so educated from infancy, and become so accustomed to this degraded condition, that many of them seem to love it.

They are excluded in most of the States from all participation in the Government; taxed without their consent and compelled to submit to unrighteous laws, strong as the nation that enacts them, and cruel as the grave.

They are also excluded from every branch of mechanical industry, the workshop, the factory, the counting-room and every avenue to wealth and respectability, is closed against them.

Colleges and Academies slowly open their doors to them, when they possess no means to avail themselves of their advantages, and when their social condition has so degraded and demoralized them as to destroy all motive or desire to.

They are by necessity constant consumers, while they produce comparatively nothing, nor derive profit from the production of others. Shut out from all these advantages, and trained to fill the lowest condition in society, their teachers and ministers as a class educate them only for the situation to which the American people have assigned them. And hence too many of them aspire no higher than the gratification of their passions and appetites, and cling with deadly tenacity to a country that hates them and offers them nothing but chains, degradation and slavery.

Since things are so, it is impossible for them while in this country to prove to the world the moral and intellectual equality of the Africans and their descendents. Before such an experiment can be fairly tested, our colored youth from childhood must be admitted to a full participation in all the privileges of our schools, academies and colleges, and in all the immunities and rights of citizenship, free from every distinction on account of color, and the degrading influences that ignorance, prejudice and Slavery have heretofore thrown around them.

The same inducements as to white Americans should engage them in agriculture, commerce, manufactures, the mechanic arts, and all the pursuits of civilized and enlightened communities. Every man of common intelligence knows this has not been done; knows, too, it can not be done, for the first time, in the United States. In the face of these facts we are compelled to admit that the Afric-Americans, in their present state, can not compete with the superior energy and cultivated intellect of long civilized and Christian Saxons.

And, hence, we are driven to the conclusion that the friendly and mutual separation of the two races is not only necessary to the peace, happiness and prosperity of both, but indispensable to the preservation of the one and the glory of the other. While we would thus promote the interests of two great continents, and build up another powerful Republic, as an asylum for the oppressed, we would, at the same time, gratify national prejudices. We should be the last to admit that the colored man here, by nature and birth, is inferior in intellect, but by education and circumstances he may be. We could name many moral and intelligent colored young men in New-York, Philadelphia, and Boston, whose talents and genius far excel our own, and those of a majority of the hundreds of Saxon students with whom we have at different times been associated—men who, if liberally educated, would operate like leaven on our whole people, waken responses in the unexplored regions of Africa, and pour new light on the Republic of letters—but who, for the want of means and an unchained intellect, will probably live and die 'unknown, unhonored and unsung.'

> Full many a gem of purest ray serene,
> The dark unfathomed caves of ocean bear.
> Full many a flower is born to blush unseen,
> And waste its sweetness on the desert air.

This may appear ridiculous to those who know the colored man only as a domestic slave in the South or a political cipher in the North. But the generations living sixty years hence will regard him in a very different light. Before that time shall have arrived American Christians, as an expiation for the past, have a great duty to discharge to a prostrate nation, pleading in silent agony to God.

> With tears more eloquent than learned tongue
> Or lyre of purest note.

We too have a great work to perform. To the Anglo and Afric-American is committed the redemption and salvation of a numerous people for ages sunk in the lowest depth of superstition and barbarism. — Who but educated and pious colored men are to lead on the van of the 'sacramental host of God's elect' to conquer by love, and bring Africa with her trackless regions, under the dominion of our Savior — to baptize her sons at the font of science and religion, and teach them to chant the praises of Liberty and God until

> One song employs all nations; and all cry,
> "Worthy the Lamb, for he was slain for us!"
> The dwellers in the vales and on the rocks
> Shout to each other, and the mountain tops
> From distant mountains catch the flying joy,
> Till, nation after nation taught the strain,
> Earth rolls the rapturous hosahna round.

Whatever may have been the objections to Colonization in former times, I call upon colored people of this country to investigate the subject now under its present auspices. When I consider the kind of treatment they have received from their professed friends in America, I do not blame them in the past for exclaiming "God deliver us from our friends and we will take care of our enemies." I can never forget the round of applause that rang through an audience when a talented colored man of New-York in an earnest harangue against Colonization, said, "Mr. President, the Colonizationists wants us to go to Liberia if we will, if we wont go there, we may go to Hell." It seemed to indicate that they felt there was too much truth in the remark. Their principal objection has been that the men who professed the greatest love for them in Africa, did the most to exclude them here from the means of education, improvement and every respectable pursuit of industry. And their personal treatment was such as colored men only are made to feel, but none can describe. When the temperance men treated the inebriate as an outcast — a wretch debased and lost, they accomplished nothing, but repelled him from their kind influences; now when they recognize him as a man and a brother their efforts are crowned with great success. In keeping with other reforms, I think that Colonizationists have become more liberal and kind than formerly. — Whether this be true or not, if I can dispose of a single objection, I shall be confident that Afric-Americans are to be benefited more by the cause they advocate and sustain, than by any other practical scheme philanthropy has yet devised. I should have been glad if this Society, consistent with its leading purpose, had done something for the improvement and education of colored youth. And this would have been a great auxiliary to their main object. They have thought that if they encouraged their education here, they would not go to Africa. This is a mistake! If they would aid and encourage them in obtaining such education as white men receive, they could not keep them in this country. They would entirely unfit them for the debased position they must here occupy. Give me but educated intellect to operate upon, and I can send Liberia more useful men in three months, than I can in five years' labor with society as I find it. I speak only from my own experience when I say that during a life of constant struggle and effort, I never have received any sympathy or encouragement in obtaining an education nor in aspirations to usefulness, from any of the advocates of Colonization, except my noble friend J. C. Potts, Esq. of Trenton, N.J. Yet from some little acquaintance with many others I believe they are good and true friends ready to do anything for colored Americans that they would for white men, in similar circumstances. I have never doubted the good motives and true benevolence of such gentlemen as Benjamin Coates, Theodore Frelinghuysen, A. G. Phelps, J. G. Pinney, John McDonough and a host of others whose sentiments and efforts in our behalf, I know only by reading. But Slavery and its consequent degradation, together with our social position have kept us further apart than if separated by the waters of the Atlantic. However good the men and worthy their cause, it cannot flourish without the cooperation of Afric-Americans here. Our brethren across the Atlantic, have been struggling thirty years and in tears and joy have laid the foundations of a free Republic with civil and religious institutions. — They now call on us to assist in sustaining them and participate in their blessings — to aid them to civilize its inhabitants and extend the rising glory of the Lone Star of Africa. We should examine their cause, and if it is just we should no longer withhold our aid, and especially when in benefiting them, we must benefit ourselves. If by my feeble efforts, I shall ever be able to do anything that shall tell in future blessings on that injured country, it will be very much owing to the sympathy and encouragement received, in the course of my education from S. H. Cox, D.D. of 1844 and Lewis Tappan, Esq. that unchanging and unflinching advocate of the slave.

But we have never been pledged to any men or set of measures. We must mark out an independent course and become the architects of our own fortunes, when neither Colonizationists nor Abolitionists have the power or the will to admit us to any honorable or profitable means of subsistence in this country. I only regret that I come to the aid of Africa, at a time when I possess less ability to speak or write in her behalf than I did five years since. Strange as it may appear, whatever may be a colored man's natural capacity and literary attainments, I believe that as soon as he leaves the academic halls to mingle in the only society he can find in the United States, unless he be a minister or lecturer, he must and will retrograde. And for the same reason, just in proportion as he increases in knowledge, will he become the more miserable.

If ignorance is bliss, 'tis folly to be wise.

He who would not rather live anywhere on earth in freedom than in this country in social and political degradation, has not attained half the dignity of his manhood. I hope our Government will justly recognize the independence of Liberia, establish that line of steamers, and thus give Africa a reinforcement of 10,000 men per annum instead of 400.

Pardon my prolixity. The subject and the occasion have compelled me to write more than I expected to. In attempting to be just to three classes, I expect to please none. While the press and our whole country is vexed and agitated on subjects pertaining to us, if I can do nothing more than provoke an inquiry among Afric-Americans, I shall have the satisfaction of hoping, at least, that I have contributed something to the interest and happiness of the citizens of the United States and the people of Africa.

AUGUSTUS WASHINGTON

Hartford, July 3, 1851

Frederick Douglass

The career of Frederick Douglass represented the depths and the heights of the career of the black American during the nineteenth century. Struggling to be a man while yet a slave; escaping to the North and joining the abolitionists; establishing his own abolitionist newspaper; securing for blacks a share in the honor of defending Union and liberty; agitating for full political and civil rights as well as freedom for blacks; and serving at last as Marshall of the District of Columbia and Minister to Haiti, Douglass more than anyone else represented the aspirations and achievements of the nineteenth century black American. He was not, of course, an "average" black or an "average" man. He was extraordinary as a political leader, as a writer and orator, as a thinker, as a human being. He was without question one of the great men of his generation.

The chief theme of Douglass' thought is that the black man is in the United States to stay. "We shall neither die out nor be driven out, but shall go with this people, either as a testimony against them, or as evidence in their favor throughout their generations." While Douglass insisted upon fundamental political and civil rights for all, he acknowledged that the United States was and, in a sense, would always be, the white man's country. The blacks were stepchildren of Abraham Lincoln and of the United States, he said in his speech at the dedication of the Freedman's Monument in Washington, D.C., one of the most profound statements ever made on the relation of blacks and whites in America. These stepchildren were, in Douglass' view, determined to remain in America, determined to make Americans live up to their own principles, and determined to fit themselves for the benefits America offered. Few men have understood the American principles, and their shocking betrayal, so well. Douglass' Fourth of July Oration in Rochester in 1852 is, in both substance and rhetoric, quite possibly the best speech of its kind ever given by a black American.

Although one of the great men of his race, Douglass was not a "race" man. His platform was the individualism of the Declaration of Independence, and he was consistent in urging the American government and society to abolish distinctions based on race and

Fourth of July Oration

• • •

This, for the purpose of this celebration, is the 4th of July. It is the birthday of your National Independence, and of your political freedom. This, to you, is what the Passover was to the emancipated people of God. It carries your minds back to the day, and to the act of your great deliverance; and to the signs, and to the wonders, associated with that act, and that day. This celebration also marks the beginning of another year of your national life; and reminds you that the Republic of America is now 76 years old. I am glad, fellow-citizens, that your nation is so young. Seventy-six years, though a good old age for a man, is but a mere speck in the life of a nation. Three score years and ten is the allotted time for individual men; but nations number their years by thousands. According

Oration Delivered in Corinthian Hall, Rochester, by Frederick Douglass, July 5, 1852. Published by Lee, Mann & Co., 1852. (Abridged)

in urging blacks to eschew "race" organizations and principles and values, except to the extent that they were forced on them by circumstances. His emphasis was on the individual—individual rights and individual duties. While demanding the removal of the external obstacles of discrimination and civil wrongs, Douglass emphasized the very great responsibility of the black to remove the inner obstacles of ignorance, sloth, and moral corruption, which enslaved and degraded too many blacks, while providing plausible justification for prejudice and discrimination.

Additional Readings: Douglass published a series of autobiographical writings during his life, the fullest of which is the *Life and Times of Frederick Douglass,* finished in 1892. The shorter *Narrative of the Life of Frederick Douglass* was first published in 1845. It covers mainly Douglass' life as a slave and is an excellent introduction to the character of Frederick Douglass and to the inner workings of slavery. The most complete collection of Douglass' writings is Philip Foner's four-volume *Life and Writings of Frederick Douglass,* now available in paperback. Carter G. Woodson's *Negro Orators and their Orations* contains much Negro thought and argument from the Douglass period.

to this fact, you are, even now only in the beginning of your national career, still lingering in the period of childhood. I repeat, I am glad this is so. There is hope in the thought, and hope is much needed, under the dark clouds which lower above the horizon. The eye of the reformer is met with angry flashes, portending disastrous times; but his heart may well beat lighter at the thought that America is young, and that she is still in the impressible stage of her existence. May he not hope that high lessons of wisdom, of justice and of truth, will yet give direction to her destiny? Were the nation older, the patriot's heart might be sadder, and the reformer's brow heavier. Its future might be shrouded in gloom, and the hope of its prophets go out in sorrow. There is consolation in the thought, that America is young.—Great streams are not easily turned from channels, worn deep in the course of ages. They may sometimes rise in quiet and stately majesty, and inundate the land, refreshing and fertilizing the earth with their mysterious properties. They may also rise in wrath and fury, and bear away, on their angry waves, the accumulated wealth of years of toil and hardship. They, however, gradually flow back to the same old channel, and flow on as serenely as ever. But, while the river may not be turned aside, it may dry up, and leave nothing behind but the withered branch, and the unsightly rock, to howl in the abyss-sweeping wind, the sad tale of departed glory. As with rivers so with nations.

. . .

Fellow Citizens, I am not wanting in respect for the fathers of this republic. The signers of the Declaration of Independence were brave men. They were great men too—great enough to give fame to a great age. It does not often happen to a nation to raise, at one time, such a number of truly great men. The point from which I am compelled to view them is not, certainly the most favorable; and yet I cannot contemplate their great deeds with less than admiration. They were statesmen, patriots and heroes, and for the good they did, and the principles they contended for, I will unite with you to honor their memory.

They loved their country better than their own private interests; and, though this is not the highest form of human excellence, all will concede that it is a rare virtue, and that when it is exhibited, it ought to command respect. He who will, intelligently, lay down his life for his country, is a man whom it is not in human nature to despise. Your fathers staked their lives, their fortunes, and their sacred honor, on the cause of their country. In their admiration of liberty, they lost sight of all other interests.

They were peace men; but they preferred revolution to peaceful submission to bondage. They were quiet men; but they did not shrink from agitating against oppression. They showed forbearance; but that they knew its limits. They believed in order; but not in the order of tyranny. With them, nothing was *"settled"* that was not right. With them, justice, liberty and humanity were *"final;"* not slavery and oppression. You may well cherish the memory of such men. They were great in their day and generation. Their solid manhood stands out the more as we contrast it with these degenerate times.

How circumspect, exact and proportionate were all their movements! How unlike the politicians of an hour! Their statesmanship looked beyond the passing moment, and stretched away in strength into the distant future. They seized upon eternal principles, and set a glorious example in their defence. Mark them!

Fully appreciating the hardships to be encountered, firmly believing in the right of their cause, honorably inviting the scrutiny of an on-looking world, reverently appealing to heaven to attest their sincerity, soundly comprehending the solemn responsibility they were about to assume, wisely measuring the terrible odds against them, your fathers, the fathers of this republic, did, most deliberately, under the inspiration of a glorious patriotism, and with a sublime faith in the great principles of justice and freedom, lay deep, the corner-stone of the national superstructure, which has risen and still rises in grandeur around you.

Of this fundamental work, this day is the anniversary. Our eyes are met with demonstrations of joyous enthusiasm. Banners and penants wave exultingly on the breeze. The din of business, too, is hushed. Even mammon seems to have quitted his grasp on this day. The ear-piercing fife and the stirring drum unite their accents with the ascending peal of a thousand church bells. Prayers are made, hymns are sung, and sermons are preached in honor of this day; while the quick martial tramp of a great and multitudinous nation, echoed back by all the hills, valleys and mountains of a vast continent, bespeak the occasion one of thrilling and universal interest—a nation's jubilee.

• • •

My business, if I have any here to-day, is with the present. The accepted time with God and his cause is the ever-living now.

> Trust no future, however pleasant,
>   Let the dead past bury its dead;
> Act, act in the living present,
>   Heart within, and God overhead.

We have to do with the past only as we can make it useful to the present and to the future. To all inspiring motives, to noble deeds which can be gained from the past, we are welcome. But now is the time, the important time. Your fathers have lived, died, and have done their work, and have done much of it well. You live and must die, and you must do your work. You have no right to enjoy a child's share in the labor of your fathers, unless your children are to be blest by your labors. You have no right to wear out and waste the hard-earned fame of your fathers to cover your indolence.

• • •

Fellow-citizens, pardon me, allow me to ask, why am I called upon to speak here to-day? What have I, or those I represent, to do with your national independence? Are the great principles of political freedom and of natural justice, embodied in that Declaration of Independence, extended to us? and am I, therefore, called upon to bring our humble offering to the national altar, and to confess the benefits and express devout gratitude for the blessings resulting from your independence to us?

Would to God, both for your sakes and ours, that an affirmative answer could be truthfully returned to these questions! Then would my task be light, and my burden easy and delightful. For *who* is there so cold, that a nation's sympathy could not warm him? Who so obdurate and dead to the claims of gratitude, that would not thankfully acknowledge such priceless benefits? Who so stolid and selfish, that would not give his voice to swell the hallelujahs of a nation's jubilee, when the chains of servitude had been torn from his limbs? I am not that man. In a case like that, the dumb might eloquently speak, and the "lame man leap as an hart."

But, such is not the state of the case. I say it with a sad sense of the disparity between us. I am not included within the pale of this glorious anniversary! ~~Your high independence only reveals the immeasurable distance between us.~~ The blessings in which you, this day, rejoice, are not enjoyed in common. — ~~The rich inheritance of justice, liberty, prosperity and independence, bequeathed by your fathers, is shared by you, not by me. The sunlight that brought life and healing to you, has brought stripes and death to me. This Fourth July is *yours*, not *mine. You may rejoice, I must mourn.~~ To drag a man in fetters into the grand illuminated temple of liberty, and call upon him to join you in joyous anthems, were inhuman mockery and sacrilegious irony. ~~Do you mean, citizens, to mock me, by asking me to speak to-day?~~ If so, there is a parallel to your conduct. And let me warn you that it is dangerous to copy the example of a nation whose crimes, towering up to heaven, were thrown down by the breath of the Almighty, burying that nation in irrecoverable ruin! I can today take up the plaintive lament of a peeled and woe-smitten people!

"By the rivers of Babylon, there we sat down. Yea! we wept when we remembered Zion. We hanged our harps upon the willows in the midst thereof. For there, they that carried us away captive, required of us a song; and they who wasted us required of us mirth, saying, Sing us one of the songs of Zion. How can we sing the Lord's song in a strange land? If I forget thee, O Jerusalem, let my right hand forget her cunning. If I do not remember thee, let my tongue cleave to the roof of my mouth."

Fellow-citizens; above your national, tumultous joy, I hear the mournful wail of millions! whose chains, heavy and grievous yesterday, are, to-day, rendered more intolerable by the jubilee shouts that reach them. If I do forget, if I do not faithfully remember those bleeding children of sorrow this day, "may my right hand forget her cunning, and may my tongue cleave to the roof of my mouth!" To forget them, to pass lightly over their wrongs, and to chime in with the popular theme, would be treason most scandalous and shocking, and would make me a reproach before God and the world. My subject, then, fellow-citizens, is AMERICAN SLAVERY. I shall see, this day, and its popular characteristics, from the slave's point of view. Standing there, identified with the American bondman, making his wrongs mine, ~~I do not hesitate to declare, with all my soul, that the character and conduct of this nation never looked blacker to me than on this 4th of July!~~ Whether we turn to the declarations of the past, or to the professions of the present, the conduct of the nation seems equally hideous and revolting. America is false to the past, false to the present, and solemnly binds herself to be false to the future. Standing with God and the crushed and bleeding slave on this occasion,

I will, in the name of humanity which is outraged, in the name of liberty which is fettered, in the name of the constitution and the Bible, which are disregarded and trampled upon, dare to call in question and to denounce, with all the emphasis I can command, everything that serves to perpetuate slavery—the great sin and shame of America! "I will not equivocate; I will not excuse;" I will use the severest language I can command; and yet not one word shall escape me that any man, whose judgment is not blinded by prejudice, or who is not at heart a slaveholder, shall not confess to be right and just.

But I fancy I hear some one of my audience say, it is just in this circumstance that you and your brother abolitionists fail to make a favorable impression on the public mind. Would you argue more, and denounce less, would you persuade more, and rebuke less, your cause would be much more likely to succeed. But, I submit, where all is plain there is nothing to be argued. What point in the anti-slavery creed would you have me argue? On what branch of the subject do the people of this country need light? Must I undertake to prove that the slave is a man? That point is conceded already. Nobody doubts it. The slaveholders themselves acknowledge it in the enactment of laws for their government. They acknowledge it when they punish disobedience on the part of the slave. There are seventy-two crimes in the State of Virginia, which, if committed by a black man (no matter how ignorant he be), subject him to the punishment of death; while only two of the same crimes will subject a white man to the like punishment.— What is this but the acknowledgement that the slave is a moral, intellectual and responsible being. The manhood of the slave is conceded. It is admitted in the fact that Southern statute books are covered with enactments forbidding, under severe fines and penalties, the teaching of the slave to read or to write.— When you can point to any such laws, in reference to the beasts of the field, then I may consent to argue the manhood of the slave. When the dogs in your streets, when the fowls of the air, when the cattle on your hills, when the fish of the sea, and the reptiles that crawl, shall be unable to distinguish the slave from a brute, *then* will I argue with you that the slave is a man!

For the present, it is enough to affirm the equal manhood of the negro race. Is it not astonishing that, while we are ploughing, planting and reaping, using all kinds of mechanical tools, erecting houses, constructing bridges, building ships, working in metals of brass, iron, copper, silver and gold; that, while we are reading, writing and cyphering, acting as clerks, merchants and secretaries, having among us lawyers, doctors, ministers, poets, authors, editors, orators and teachers; that, while we are engaged in all manner of enterprises common to other men, digging gold in California, capturing the whale in the Pacific, feeding sheep and cattle on the hill-side, living, moving, acting, thinking, planning, living in families as husbands, wives and children, and, above all, confessing and worshipping the Christian's God, and looking hopefully for life and immortality beyond the grave, we are called upon to prove that we are men!

Would you have me argue that man is entitled to liberty? that he is the rightful owner of his own body? You have already declared it. Must I argue the wrongfulness of slavery? Is that a question for Republicans? Is it to be settled by the rules of logic and argumentation, as a matter beset with great difficulty, involving a doubtful application of the principle of justice, hard to be understood? How should I look to-day, in the presence of Americans, dividing, and subdividing a discourse, to show that men have a natural right to freedom? speaking of it relatively, and positively, negatively, and affirmatively. To do so, would be to make myself ridiculous, and to offer an insult to your understanding.— There is not a man beneath the canopy of heaven, that does not know that slavery is wrong *for him.*

What, am I to argue that it is wrong to make men brutes, to rob them of their liberty, to work them without wages, to keep them ignorant of their relations to their fellow men, to beat them with sticks, to flay their flesh with the lash, to load their limbs with irons, to hunt them with dogs, to sell them at auction, to sunder their families, to knock out their teeth, to burn their flesh, to starve them into obedience and submission to their masters? Must I argue that a system thus marked with blood, and stained with pollution, is *wrong?* No! I will not. I have better employment for my time and strength, than such arguments would imply.

What, then, remains to be argued? Is it that slavery is not divine; that God did not establish it; that our doctors of divinity are mistaken? There is blasphemy in the thought. That which is inhuman, cannot be divine! *Who* can reason on such a proposition? They that can, may; I cannot. The time for such argument is past.

At a time like this, scorching irony, not convincing argument, is needed. O! had I the ability, and could I reach the nation's ear, I would, to-day, pour out a fiery stream of biting ridicule, blasting reproach, withering sarcasm, and stern rebuke. For it is not light that is needed, but fire; it is not the gentle shower, but thunder. We need the storm, the whirlwind, and the earthquake. The feeling of the nation must be quickened; the conscience of the nation must be roused; the propriety of the nation must be startled; the hypocrisy of the nation must be exposed; and its crimes against God and man must be proclaimed and denounced.

What, to the American slave, is your 4th of July? I answer; a day that reveals to him, more than all other days in the year, the gross injustice and cruelty to which he is the constant victim. To him, your celebration is a sham; your boasted liberty, an unholy license; your national greatness, swelling vanity; your sounds of rejoicing are empty and heartless; your denunciations of tyrants, brass fronted impudence; your shouts of liberty and equality, hollow mockery; your prayers and hymns, your sermons and thanksgivings, with all your religious parade, and solemnity, are, to him, mere bombast, fraud, deception, impiety, and hypocrisy—a thin veil to cover up crimes which would disgrace a nation of savages. There is not a nation on the earth guilty of practices, more shocking and bloody, than are the people of these United States, at this very hour.

Go where you may, search where you will, roam through all the monarchies and despotisms of the old world, travel through South America, search out every abuse, and when you have found the last, lay your facts by the side of the every day practices of this nation, and you will say with me, that, for revolting barbarity and shameless hypocrisy, America reigns without a rival.

. . .

Americans! your republican politics, not less than your republican religion, are flagrantly inconsistent. You boast of your love of liberty, your superior civilization, and your pure christianity, while the whole political power of the nation, as embodied in the two great political parties, is solemnly pledged to support and perpetuate the enslavement of three millions of your countrymen. You hurl your anathemas at the crowned headed tyrants of Russia and Austria, and pride yourselves on your Democratic institutions, while you yourselves consent to be the mere *tools* and *body-guards* of the tyrants of Virginia and Carolina. You invite to your shores fugitives of oppression from abroad, honor them with banquets, greet them with ovations, cheer them, toast them, salute them, protect them, and pour out your money to them like water; but the fugitives from your own land, you advertise, hunt, arrest, shoot and kill. You glory in your refinement, and your universal education; yet you maintain a system as barbarous and dreadful, as ever stained the character of a nation—a system begun in avarice, supported in pride, and perpetuated in cruelty. You shed tears over fallen Hungary, and make the sad story of her wrongs the theme of your poets, statesmen and orators, till your gallant sons are ready to fly to arms to vindicate her cause against her oppressors; but, in regard to the ten thousand wrongs of the American slave, you would enforce the strictest silence, and would hail him as an enemy of the nation who dares to make those wrongs the subject of public discourse! You are all on fire at the mention of liberty for France or for Ireland; but are as cold as an iceberg at the thought of liberty for the enslaved of America.—You discourse eloquently on the dignity of labor; yet, you sustain a system which, in its very essence, casts a stigma upon labor. You can bare your bosom to the storm of British artillery, to throw off a three-penny tax on tea; and yet wring the last hard earned farthing from the grasp of the black laborers of your country. You profess to believe "that, of one blood, God made all nations of men to dwell on the face of all the earth," and hath commanded all men, everywhere to love one another; yet you notoriously hate, (and glory in your hatred,) all men whose skins are not colored like your own. You declare, before the world, and are understood by the world to declare, that you *"hold these truths to be self evident, that all men are created equal; and are endowed by their Creator with certain inalienable rights; and that, among these are, life, liberty, and the pursuit of happiness;"* and yet, you hold securely, in a bondage, which according to your own Thomas Jefferson, *"is worse than ages of that which your fathers rose in rebellion to oppose,"* a seventh part of the inhabitants of your country.

Fellow-citizens! I will not enlarge further on your national inconsistencies. The existence of slavery in this country brands your republicanism as a sham, your humanity as a base pretence, and your christianity as a lie. It destroys your moral power abroad [;] it corrupts your politicians at home. It saps the foundation of religion; it makes your name a hissing, and a bye-word to a mocking earth. It is the antagonistic force in your government, the only thing that seriously disturbs and endangers your *Union.* It fetters your progress; it is the enemy of improvement, the deadly foe of education; it fosters pride; it breeds insolence; it promotes vice; it shelters crime; it is a curse to the earth that supports it; and yet, you cling to it, as if it were the sheet anchor of all your hopes. Oh! be warned! be warned! a horrible reptile is coiled up in your nation's bosom; the venomous creature is nursing at the tender breast of your youthful republic; *for the love of God, tear away,* and fling from you the hidious monster, and *let the weight of twenty millions, crush and destroy it forever!*

But it is answered in reply to all this, that precisely what I have now denounced is, in fact, guaranteed and sanctioned by the Constitution of the United States; that, the right to hold, and to hunt slaves is a part of that Constitution framed by the illustrious Fathers of this Republic.

Then, I dare to affirm, notwithstanding all I have said before, your fathers stooped, basely stooped

> To palter with us in a double sense:
> And keep the word of promise to the ear,
> But break it to the heart.

And instead of being the honest men I have before declared them to be, they were the veriest imposters that ever practised on mankind. *This* is the inevitable conclusion, and from it there is no escape; but I differ from those who charge this baseness on the framers of the Constitution of the United States. *It is a slander upon their memory,* at least, so I believe. There is not time now to argue the constitutional question at length; nor have I the ability to discuss it as it ought to be discussed. The subject has been handled with masterly power by Lysander Spooner, Esq., by William Goodell, by Samuel E. Sewall, Esq., and last, though not least, by Gerritt Smith, Esq. These gentlemen have, as I think, fully and clearly vindicated the Constitution from any design to support slavery for an hour.

Fellow-citizens! there is no matter in respect to which, the people of the North have allowed themselves to be so ruinously imposed upon, as that of the pro-slavery character of the Constitution. In *that* instrument I hold there is neither warrant, license, nor sanction of the hateful thing; but interpreted, as it *ought* to be interpreted, the Constitution is a GLORIOUS LIBERTY DOCUMENT. Read its preamble, consider its purposes. Is slavery among them? Is it at the gateway? or is it in the temple? it is neither. While I do not intend to argue this question on the present occasion, let me ask, if it be not somewhat singular that, if the Constitution were intended to be, by its framers and adopters, a slaveholding instrument, why neither *slavery, slaveholding,* nor *slave* can anywhere be found in it. What would be thought of an instrument, drawn up, *legally* drawn up, for the purpose of entitling the city of Rochester to a track of land, in which no mention of land was made? Now, there are certain rules of interpretation, for the proper understanding of all legal instruments. These rules are well established. They are plain, common-sense rules, such as you and I, and all of us, can understand and apply, without having passed years in the study of law. I scout the idea that the question of the constitutionality, or unconstitutionality of slavery, is not a question for the people. I hold that every American citizen has a right to form an opinion of the constitution, and to propagate that opinion, and to use all honorable means to make his opinion the prevailing one. Without this right, the liberty of an American citizen would be as insecure as that of a Frenchman. Ex-Vice-President Dallas tells us that the constitution is an object to which no American mind can be too attentive, and no American heart too devoted. He further says, the constitution, in its words, is plain and intelligible, and is meant for the home-bred, unsophisticated understandings of our fellow-citizens. Senator Berrien tells us that the Constitution is the fundamental law, that which controls all others. The charter of our liberties, which every citizen has a personal interest in understanding thoroughly. The testimony of Senator Breese, Lewis Cass, and many others that might be named, who are everywhere esteemed as sound lawyers, so regard the constitution. I take it, therefore, that it is not presumption in a private citizen to form an opinion of that instrument.

Now, take the constitution according to its plain reading, and I defy the presentation of a single pro-slavery clause in it. On the other hand it will be found to contain principles and purposes, entirely hostile to the existence of slavery.

I have detained my audience entirely too long already. At some future period I will gladly avail myself of an opportunity to give this subject a full and fair discussion.

Allow me to say, in conclusion, notwithstanding the dark picture I have this day presented, of the state of the nation, I do not despair of this country. There are forces in operation, which must inevitably, work the downfall of slavery. *"The arm of the Lord is not shortened,"* and the doom of slavery is certain. I, therefore, leave off where I began, with *hope.* While drawing encouragement from "the Declaration of Independence," the great principles it contains, and the genius of American Institutions, my spirit is also cheered by the obvious tendencies of the age. Nations do not now stand in the same relation to each other that they did ages ago. No nation can now shut itself up, from the surrounding world, and trot round in the same old path of its fathers without interference. The time *was* when such could be done. Long established customs of hurtful character could formerly fence themselves in, and do their evil work with social impunity. Knowledge was then confined and enjoyed by the privileged few, and the multitude walked on in mental darkness. But a change has now come over the affairs of mankind. Walled cities and empires have become unfashionable. The arm of commerce has borne away the gates of the strong city. Intelligence is penetrating the darkest corners of the globe. It makes its pathway over and under the sea, as well as on the earth. Wind, steam, and lightning are its chartered agents. Oceans no longer divide, but link nations together. From Boston to London is now a holiday excursion. Space is comparatively annihilated. — Thoughts expressed on one side of the Atlantic, are distinctly heard on the other.

The far off and almost fabulous Pacific rolls in grandeur at our feet. The Celestial Empire, the mystery of ages, is being solved. The fiat of the Almighty, *"Let there be Light,"* has not yet spent its force. No abuse, no outrage whether in taste, sport or avarice, can now hide itself from the all-pervading light. The iron shoe, and crippled foot of China must be seen, in contrast with nature. *Africa must rise and put on her yet unwoven garment. "Ethiopia shall stretch out her hand unto God."* . . .

The Destiny of Colored Americans

It is impossible to settle, by the light of the present, and by the experience of the past, any thing, definitely and absolutely, as to the future condition of the colored people of this country; but, so far as present indications determine, it is clear that this land must continue to be the home of the colored man so long as it remains the abode of civilization and religion. For more than two hundred years we have been identified with its soil, its products, and its institutions; under the sternest and bitterest circumstances of slavery and oppression—under the lash of Slavery at the South—under the sting of prejudice and malice at the North—and under hardships the most unfavorable to existence and population, we have lived, and continue to live and increase. The persecuted red man of the forest, the original owner of the soil, has, step by step, retreated from the Atlantic lakes and rivers; escaping, as it were, before the footsteps of the white man, and gradually disappearing from the face of the country. He looks upon the steamboats, the railroads, and canals, cutting and crossing his former hunting grounds; and upon the ploughshare, throwing up the bones of his venerable ancestors, and beholds his glory departing—and his heart sickens at the desolation. He spurns the civilization—he hates the race which has despoiled him, and unable to measure arms with his superior foe, he dies.

Not so with the black man. More unlike the European in form, feature and color—called to endure greater hardships, injuries and insults than those to which the Indians have been subjected, he yet lives and prospers under every disadvantage. Long have his enemies sought to expatriate him, and to teach his children that this is not their home, but in spite of all their cunning schemes, and subtle contrivances, his footprints yet mark the soil of his birth, and he gives every indication that America will, for ever, remain the home of his posterity. We deem it a settled point that the destiny of the colored man is bound up with that of the white people of this country; be the destiny of the latter what it may.

It is idle—worse than idle, ever to think of our expatriation, or removal. The history of the colonization society must extinguish all such speculations. We are rapidly filling up the number of four millions; and all the gold of California combined, would be insufficient to defray the expenses attending our colonization. We are, as laborers, too essential to

From *The North Star,* November 16, 1849.

the interests of our white fellow-countrymen, to make a very grand effort to drive us from this country among probable events. While labor is needed, the laborer cannot fail to be valued; and although passion and prejudice may sometimes vociferate against us, and demand our expulsion, such efforts will only be spasmodic, and can never prevail against the sober second thought of self-interest. *We are here,* and here we are likely to be. To imagine that we shall ever be eradicated is absurd and ridiculous. We can be remodified, changed, and assimilated, but never extinguished. We repeat, therefore, that *we are here;* and that this is *our* country; and the question for the philosophers and statesmen of the land ought to be, What principles should dicate the policy of the action towards us? We shall neither die out, nor be driven out; but shall go with this people, either as a testimony against them, or as an evidence in their favor throughout their generations. We are clearly on their hands, and must remain there for ever. All this we say for the benefit of those who hate the negro more than they love their country. In an article, under the caption of "Government and its Subjects," (published in our last week's paper,) we called attention to the unwise, as well as the unjust policy usually adopted, by our Government, towards its colored citizens. We would continue to direct attention to that policy, and in our humble way, we would remonstrate against it, as fraught with evil to the white man, as well as to his victim.

The white man's happiness cannot be purchased by the black man's misery. Virtue cannot prevail among the white people, by its destruction among the black people, who form a part of the whole community. It is evident that white and black "must fall or flourish together." In the light of this great truth, laws ought to be enacted, and institutions established — all distinctions, founded on complexion, ought to be repealed, repudiated, and for ever abolished — and every right, privilege, and immunity, now enjoyed by the white man, ought to be as freely granted to the man of color.

Where "knowledge is power," that nation is the most powerful which has the largest population of intelligent men; for a nation to cramp, and circumscribe the mental faculties of a class of its inhabitants, is as unwise as it is cruel, since it, in the same proportion, sacrifices its power and happiness. The American people, in the light of this reasoning, are, at this moment, in obedience to their pride and folly, (we say nothing of the wickedness of the act,) wasting one sixth part of the energies of the entire nation by transforming three millions of its men into beasts of burden. — What a loss to industry, skill, invention, (to say nothing of its foul and corrupting influence,) is *Slavery!* How it ties the hand, cramps the mind, darkens the understanding, and paralyses the whole man! Nothing is more evident to a man who reasons at all, than that America is acting an irrational part in continuing the slave system at the South, and in oppressing its free colored citizens at the North. Regarding the nation as an individual, the act of enslaving and oppressing thus, is as wild and senseless as it would be for Nicholas to order the amputation of the right arm of every Russian soldier before engaging in a war with France. We again repeat that Slavery is the peculiar weakness of America, as well as its peculiar crime; and the day may yet come when this visionary and oft repeated declaration will be found to contain a great truth.

What are the Colored People Doing for Themselves?

The present is a time when every colored man in the land should bring this important question home to his own heart. It is not enough to know that white men and women are nobly devoting themselves to our cause; we should know what is being done among ourselves. That our white friends have done, and are still doing, a great and good work for us, is a fact which ought to excite in us sentiments of the profoundest gratitude; but it must never be forgotten that when they have exerted all their energies, devised every scheme, and done all they can do in asserting our rights, proclaiming our wrongs, and rebuking our foes, their labor is lost—yea, worse than lost, unless we are found in the faithful discharge of our anti-slavery duties. If there be one evil spirit among us, for the casting out of which we pray more earnestly than another, it is that lazy, mean and cowardly spirit, that robs us of all manly self-reliance, and teaches us to depend upon others for the accomplishment of that which we should achieve with our own hands. Our white friends can and are rapidly removing the barriers to our improvement, which themselves have set up; but the main work must be commenced, carried on, and concluded by ourselves. While in no circumstances should we undervalue or fail to appreciate the self-sacrificing efforts of our friends, it should never be lost sight of, that our destiny, for good or for evil, for time and for eternity, is, by an all-wise God, committed to us; and that all the helps or hindrances with which we may meet on earth, can never release us from this high and heaven-imposed responsibility. It is evident that we can be improved and elevated only just so fast and far as we shall improve and elevate ourselves. We must rise or fall, succeed or

From *The North Star*, July 14, 1848.

fail, by our own merits. If we are careless and unconcerned about our own rights and interests, it is not within the power of all the earth combined to raise us from our present degraded condition.

> Hereditary bondmen, know ye not
> Who would be free, themselves must strike the blow?

We say the present is a time when every colored man should ask himself the question, What am I doing to elevate and improve my condition, and that of my brethren at large? While the oppressed of the old world are making efforts, by holding public meetings, putting forth addresses, passing resolutions, and in various other ways making their wishes known to the world, and the working men of our own country are pressing their cause upon popular attention, it is a shame that we, who are enduring wrongs far more grievous than any other portion of the great family of man, are comparatively idle and indifferent about our welfare. We confess, with the deepest mortification, that out of the five hundred thousand free colored people in this country, not more than two thousand can be supposed to take any special interest in measures for our own elevation; and probably not more than fifteen hundred take, read and pay for an anti-slavery paper. We say this in sorrow, not in anger. It cannot be said that we are too poor to patronize our own press to any greater extent than we now do; for in popular demonstrations of odd-fellowship, free-masonry and the like, we expend annually from ten to twelve thousand dollars. If we put forth a call for a National Convention, for the purpose of considering our wrongs, and asserting our rights, and adopting measures for our mutual elevation and the emancipation of our enslaved fellow-countrymen, we shall bring together about *fifty*; but if we call a grand celebration of odd-fellowship, or free-masonry, we shall assemble, as was the case a few days ago in New York, from *four to five thousand* — the expense of which alone would be from seventeen to twenty thousand dollars, a sum sufficient to maintain four or five efficient presses, devoted to our elevation and improvement. We should not say this of odd-fellowship and free-masonry, but that it is swallowing up the best energies of many of our best men, contenting them with the glittering follies of artificial display, and indisposing them to seek for solid and important realities. The enemies of our people see this tendency in us, and encourage it. The same persons who would puff such demonstrations in the newspapers, would mob us if we met to adopt measures for obtaining our just rights. They see our weak points, and avail themselves of them to crush us. We are imitating the inferior qualities and examples of white men, and neglecting superior ones. We do not pretend that all the members of odd-fellow societies and masonic lodges are indifferent to their rights and the means of obtaining them; for we know the fact to be otherwise. Some of the best and brightest among us are numbered with those societies; and it is on this account that we make these remarks. We desire to see these noble men expending their time, talents and strength for higher and nobler objects than any that can be attained by the weak and glittering follies of odd-fellowship and free-masonry.

We speak plainly on this point, for we feel deeply. We have dedicated ourself, heart and soul, without reserve, to the elevation and improve-ment of our race, and have resolved to sink or swim with them. Our inmost soul is fired with a sense of the various forms of injustice to which we are daily subjected, and we must and will speak out against any-thing, within ourselves or our guilty oppressors, which may tend to pro-long this reign of injustice. To be faithful to our oppressors, we must be faithful to ourselves; and shame on any colored man who would have us do otherwise. For this very purpose the North Star was established— that it might be as faithful to ourselves as to our oppressors. In this re-spect, we intend that it shall be different from most of its predecessors, and if it cannot be sustained in its high position, its death will be wel-comed by us. But to return.

It is a doctrine held by many good men, in Europe as well as in Amer-ica, that every oppressed people will gain their rights just as soon as they prove themselves worthy of them; and although we may justly object to the extent to which this doctrine is carried, especially in reference to ourselves as a people, it must still be evident to all that there is a great truth in it.

One of the first things necessary to prove the colored man worthy of equal freedom, is an earnest and persevering effort on his part to gain it. We deserve no earthly or heavenly blessing, for which we are unwilling to labor. For our part, we despise a freedom and equality obtained for us by others, and for which we have been unwilling to labor. A man who will not labor to gain his rights, is a man who would not, if he had them, prize and defend them. What is the use of standing a man on his feet, if, when we let him go, his head is again brought to the pavement? Look out of ourselves as we will—beg and pray to our white friends for assist-ance as much as we will—and that assistance may come, and come at the needed time; but unless we, the colored people of America, shall set about the work of our own regeneration and improvement, we are doomed to drag on in our present miserable and degraded condition for ages. Would that we could speak to every colored man, woman and child in the land, and, with the help of Heaven, we would thunder into their ears their duties and responsibilities, until a spirit should be roused among them, never to be lulled till the last chain is broken.—But here we are mortified to think that we are now speaking to tens where we ought to speak to thousands. Unfortunately, those who have the ear of our people on Sundays, have little sympathy with the anti-slavery cause, or the cause of progress in any of its phases. ~~They are too frequently disposed to follow the beaten paths of their fathers.~~ — The most they aim at, ~~is to get to heaven when they die.~~ They reason thus: Our fathers got along pretty well through the world without learning and without meddling with abolitionism, and we can do the same. — We have in our minds three pulpits among the colored people in the North, which have the power to produce a revolution in the condition of the colored people in this country in three years.

First among these, we may mention the great Bethel Church in Philadelphia. That church is the largest colored church in this Union, and from two to three thousand persons worship there every Sabbath. It has its branches in nearly all parts of the North and West, and a few in the South. It is surrounded by numerous little congregations in Philadelphia. Its ministers and bishops travel in all directions, and vast numbers of colored people belong to its branches all over the country. The Bethel pulpit in Philadelphia may be said to give tone to the entire denomination—"as goes large Bethel, so go the small Bethels throughout the Union." Here is concentrated the talent of the church, and here is the central and ruling power. — Now, if that pulpit would but speak the right word—the word for progress—the word for mental culture—encourage reading, and would occasionally take up contributions to aid those who are laboring for their elevation, as the white churches do to aid the colonization society to send us out of the country—there is no telling the good that would result from such labors. An entire change might soon take place in that denomination; loftier views of truth and duty would be presented; a nobler destiny would be opened up to them, and a deeper happiness would at once be enjoyed through all the ramifications of that church.

Similarly situated is the "Zion Church" in New York. That church exerts a controlling influence over the next largest colored denomination in this country. It, too, is a unit—has its branches in all directions in the North rather than in the South. Its ministers are zealous men, and some of them powerful preachers. There is no estimating the good these men might do, if they would only encourage their congregations to take an interest in the subject of reform.

The next church in importance, is St. Phillip's, in New York. This church is more important on account of the talent and respectability which it comprises, than for its numbers. Now, could the influence of these churches be enlisted in exciting our people to a constant and persevering effort at self-elevation, a joyful change would soon come over us.

What we, the colored people, want, is *character,* and this nobody can give us. It is a thing we must get for ourselves. We must labor for it. It is gained by toil—hard toil. Neither the sympathy nor the generosity of our friends can give it to us. It is attainable—yes, thank God, it is attainable. "There is gold in the earth, but we must dig it"—so with character. It is attainable; but we must attain it, and attain it each for himself. I cannot for you, and you cannot for me.—What matters it to the mass of colored people of this country that they are able to point to their Peningtons, Garnets, Remonds, Wards, Purvises, Smiths, Whippers, Sandersons, and a respectable list of other men of character, which we might name, while our general ignorance makes these men exceptions to our race? Their talents can do little to give us character in the eyes of the world. We must get character for ourselves, as a people. A change in our political condition would do very little for us without this. Character is the important thing, and without it we must continue to be marked for degradation and stamped with the brand of inferiority. With character, we shall be powerful. Nothing can harm us long when we get character.—There are certain great elements of character in us which may be hated, but never despised. Industry, sobriety, honesty, combined with intelligence and a due self-respect, find them where you will, among black or white, must be *looked up to*—can never be *looked down upon*. In their presence, prejudice is abashed, confused and mortified. Encountering this solid mass of living character, our vile oppressors are ground to atoms. In its presence, the sneers of a caricaturing press, the taunts of natural inferiority, the mischievous assertions of Clay, and fine-spun sophisms of Calhoun, are innoxious, powerless and unavailing. In answer to these men and the sneers of the multitude, there is nothing in the wide world half so effective as the presentation of a character precisely the opposite of all their representations. We have it in our power to convert the weapons intended for our injury into positive blessings. That we may sustain temporary injury from gross and general misrepresentation, is most true; but the injury is but temporary, and must disappear at the approach of light, like mist from the vale. The offensive traits of character imputed to us, can only be injurious while they are true of us. For a man to say that sweet is bitter—that right is wrong—that light is darkness—is not to injure the truth, but to stamp himself a liar; and the like is true when they impute to us that of which we are not guilty. We have the power of making our enemies slanderers, and this we must do by showing ourselves worthy and respectable men.

We are not insensible to the various obstacles that throng the colored man's pathway to respectability. Embarrassments and perplexities, unknown to other men, are common to us. Though born on American soil, we have fewer privileges than aliens. The school-house, the work-shop, counting-house, attorney's office, and various professions, are opened to them, but closed to us. This, and much more, is true. A general and withering prejudice—a malignant and active hate, pursues us even in the best parts of this country. But a few days ago, one of our best and most talented men—and he a *lame man*, having lost an important limb—was furiously hurled from a car on the Niagara & Buffalo Railroad, by a band of white ruffians, who claim impunity for their atrocious outrage on the plea that New York law does not protect the rights of colored against a company of white men, and the sequel has proved them right; for the case, it appears, was brought before the grand jury, but that jury found no bill. We cannot at this time dwell on this aspect of the subject.

The fact that we are limited and circumscribed, ought rather to incite us to a more vigorous and persevering use of the elevating means within our reach, than to dishearten us. The means of education, though not so free and open to us as to white persons, are nevertheless at our command to such an extent as to make education possible; and these, thank God, are increasing. Let us educate our children, even though it should us subject to a coarser and scantier diet, and disrobe us of our few fine garments. "For the want of knowledge we are killed all the day." Get wisdom — get understanding, is a peculiarly valuable exhortation to us, and the compliance with it is our only hope in this land. — It is idle, a hollow mockery, for us to pray to God to break the oppressor's power, while we neglect the means of knowledge which will give us the ability to break this power. — God will help us when we help ourselves. Our oppressors have divested us of many valuable blessings and facilities for improvement and elevation; but, thank heaven, they have not yet been able to take from us the privilege of being honest, industrious, sober and intelligent. We may read and understand — we may speak and write — we may expose our wrongs — we may appeal to the sense of justice yet alive in the public mind, and by an honest, upright life, we may at last wring from a reluctant public the all-important confession, that we are men, worthy men, good citizens, good Christians, and ought to be treated as such.

Oration in Memory of Abraham Lincoln

Friends and Fellow-citizens:

I warmly congratulate you upon the highly interesting object which has caused you to assemble in such numbers and spirit as you have to-

From *Oration by Frederick Douglass delivered on the occasion of the unveiling of the Freedmen's Monument in memory of Abraham Lincoln,* in Lincoln Park, Washington, D.C., April 14, 1876. Gibson Brothers, Printers, 1876.

day. This occasion is in some respects remarkable. Wise and thoughtful men of our race, who shall come after us, and study the lesson of our history in the United States; who shall survey the long and dreary spaces over which we have traveled; who shall count the links in the great chain of events by which we have reached our present position, will make a note of this occasion; they will think of it and speak of it with a sense of manly pride and complacency.

I congratulate you, also, upon the very favorable circumstances in which we meet to-day. They are high, inspiring, and uncommon. They lend grace, glory, and significance to the object for which we have met. Nowhere else in this great country, with its uncounted towns and cities, unlimited wealth, and immeasurable territory extending from sea to sea, could conditions be found more favorable to the success of this occasion than here.

We stand to-day at the national centre to perform something like a national act—an act which is to go into history; and we are here where every pulsation of the national heart can be heard, felt, and reciprocated. A thousand wires, fed with thought and winged with lightning, put us in instantaneous communication with the loyal and true men all over this country.

Few facts could better illustrate the vast and wonderful change which has taken place in our condition as a people than the fact of our assembling here for the purpose we have to-day. Harmless, beautiful, proper, and praiseworthy as this demonstration is, I cannot forget that no such demonstration would have been tolerated here twenty years ago. The spirit of slavery and barbarism, which still lingers to blight and destroy in some dark and distant parts of our country, would have made our assembling here the signal and excuse for opening upon us all the flood-gates of wrath and violence. That we are here in peace to-day is a compliment and a credit to American civilization, and a prophecy of still greater national enlightenment and progress in the future. I refer to the past not in malice, for this is no day for malice; but simply to place more distinctly in front the gratifying and glorious change which has come both to our white fellow-citizens and ourselves, and to congratulate all upon the contrast between now and then; the new dispensation of freedom with its thousand blessings to both races, and the old dispensation of slavery with its ten thousand evils to both races—white and black. In view, then, of the past, the present, and the future, with the long and dark history of our bondage behind us, and with liberty, progress, and enlightenment before us, I again congratulate you upon this auspicious day and hour.

Friends and fellow-citizens, the story of our presence here is soon and easily told. We are here in the District of Columbia, here in the city of Washington, the most luminous point of American territory; a city recently transformed and made beautiful in its body and in its spirit; we are here in the place where the ablest and best men of the country are sent to devise the policy, enact the laws, and shape the destiny of the Republic; we are here, with the stately pillars and majestic dome of the Capitol of the nation looking down upon us; we are here, with the broad earth freshly adorned with the foliage and flowers of spring for our church, and all races, colors, and conditions of men for our congregation—in a word, we are here to express, as best we may, by appropriate forms and ceremonies, our grateful sense of the vast, high, and pre-eminent services rendered tc ourselves, to our race, to our country, and to the whole world by Abraham Lincoln.

The sentiment that brings us here to-day is one of the noblest that can stir and thrill the human heart. It has crowned and made glorious the high places of all civilized nations with the grandest and most enduring works of art, designed to illustrate the characters and perpetuate the memories of great public men. It is the sentiment which from year to year adorns with fragrant and beautiful flowers the graves of our loyal, brave, and patriotic soldiers who fell in defence of the Union and liberty. It is the sentiment of gratitude and appreciation, which often, in the presence of many who hear me, has filled yonder heights of Arlington with the eloquence of eulogy and the sublime enthusiasm of poetry and song; a sentiment which can never die while the Republic lives.

For the first time in the history of our people, and in the history of the whole American people, we join in this high worship, and march conspicuously in the line of this time-honored custom. First things are always interesting, and this is one of our first things. It is the first time that, in this form and manner, we have sought to do honor to an American great man, however deserving and illustrious. I commend the fact to notice; let it be told in every part of the Republic; let men of all parties and opinions hear it; let those who despise us, not less than those who respect us, know that now and here, in the spirit of liberty, loyalty, and gratitude, let it be known everywhere, and by everybody who takes an interest in human progress and in the amelioration of the condition of mankind, that, in the presence and with the approval of the members of the American House of Representatives, reflecting the general sentiment of the country; that in the presence of that august body, the American Senate, representing the highest intelligence and the calmest judgment of the country; in the presence of the Supreme Court and Chief-Justice of the United States, to whose decisions we all patriotically bow; in the presence and under the steady eye of the honored and trusted President of the United States, with the members of his wise and patriotic Cabinet, we, the colored people, newly emancipated and rejoicing in our blood-bought freedom, near the close of the first century in the life of this Republic, have now and here unveiled, set apart, and dedicated a monument of enduring granite and bronze, in every line, feature, and figure of which the men of this generation may read, and those of after-coming generations may read, something of the exalted character and great works of Abraham Lincoln, the first martyr President of the United States.

Fellow-citizens, in what we have said and done to-day, and in what we may say and do hereafter, we disclaim everything like arrogance and assumption. We claim for ourselves no superior devotion to the character, history, and memory of the illustrious name whose monument we have here dedicated to-day. We fully comprehend the relation of Abraham Lincoln both to ourselves and to the white people of the United States. Truth is proper and beautiful at all times and in all places, and it is never more proper and beautiful in any case than when speaking of a great public man whose example is likely to be commended for honor and imitation long after his departure to the solemn shades, the silent continents of eternity. It must be admitted, truth compels me to admit, even here in the presence of the monument we have erected to his memory, Abraham Lincoln was not, in the fullest sense of the word, either our man or our model. In his interests, in his associations, in his habits of thought, and in his prejudices, he was a white man.

He was pre-eminently the white man's President, entirely devoted to the welfare of white men. He was ready and willing at any time during the first years of his administration to deny, postpone, and sacrifice the rights of humanity in the colored people to promote the welfare of the white people of this country. In all his education and feeling he was an American of the Americans. He came into the Presidential chair upon one principle alone, namely, opposition to the extension of slavery. His arguments in furtherance of this policy had their motive and mainspring in his patriotic devotion to the interests of his own race. To protect, defend, and perpetuate slavery in the states where it existed Abraham Lincoln was not less ready than any other President to draw the sword of the nation. He was ready to execute all the supposed guarantees of the United States Constitution in favor of the slave system anywhere inside the slave States. He was willing to pursue, recapture, and send back the fugitive slave to his master, and to suppress a slave rising for liberty, though his guilty master were already in arms against the Government. The race to which we belong were not the special objects of his consideration. Knowing this, I concede to you, my white fellow-citizens, a pre-eminence in this worship at once full and supreme. First, midst, and last, you and yours were the objects of his deepest affection and his most earnest solicitude. You are the children of Abraham Lincoln. We are at best only his step-children; children by adoption, children by force of circumstances and necessity. To you it especially belongs to sound his praises, to preserve and perpetuate his memory, to multiply his statues, to hang his pictures high upon your walls, and commend his example, for to you he was a great and glorious friend and benefactor. Instead of supplanting you at his altar, we would exhort you to build high his monuments; let them be of the most costly material, of the most cunning workmanship; let their forms be symmetrical, beautiful, and perfect; let their bases be upon solid rocks, and their summits lean against the unchanging blue, overhanging sky, and let them endure forever! But while in the abundance of your wealth, and in the fullness of your just and patriotic devotion, you do all this, we entreat you to despise not the humble offering we this day unveil to view; for while Abraham Lincoln saved for you a country, he delivered us from a bondage, according to Jefferson, one hour of which was worse than ages of the oppression your fathers rose in rebellion to oppose.

Fellow-citizens, ours is no new-born zeal and devotion—merely a thing of this moment. The name of Abraham Lincoln was near and dear to our hearts in the darkest and most perilous hours of the Republic. We were no more ashamed of him when shrouded in clouds of darkness, of doubt, and defeat than when we saw him crowned with victory, honor, and glory. Our faith in him was often taxed and strained to the uttermost, but it never failed. When he tarried long in the mountain; when he strangely told us that we were the cause of the war; when he still more strangely told us to leave the land in which we were born; when he refused to employ our arms in defence of the Union; when, after accepting our services as colored soldiers, he refused to retaliate our murder and torture as colored prisoners; when he told us he would save the Union if he could with slavery; when he revoked the Proclamation of Emancipation of General Fremont; when he refused to remove the popular commander of the Army of the Potomac, in the days of its inaction and defeat, who was more zealous in his efforts to protect slavery than to suppress rebellion; when we saw all this, and more, we were at times grieved, stunned, and greatly bewildered; but our hearts believed while they ached and bled. Nor was this, even at that time, a blind and unreasoning superstition. Despite the mist and haze that surrounded him; despite the tumult, the hurry, and confusion of the hour, we were able to take a comprehensive view of Abraham Lincoln, and to make reasonable allowance for the circumstances of his position. We saw him, measured him, and estimated him; not by stray utterances to injudicious and tedious delegations, who often tried his patience; not by isolated facts torn from their connection; not by any partial and imperfect glimpses, caught at inopportune moments; but by a broad survey, in the light of the stern logic of great events, and in view of that divinity which shapes our ends, rough hew them how we will, we came to the conclusion that the hour and the man of our redemption had somehow met in the person of Abraham Lincoln. It mattered little to us what language he might employ on special occasions; it mattered little to us, when we fully knew him, whether he was swift or slow in his movements; it was enough for us that Abraham Lincoln was at the head of a great movement, and was in living and earnest sympathy with that movement, which, in the nature of things, must go on until slavery should be utterly and forever abolished in the United States.

When, therefore, it shall be asked what we have to do with the memory of Abraham Lincoln, or what Abraham Lincoln had to do with us, the answer is ready, full, and complete. Though he loved Caesar less than Rome, though the Union was more to him than our freedom or our future, under his wise and beneficent rule we saw ourselves gradually lifted from the depths of slavery to the heights of liberty and manhood; under his wise and beneficent rule, and by measures approved and vigorously pressed by him, we saw that the handwriting of ages, in the form of prejudice and proscription, was rapidly fading away from the face of our whole country; under his rule, and in due time, about as soon after all as the country could tolerate the strange spectacle, we saw our brave sons and brothers laying off the rags of bondage, and being clothed all over in the blue uniforms of the soldiers of the United States; under his rule we saw two hundred thousand of our dark and dusky people responding to the call of Abraham Lincoln, and with muskets on their shoulders, and eagles on their buttons, timing their high footsteps to liberty and union under the national flag; under his rule we saw the independence of the black republic of Hayti, the special object of slaveholding aversion and horror, fully recognized, and her minister, a colored gentleman, duly received here in the city of Washington; under his rule we saw the internal slave-trade, which so long disgraced the nation, abolished, and slavery abolished in the District of Columbia; under his rule we saw for the first time the law enforced against the foreign slave-trade, and the first slave-trader hanged like any other pirate or murderer; under his rule, assisted by the greatest captain of our age, and his inspiration, we saw the Confederate States, based upon the idea that our race must be slaves, and slaves forever, battered to pieces and scattered to the four winds; under his rule, and in the fullness of time, we saw Abraham Lincoln, after giving the slaveholders three months' grace in which to save their hateful slave system, penning the immortal paper, which, though special in its language, was general in its principles and effect, making slavery forever impossible in the United States. Though we waited long, we saw all this and more.

Can any colored man, or any white man friendly to the freedom of all men, ever forget the night which followed the first day of January, 1863, when the world was to see if Abraham Lincoln would prove to be as good as his word? I shall never forget that memorable night, when in a distant city I waited and watched at a public meeting, with three thousand others not less anxious than myself, for the word of deliverance which we have heard read today. Nor shall I ever forget the outburst of joy and thanksgiving that rent the air when the lightning brought to us the emancipation proclamation. In that happy hour we forgot all delay, and forgot all tardiness, forgot that the President had bribed the rebels to lay down their arms by a promise to withhold the bolt which would smite the slave-system with destruction; and we were thenceforward willing to allow the President all the latitude of time, phraseology, and every honorable device that statesmanship might require for the achievement of a great and beneficent measure of liberty and progress.

Fellow-citizens, there is little necessity on this occasion to speak at length and critically of this great and good man, and of his high mission in the world. That ground has been fully occupied and completely covered both here and elsewhere. The whole field of fact and fancy has been gleaned and garnered. Any man can say things that are true of Abraham Lincoln, but no man can say anything that is new of Abraham Lincoln. His personal traits and public acts are better known to the American people than are those of any other man of his age. He was a mystery to no man who saw him and heard him. Though high in position, the humblest could approach him and feel at home in his presence. Though deep, he was transparent; though strong, he was gentle; though decided and pronounced in his convictions, he was tolerant towards those who differed from him, and patient under reproaches. Even those who only knew him through his public utterances obtained a tolerably clear idea of his character and his personality. The image of the man went out with his words, and those who read them, knew him.

I have said that President Lincoln was a white man, and shared the prejudices common to his countrymen towards the colored race. Looking back to his times and to the condition of his country, we are compelled to admit that this unfriendly feeling on his part may be safely set down as one element of his wonderful success in organizing the loyal American people for the tremendous conflict before them, and bringing them safely through that conflict. His great mission was to accomplish two things: first, to save his country from dismemberment and ruin; and, second, to free his country from the great crime of slavery. To do one or the other, or both, he must have the earnest sympathy and the powerful co-operation of his loyal fellow-countrymen. Without this primary and essential condition to success his efforts must have been vain and utterly fruitless. Had he put the abolition of slavery before the salvation of the

Union, he would have inevitably driven from him a powerful class of the American people and rendered resistance to rebellion impossible. Viewed from the genuine abolition ground, Mr. Lincoln seemed tardy, cold, dull, and indifferent; but measuring him by the sentiment of his country, a sentiment he was bound as a statesman to consult, he was swift, zealous, radical, and determined.

Though Mr. Lincoln shared the prejudices of his white fellow-country-men against the negro, it is hardly necessary to say that in his heart of hearts he loathed and hated slavery.* The man who could say, "Fondly do we hope, fervently do we pray, that this mighty scourge of war shall soon pass away, yet if God wills it continue till all the wealth piled by two hundred years of bondage shall have been wasted, and each drop of blood drawn by the lash shall have been paid for by one drawn by the sword, the judgments of the Lord are true and righteous alto-gether," gives all needed proof of his feeling on the subject of slavery. He was willing, while the South was loyal, that it should have its pound of flesh, because he thought that it was so nominated in the bond; but farther than this no earthly power could make him go.

Fellow-citizens, whatever else in this world may be partial, unjust, and uncertain, time, time! is impartial, just, and certain in its action. In the realm of mind, as well as in the realm of matter, it is a great worker, and often works wonders. The honest and comprehensive statesman, clearly discerning the needs of his country, and earnestly endeavoring to do his whole duty, though covered and blistered with reproaches, may safely leave his course to the silent judgment of time. Few great public men have ever been the victims of fiercer denunciation than Abraham Lincoln was during his administration. He was often wounded in the house of his friends. Reproaches came thick and fast upon him from within and from without, and from opposite quarters. He was assailed by Abolitionists; he was assailed by slaveholders; he was assailed by the men who were for peace at any price; he was assailed by those who were for a more vigorous prosecution of the war; he was assailed for not making the war an abolition war; and he was bitterly assailed for making the war an abolition war.

But now behold the change: the judgment of the present hour is, that taking him for all in all, measuring the tremendous magnitude of the work before him, considering the necessary means to ends, and surveying the end from the beginning, infinite wisdom has seldom sent any man into the world better fitted for his mission than Abraham Lincoln. His birth, his training, and his natural endowments, both mental and physi-

---

*"I am naturally anti-slavery. If slavery is not wrong, nothing is wrong. I cannot remember when I did not so think and feel."—*Letter of Mr. Lincoln to Mr. Hodges, of Kentucky,* April 4, 1864.

cal, were strongly in his favor. Born and reared among the lowly, a stranger to wealth and luxury, compelled to grapple single-handed with the flintiest hardships of life, from tender youth to sturdy manhood, he grew strong in the manly and heroic qualities demanded by the great mission to which he was called by the votes of his countrymen. The hard condition of his early life, which would have depressed and broken down weaker men, only gave greater life, vigor, and buoyancy to the heroic spirit of Abraham Lincoln. He was ready for any kind and any quality of work. What other young men dreaded in the shape of toil, he took hold of with the utmost cheerfulness.

> A spade, a rake, a hoe,
> A pick-axe, or a bill;
> A hook to reap, a scythe to mow,
> A flail, or what you will.

All day long he could split heavy rails in the woods, and half the night long he could study his English Grammar by the uncertain flare and glare of the light made by a pine-knot. He was at home on the land with his axe, with his maul, with gluts, and his wedges; and he was equally at home on water, with his oars, with his poles, with his planks, and with his boat-hooks. And whether in his flat-boat on the Mississippi river, or at the fireside of his frontier cabin, he was a man of work. A son of toil himself, he was linked in brotherly sympathy with the sons of toil in every loyal part of the Republic. This very fact gave him tremendous power with the American people, and materially contributed not only to selecting him to the Presidency, but in sustaining his administration of the Government.

Upon his inauguration as President of the United States, an office, even where assumed under the most favorable conditions, fitted to tax and strain the largest abilities, Abraham Lincoln was met by a tremendous crisis. He was called upon not merely to administer the Government, but to decide, in the face of terrible odds, the fate of the Republic.

A formidable rebellion rose in his path before him; the Union was already practically dissolved; his country was torn and rent asunder at the centre. Hostile armies were already organized against the Republic, armed with the munitions of war which the Republic had provided for its own defence. The tremendous question for him to decide was whether his country should survive the crisis and flourish, or be dismembered and perish. His predecessor in office had already decided the question in favor of national dismemberment, by denying to it the right of self-defence and self-preservation—a right which belongs to the meanest insect.

Happily for the country, happily for you and for me, the judgment of James Buchanan, the patrician, was not the judgment of Abraham Lincoln, the plebeian. He brought his strong common sense, sharpened in the school of adversity, to bear upon the question. He did not hesitate, he did not doubt, he did not falter; but at once resolved that at whatever peril, at whatever cost, the union of the States should be preserved. A patriot himself, his faith was strong and unwavering in the patriotism of his countrymen. Timid men said before Mr. Lincoln's inauguration, that we had seen the last President of the United States. A voice in influential quarters said, "Let the Union slide." Some said that a Union maintained by the sword was worthless. Others said a rebellion of 8,000,000 cannot be suppressed; but in the midst of all this tumult and timidity, and against all this, Abraham Lincoln was clear in his duty, and had an oath in heaven. He calmly and bravely heard the voice of doubt and fear all around him; but he had an oath in heaven, and there was not power enough on the earth to make this honest boatman, backwoodsman, and broad-handed splitter of rails evade or violate that sacred oath. He had not been schooled in the ethics of slavery; his plain life had favored his love of truth. He had not been taught that treason and perjury were the proof of honor and honesty. His moral training was against his saying one thing when he meant another. The trust which Abraham Lincoln had in himself and in the people was surprising and grand, but it was also enlightened and well founded. He knew the American people better than they knew themselves, and his truth was based upon this knowledge.

Fellow-citizens, the fourteenth day of April, 1865, of which this is the eleventh anniversary, is now and will ever remain a memorable day in the annals of this Republic. It was on the evening of this day, while a fierce and sanguinary rebellion was in the last stages of its desolating power; while its armies were broken and scattered before the invincible armies of Grant and Sherman; while a great nation, torn and rent by war, was already beginning to raise to the skies loud anthems of joy at the dawn of peace, it was startled, amazed, and overwhelmed by the crowning crime of slavery—the assassination of Abraham Lincoln. It was a new crime, a pure act of malice. No purpose of the rebellion was to be served by it. It was the simple gratification of a hell-black spirit of revenge. But it has done good after all. It has filled the country with a deeper abhorrence of slavery and a deeper love for the great liberator.

Had Abraham Lincoln died from any of the numerous ills to which flesh is heir; had he reached that good old age of which his vigorous constitution and his temperate habits gave promise; had he been permitted to see the end of his great work; had the solemn curtain of death come down but gradually—we should still have been smitten with a heavy grief, and treasured his name lovingly. But dying as he did die, by the red hand of violence, killed, assassinated, taken off without warning, not because of personal hate—for no man who knew Abraham Lincoln could hate him—but because of his fidelity to union and liberty, he is doubly dear to us, and his memory will be precious forever.

Fellow-citizens, I end, as I began, with congratulations. We have done a good work for our race to-day. In doing honor to the memory of our friend and liberator, we have been doing highest honors to ourselves and those who come after us; we have been fastening ourselves to a name and fame imperishable and immortal; we have also been defending ourselves from a blighting scandal. When now it shall be said that the colored man is soulless, that he has no appreciation of benefits or benefactors; when the foul reproach of ingratitude is hurled at us, and it is attempted to scourge us beyond the range of human brotherhood, we may calmly point to the monument we have this day erected to the memory of Abraham Lincoln.

Booker T. Washington

Booker T. Washington is usually thought of as a practical politician or a compromiser rather than as a political theorist. Yet a good case can be made that his vision of the place of the black man in the United States was broader and deeper than that of any other thinker. This does not mean of course that he was necessarily right; but it does suggest that his arguments ought to be taken seriously, free of the prejudices, pro and con, that have encrusted the reputation of the founder of Tuskegee.

Fortunately there is a greater disposition now than there was a few years ago to see that Washington's educational, political, and moral principles deserve the attention of thoughtful men. Washington's acceptance of an "equal but separate" status for blacks seems again not unreasonable to many blacks disillusioned with "integration" and doubtful about its political and moral implications. Washington's principles of education, beginning with training to meet the immediate needs of earning a living and do-

mestic economy and broadening out to moral and liberal education, are seen to have relevance to some of the educational
problems that our schools have yet to solve. Washington's emphasis on economic activity as a source of strength and economic
exchange as a relatively available mode of black advancement
and integration are echoed today from all parts of the political
spectrum. Even Washington's emphasis on the individual's responsibility for himself—on the need of the black man to concern
himself principally, though not exclusively, with the inner obstacles to independence and dignity—is enjoying a kind of renaissance among some black thinkers. "Character, not circumstances,
makes the man." Washington's ideas are again at least controver-
sial.

Perhaps the most criticized part of Washington's outlook is his
determination to find things to praise in those who deserve so
much blame for the blacks' condition. The reader should carefully consider the rationale of Washington's rhetoric. It was based
partly on the general principle of appealing to the best in men.
More fundamental, however, was Washington's opinion that the
deepest harm of the institution of slavery was done not to the
enslaved but to the enslaver. "No race can wrong another without
being permanently injured in morals." The black man's noblest
task was to help these injured men to recover, so far as possi-

Atlanta Exposition Address

Mr. President and Gentlemen of the Board of Directors and Citizens:

One-third of the population of the South is of the Negro race. No enterprise seeking the material, civil, or moral welfare of this section can disregard this element of our population and reach the highest success. I but
convey to you, Mr. President and Directors, the sentiment of the masses
of my race when I say that in no way have the value and manhood of the
American Negro been more fittingly and generously recognized than by
the managers of this magnificent Exposition at every stage of its progress.
It is a recognition that will do more to cement the friendship of the two
races than any occurrence since the dawn of our freedom.

Not only this, but the opportunity here afforded will awaken among us

From *Up From Slavery: An Autobiography* by Booker T. Washington, pp. 218–225.
Published by Doubleday, Page & Co., 1901.

ble, from the degradation caused by their participation in slavery. It was a task that required understanding and, Washington thought, compassion. "If the Negro who has been oppressed, ostracized, denied rights in a Christian land, can help you, North and South, to rise, can be the medium of your rising to these sublime heights of unselfishness and self-forgetfulness, who may say that the Negro, this new citizen, will not see in it, a recompense for all that he has suffered and will have performed a mission that will be placed beside that of the lowly Nazarine?"

Additional Readings: The principal source of Washington's thought, in addition to the materials here, is his autobiographical *Up From Slavery,* written in 1901 and available in a number of paperback editions. *Up From Slavery,* is intended not merely to recount the events of a life but to teach, to give concrete form to the general principles expressed in other writings. Washington's other autobiographical works have the same intention; see *Working with the Hands* and *My Larger Education.* Some of Washington's most significant thoughts are expressed in the addresses collected in *Selected Speeches of Booker T. Washington,* edited by E. Davidson Washington, and in his two-volume *Story of the Negro,* which have unfortunately, not been reprinted. Brotz's *Negro Social and Political Thought* contains an excellent selection of Washington's writings.

a new era of industrial progress. Ignorant and inexperienced, it is not strange that in the first years of our new life we began at the top instead of at the bottom; that a seat in Congress or the state legislature was more sought than real estate or industrial skill; that the political convention or stump speaking had more attractions than starting a dairy farm or truck garden.

A ship lost at sea for many days suddenly sighted a friendly vessel. From the mast of the unfortunate vessel was seen a signal, "Water, water; we die of thirst!" The answer from the friendly vessel at once came back, "Cast down your bucket where you are." A second time the signal, "Water, water; send us water!" ran up from the distressed vessel, and was answered, "Cast down your bucket where you are." And a third and fourth signal for water was answered, "Cast down your bucket where you are." The captain of the distressed vessel, at last heeding the injunction, cast down his bucket, and it came up full of fresh, sparkling water from the mouth of the Amazon River. To those of my race who depend on bettering their condition in a foreign land or who underestimate the importance of cultivating friendly relations with the Southern white man, who is their next-door neighbour, I would say: "Cast down your bucket where you are"—cast it down in making friends in every manly way of the people of all races by whom we are surrounded.

Cast it down in agriculture, mechanics, in commerce, in domestic service, and in the professions. And in this connection it is well to bear in mind that whatever other sins the South may be called to bear, when it comes to business, pure and simple, it is in the South that the Negro is given a man's chance in the commercial world, and in nothing is this Exposition more eloquent than in emphasizing this chance. Our greatest danger is that in the great leap from slavery to freedom we may overlook the fact that the masses of us are to live by the productions of our hands, and fail to keep in mind that we shall prosper in proportion as we learn to dignify and glorify common labour and put brains and skill into the common occupations of life; shall prosper in proportion as we learn to draw the line between the superficial and the substantial, the ornamental gewgaws of life and the useful. No race can prosper till it learns that there is as much dignity in tilling a field as in writing a poem. It is at the bottom of life we must begin, and not at the top. Nor should we permit our grievances to overshadow our opportunities.

To those of the white race who look to the incoming of those of foreign birth and strange tongue and habits for the prosperity of the South, were I permitted I would repeat what I say to my own race, "Cast down your bucket where you are." Cast it down among the eight millions of Negroes whose habits you know, whose fidelity and love you have tested in days when to have proved treacherous meant the ruin of your firesides. Cast down your bucket among these people who have, without strikes and labour wars, tilled your fields, cleared your forests, builded your railroads and cities, and brought forth treasures from the bowels of the earth, and helped make possible this magnificent representation of the progress of the South. Casting down your bucket among my people, helping and encouraging them as you are doing on these grounds, and to education of head, hand, and heart, you will find that they will buy your surplus land, make blossom the waste places in your fields, and run your factories. While doing this, you can be sure in the future, as in the past, that you and your families will be surrounded by the most patient, faithful, law-abiding, and unresentful people that the world has seen. As we have proved our loyalty to you in the past, in nursing your children, watching by the sick-bed of your mothers and fathers, and often following them with tear-dimmed eyes to their graves, so in the future, in our humble way, we shall stand by you with a devotion that no foreigner can approach, ready to lay down our lives, if need be, in defence of yours, interlacing our industrial, commercial, civil, and religious life with yours in a way that shall make the interests of both races one. In all things that are purely social we can be as separate as the fingers, yet one as the hand in all things essential to mutual progress.

There is no defence or security for any of us except in the highest intelligence and development of all. If anywhere there are efforts tending to curtail the fullest growth of the Negro, let these efforts be turned into stimulating, encouraging, and making him the most useful and intelligent citizen. Effort or means so invested will pay a thousand per cent interest. These efforts will be twice blessed—"blessing him that gives and him that takes."

There is no escape through law of man or God from the inevitable:—

> The laws of changeless justice bind
> Oppressor with oppressed;
> And close as sin and suffering joined
> We march to fate abreast.

Nearly sixteen millions of hands will aid you in pulling the load upward, or they will pull against you the load downward. We shall constitute one-third and more of the ignorance and crime of the South, or one-third its intelligence and progress; we shall contribute one-third to the business and industrial prosperity of the South, or we shall prove a veritable body of death, stagnating, depressing, retarding every effort to advance the body politic.

Gentlemen of the Exposition, as we present to you our humble effort at an exhibition of our progress, you must not expect overmuch. Starting thirty years ago with ownership here and there in a few quilts and pumpkins and chickens (gathered from miscellaneous sources), remember the path that has led from these to the inventions and production of agricultural implements, buggies, steam-engines, newspapers, books, statuary, carving, paintings, the management of drug-stores and banks, has not been trodden without contact with thorns and thistles. While we take pride in what we exhibit as a result of our independent efforts, we do not for a moment forget that our part in this exhibition would fall far short of your expectations but for the constant help that has come to our educational life, not only from the Southern states, but especially from Northern philanthropists, who have made their gifts a constant stream of blessing and encouragement.

The wisest among my race understand that the agitation of questions of social equality is the extremest folly, and that progress in the enjoyment of all the privileges that will come to us must be the result of severe and constant struggle rather than of artificial forcing. No race that has anything to contribute to the markets of the world is long in any degree ostracized. It is important and right that all privileges of the law be ours, but it is vastly more important that we be prepared for the exercises of these privileges. The opportunity to earn a dollar in a factory just now is worth infinitely more than the opportunity to spend a dollar in an opera-house.

In conclusion, may I repeat that nothing in thirty years has given us more hope and encouragement, and drawn us so near to you of the white race, as this opportunity offered by the Exposition; and here bending, as it were, over the altar that represents the results of the struggles of your race and mine, both starting practically empty-handed three decades ago, I pledge that in your effort to work out the great and intricate problem which God has laid at the doors of the South, you shall have at all times the patient, sympathetic help of my race; only let this be constantly in mind, that, while from representations in these buildings of the product of field, of forest, of mine, of factory, letters, and art, much good will come, yet far above and beyond material benefits will be that higher good, that, let us pray God, will come, in a blotting out of sectional differences and racial animosities and suspicions, in a determination to administer absolute justice, in a willing obedience among all classes to the mandates of law. This, coupled with our material prosperity, will bring into our beloved South a new heaven and a new earth.

Our New Citizen

Gentlemen of the Hamilton Club:

From whence came our new citizen? Who is he? And what is his mission? It is interesting to note that the Negro is the only citizen of this country who came here by special invitation and by reason of special provision. The Caucasian came here against the protest of the leading citizens of this country in 1492. We were so important to the prosperity of this country that special vessels were sent to convey us hither.

Shall we be less important in the future than in the past? The Negroes are one eighth of your population. Our race is larger than the population of the Argentine Republic, larger than Chile, larger than Peru and Venezuela combined — nearly as large as Mexico.

Whether the call has come for us to clear the forests of your country, to make your cotton, rice, and sugar cane, build houses or railroads, or to

Address delivered before the Hamilton Club, Chicago, Illinois, January 31, 1896. From *Selected Speeches of Booker T. Washington*, edited by E. Davidson Washington. Published by Doubleday, Doran & Co., 1932. Reprinted by permission of Mrs. Portia Washington Pitman.

shoulder arms in defense of our country, have we not answered that call? When the call has come to educate our children, to teach them thrift, habits of industry, have we not filled every school that has been opened for us? When with others there have been labor wars, strikes, and destruction of property, have we not set the world an example in each one quietly attending to his own business? When, even here in the North, the shop, the factory, the trades have closed against us, have we not patiently, faithfully gone on taking advantage of our disadvantages, and through it all have we not continued to rise, to increase in numbers and prosperity? If in the past we have thus proven our right to your respect and confidence, shall it be less so in the future? If in proportion as we contribute, by the exercise of the higher virtues, by the product of brain and skilled hand, to the common prosperity of our country, shall we not receive all the privileges of any other citizen, whether born out of this country or under the Stars and Stripes?

You of the great and prosperous North still owe a serious and uncompleted duty to your less fortunate brothers of the white race [in the] South who suffered and are still suffering the consequences of American slavery. What was the task you asked them to perform? Returning to their destitute homes after years of war, to face blasted hopes, devastation, a shattered industrial system, you asked them to add to their burdens that of preparing in education, politics, and economics, in a few short years, for citizenship four or five millions of former slaves. That the South, staggering under the burden, made blunders, that in some measure there has been disappointment, no one need be surprised.

And yet, taking it all in all, we may, I think, safely challenge history to find a case where two races, but yesterday master and slave, today citizen and citizen, have made such marvelous progress in the adjustment of themselves to new conditions, where each has traveled so fast in the divine science of forgetting and forgiving; and yet do not misunderstand me that all is done or that there are not serious wrongs yet to be blotted out.

In making these observations I do not, I cannot, forget as an humble representative of my race the vacant seat, the empty sleeve, the lives offered up on Southern battlefields, that we might have a united country and that our flag should shelter none save freemen, nor do I forget the millions of dollars that have gone into the South from the hands of philanthropic individuals and religious organizations.

Nor are we of the black race leaving the work alone to your race in the North or your race in the South—mark what this new citizen is doing. Go with me tonight to the Tuskegee Institute in the Black Belt of Alabama, in an old slave plantation where a few years ago my people were bought and sold, and I will show you an industrial village, which is an example of others, with nearly eight hundred young men and women working with head and hand by night and by day, preparing themselves, in literature, in science, in agriculture, in dairying, in fruit-growing, in stock-raising, in brick-making, in brick masonry, in woodwork, in iron-work, in tinwork, in leatherwork, in cloth, in cooking, in laundrying, in printing, in household science — in the duties of Christian citizenship — preparing themselves that they may prepare thousands of others of our race that they may contribute their full quota of virtue, of thrift and intelligence to the prosperity of our beloved country. It is said that we will be hewers of wood and drawers of water, but we shall be more, we shall turn the wood into houses, into machinery, into implements of commerce and civilization. We shall turn the water into steam, into electricity, into dairy and agricultural products, into food and raiment — and thus wind our life about yours, thus knit our civil and commercial interests into yours in a way that shall make us all realize anew that "of one blood hath God made all men to dwell and prosper on the face of the earth."

But when all this is said, I repeat, gentlemen of the club, that you of this generation owe to the South, not less than to yourselves, an unful-filled duty. Surely, surely, if the Negro, with all that is behind him, can forget the past, you ought to rise above him in this regard. When the South is poor you are poor, when the South commits crime you commit crime, when the South prospers you prosper. There is no power that can separate our destiny. Let us ascend in this matter above color or race or party or sectionalism into the region of duty of man to man, American to American, Christian to Christian. If the Negro who has been oppressed, ostracized, denied rights in a Christian land, can help you, North and South, to rise, can be the medium of your rising to these sublime heights of unselfishness and self-forgetfulness, who may say that the Negro, this new citizen, will not see in it a recompense for all that he has suffered and will have performed a mission that will be placed beside that of the lowly Nazarine?

Let the Negro, the North, and the South do their duty with a new spirit and a new determination during this, the dawning of a new cen-tury, and at the end of fifty years a picture will be painted — what is it? A race dragged from its native land in chains, three hundred years of slavery, years of fratricidal war, thousands of lives laid down, freedom for the slave, reconstruction, blunders, bitterness between North and South. The South staggers under the burden; the North forgets the past and comes to the rescue; the Negro, in the midst, teaching North and South patience, forbearance, long-suffering, obedience to law, develop-ing in intellect, character and property, skill and habits of industry. The North and South, joining hands with the Negro, take him whom they have wronged, help him, encourage him, stimulate him in self-help, give him the rights of man, and, in lifting up the Negro, lift themselves up into that atmosphere where there is a new North, a new South—a new citizen—a new republic.

Democracy and Education

Mr. Chairman, Ladies and Gentlemen:

It is said that the strongest chain is no stronger than its weakest link. In the Southern part of our country there are twenty-two millions of your brethren who are bound to you by ties which you cannot tear asunder if you would. The most intelligent man in your community has his intelligence darkened by the ignorance of a fellow citizen in the Mississippi bottoms. The most wealthy in your city would be more wealthy but for the poverty of a fellow being in the Carolina rice swamps. The most moral and religious among you has his religion and morality modified by the degradation of the man in the South whose religion is a mere matter of form or emotionalism.

The vote in your state that is cast for the highest and purest form of government is largely neutralized by the vote of the man in Louisiana whose ballot is stolen or cast in ignorance. When the South is poor, you are poor; when the South commits crime, you commit crime. My friends, there is no mistake; you must help us to raise the character of our civilization or yours will be lowered. No member of your race in any part of our country can harm the weakest and meanest member of mine without the proudest and bluest blood in the city of Brooklyn being degraded. The central ideal which I wish you to help me consider is the reaching and lifting up of the lowest, most unfortunate, negative element that occupies so large a proportion of our territory and composes so large a percentage of our population. It seems to me that there never was a time in the history of our country when those interested in education should more earnestly consider to what extent the mere acquiring of a knowledge of literature and science makes producers, lovers of labor, independent, honest, unselfish, and, above all, supremely good. Call education by what name you please, and if it fails to bring about

Address delivered before the Institute of Arts and Sciences, Brooklyn, New York, September 30, 1896. From *Selected Speeches of Booker T. Washington*, edited by E. Davidson Washington. Published by Doubleday, Doran & Co., 1932. Reprinted by permission of Mrs. Portia Washington Pitman.

these results among the masses it falls short of its highest end. The science, the art, the literature that fails to reach down and bring the humblest up to the fullest enjoyment of the blessings of our government is weak, no matter how costly the buildings or apparatus used, or how modern the methods in instruction employed. The study of arithmetic that does not result in making someone more honest and self-reliant is defective. The study of history that does not result in making men conscientious in receiving and counting the ballots of their fellow men is most faulty. The study of art that does not result in making the strong less willing to oppress the weak means little. How I wish that from the most humble log cabin schoolhouse in Alabama we could burn it, as it were, into the hearts and heads of all, that usefulness, service to our brother, is the supreme end of education. Putting the thought more directly as it applies to conditions in the South: Can you make your intelligence affect us in the same ratio that our ignorance affects you? Let us put a not improbable case. A great national question is to be decided, one that involves peace or war, the honor or dishonor of our nation—yea, the very existence of the government. The North and West are divided. There are five million votes to be cast in the South, and of this number one half are ignorant. Not only are one half the voters ignorant, but, because of this ignorant vote, corruption, dishonesty in a dozen forms have crept into the exercise of the political franchise, to the extent that the conscience of the intelligent class is soured in its attempts to defeat the will of the ignorant voters. Here, then, on the one hand you have an ignorant vote, and on the other hand an intelligent vote minus a conscience. The time may not be far off when to this kind of jury we shall have to look for the verdict that is to decide the course of our democratic institutions.

When a great national calamity stares us in the face, we are, I fear, too much given to depending on a short campaign of education to do on the hustings what should have been accomplished in the schoolroom. With this preliminary survey, let us examine with more care the work to be done in the South before all classes will be fit for the highest duties of citizenship. In reference to my own race I am confronted with some embarrassment at the outset because of the various and conflicting opinions as to what is to be its final place in our economic and political life. Within the last thirty years—and, I might add, within the last three months—it has been proven by eminent authority that the Negro is increasing in numbers so fast that it is only a question of a few years before he will far outnumber the white race in the South, and it has also been proven that the Negro is fast dying out and it is only a question of a few years before he will have completely disappeared. It has also been proven that crime among us is on the increase and that crime is on the decrease; that education helps the Negro, that education also hurts him; that he is fast leaving the South and taking up his residence in the North and West, and that the tendency of the Negro is to drift to the lowlands of the Mississippi bottoms. It has been proven that as a slave laborer he produced less cotton than a free man. It has been proven that education unfits the Negro for work, and that education also makes him more valuable as a laborer; that he is our greatest criminal and that he is our most law-abiding citizen. In the midst of these opinions, in the words of a modern statesman, "I hardly know where I am at." I hardly know whether I am myself or the other fellow. But in the midst of this confusion there are a few things of which I feel certain that furnish a basis for thought and action. I know that, whether we are increasing or decreasing, whether we are growing better or worse, whether we are valuable or valueless, a few years ago fourteen of us were brought into this country and now there are eight million of us. I know that, whether in slavery or freedom, we have always been loyal to the Stars and Stripes, that no schoolhouse has been opened for us that has not been filled; that 1,500,000 ballots that we have the right to cast are as potent for weal and woe as the ballot cast by the whitest and most influential man in your commonwealth. I know that wherever our life touches yours we help or hinder; that wherever your life touches ours you make us stronger or weaker. Further I know that almost every other race that tried to look the white man in the face has disappeared. With all the conflicting opinions, and with the full knowledge of all our weaknesses, I know that only a few centuries ago in this country we went into slavery pagans: we came out Christians; we went into slavery pieces of property: we came out American citizens; we went into slavery without a language: we came out speaking the proud Anglo-Saxon tongue; we went into slavery with the slave chains clanking about our wrists: we came out with the American ballot in our hands. My friends, I submit it to your sober and candid judgment, if a race that is capable of such a test, such a transformation, is not worth saving and making a part, in reality as well as in name, of our democratic government. It is with an ignorant race as it is with a child: it craves at first the superficial, the ornamental, the signs of progress rather than the reality. The ignorant race is tempted to jump, at one bound, to the position that it has required years of hard struggle for others to reach. It seems to me that the temptation in education and missionary work is to do for a people a thousand miles away without always making a careful study of the needs and conditions of the people whom we are trying to help. The temptation is to run all people through a certain educational mold regardless of the condition of the subject or the end to be accomplished. Unfortunately for us as a race, our education was begun, just after the war, too nearly where New England education ended. We seemed to overlook the fact that we were dealing with a race that has little love for labor in their native land and consequently brought little love for labor with them to America. Added to this was the fact that they had been forced for two hundred and fifty years to labor without compensation under circumstances that were calculated to do anything but teach them the dignity, beauty, and civilizing power of intelligent labor. We forgot the industrial education that was given the Pilgrim Fathers of New England in clearing and planting its cold, bleak, and snowy hills and valleys, in providing shelter, founding the small mills and factories, in supplying themselves with home-made products, thus laying the foundation of an industrial life that now keeps going a large part of the colleges and missionary effort of the world. May I be tempted one step further in showing how prone we are to make our education formal, technical, instead of making it meet the needs of conditions regardless of formality and technicality? At least eighty per cent of my pupils in the South are found in the rural districts, and they are dependent on agriculture in some form for their support. Notwithstanding in this instance we have a whole race depending upon agriculture, and notwithstanding thirty years have passed since our freedom, aside from what we have done at Hampton and Tuskegee and one or two other institutions, not a thing has been attempted by state or philanthropy in the way of educating the race in this industry on which their very existence depends. Boys have been taken from the farms and educated in law, theology, Hebrew, and Greek—educated in everything else but the very subject they should know the most about. I question whether or not among all the educated colored people in the United States you can find six, if we except the institutions named, that have received anything like a thorough training in agriculture. It would have seemed, since self-support and industrial independence are the first conditions for lifting up any race, that education in theoretical and practical agriculture, horticulture, dairying, and stock-raising should have occupied the first place in our system. Some time ago when we decided to make tailoring a part of our training at the Tuskegee Institute, I was amazed to find that it was almost impossible to find in the whole country an educated colored man who could teach the making of clothing. I could find them by the score who could teach astronomy, theology, Greek, or Latin, but almost none who could instruct in the making of clothing, something that has to be used by every one of us every day in the year. How often has my heart been made to sink as I have gone through the South and into the homes of the people and found women who could converse intelligently on Grecian history, who had studied geometry, could analyze the most complex sentences, and yet could not analyze the poorly cooked and still more poorly served bread and fat meat that they and their families were eating three times a day. It is little trouble to find girls who can locate Pekin and the Desert of Sahara on an artificial globe; but seldom can you find one who can locate on an actual dinner table the proper place for the carving knife and fork or the meat and vegetables. A short time ago, in one of our Southern cities, a colored man died who had received training as a skilled mechanic during the days of slavery. By his skill and industry he had built up a great business as a house contractor and builder. In this same city there are thirty-five thousand colored people, among them young men who have been well educated in languages and literature, but not a single one could be found who had been trained in architectural and mechanical drawing that could carry on the business which this ex-slave had built up, and so it was soon scattered to the wind. Aside from the work done in the institutions that I have mentioned, you will find no colored men who have been trained in the principles of architecture, notwithstanding the vast majority of the race is without homes. Here, then, are the three prime conditions for growth, for civilization—food, clothing, shelter— yet we have been the slaves of form and custom to such an extent that we have failed in a large measure to look matters squarely in the face and meet actual needs. You cannot graft a fifteenth-century civilization onto a twentieth-century civilization by the mere performance of mental gymnastics. Understand, I speak in no fault-finding spirit, but with a feeling of deep regret for what has been done; but the future must be an improvement on the past.

I have endeavored to speak plainly in regard to the past, because I fear that the wisest and most interested have not fully comprehended the task which American slavery has laid at the doors of the Republic. Few, I fear, realize what is to be done before the seven million of my people in the South can be made a safe, helpful, progressive part of our institutions. The South, in proportion to its ability, has done well, but this does not change facts. Let me illustrate what I mean by a single example. In spite of all that has been done, I was in a county in Alabama a few days ago where there are some thirty thousand colored people and about seven thousand whites; in this county not a single public school for Negroes has been open this year longer than three months, not a single colored teacher has been paid more than fifteen dollars a month for his teaching. Not one of these schools was taught in a building worthy of the name of schoolhouse. In this county the state or public authorities do not own a dollar's worth of school property—not a schoolhouse, a blackboard, or a piece of crayon. Each colored child had spent on him this year for his education about fifty cents, while one of your children had spent on him this year for education not far from twenty dollars.

And yet each citizen of this county is expected to share the burdens and privileges of our democratic form of government just as intelligently and conscientiously as the citizens of your beloved Kings County. A vote in this county means as much to the nation as a vote in the city of Boston. Crime in this county is as truly an arrow aimed at the heart of the government as crime committed in your own streets. Do you know that a single schoolhouse built this year in a town near Boston to shelter about three hundred students has cost more for building alone than will be spent for the education, including buildings, apparatus, teachers, of the whole colored school population of Alabama? The commissioner of education for the state of Georgia recently reported to the state legislature that in the state there were two hundred thousand children that had entered no school the past year, and one hundred thousand more who were in school but a few days, making practically three hundred thousand children between six and sixteen years of age that are growing up in ignorance in one Southern state. The same report states that outside of the cities and towns, while the average number of schoolhouses in a county is sixty, all of these sixty schoolhouses are worth in a lump sum less than $2,000, and the report further adds that many of the schoolhouses in Georgia are not fit for horse stables. These illustrations, my friends, as far as concerns the Gulf states, are not exceptional cases or overdrawn.

I have referred to industrial education as a means of fitting the millions of my people in the South for the duties of citizenship. Until there is industrial independence it is hardly possible to have a pure ballot. In the country districts of the Gulf states it is safe to say that not more than one black man in twenty owns the land he cultivates. Where so large a proportion of the people are dependent, live in other people's houses, eat other people's food, and wear clothes they have not paid for, it is a pretty hard thing to tell how they are going to vote. My remarks thus far have referred mainly to my own race. But there is another side. The longer I live and the more I study the question, the more I am convinced that it is not so much a problem as to what you will do with the Negro as what the Negro will do with you and your civilization. In considering this side of the subject, I thank God that I have grown to the point where I can sympathize with a white man as much as I can sympathize with a black man. I have grown to the point where I can sympathize with a Southern white man as much as I can sympathize with a Northern white man. To me "a man's a man for a' that and a' that." As bearing upon democracy and education, what of your white brethren in the South, those who suffered and are still suffering the consequences of American slavery for which both you and they are responsible? You of the great and prosperous North still owe to your unfortunate brethren of the Caucasian race in the South, not less than to yourselves, a serious and uncompleted duty. What was the task you asked them to perform? Returning to their destitute homes after years of war to face blasted hopes, devastation, a shattered industrial system, you asked them to add to their own burdens that of preparing in education, politics, and economics in a few short years, for citizenship, four millions of former slaves. That the South, staggering under the burden, made blunders, and that in a measure there has been disappointment, no one need be surprised.

The educators, the statesmen, the philanthropists have never comprehended their duty toward the millions of poor whites in the South who were buffeted for two hundred years between slavery and freedom, between civilization and degradation, who were disregarded by both master and slave. It needs no prophet to tell the character of our future civilization when the poor white boy in the country districts of the South receives one dollar's worth of education and your boy twenty dollars' worth, when one never enters a library or reading room and the other has libraries and reading rooms in every ward and town. When one hears lectures and sermons once in two months and the other can hear a lecture or sermon every day in the year. When you help the South you help yourselves. Mere abuse will not bring the remedy. The time has come, it seems to me, when in this matter we should rise above party or race or sectionalism into the region of duty of man to man, citizen to citizen, Christian to Christian, and if the Negro who has been oppressed and denied rights in a Christian land can help you North and South to rise, can be the medium of your rising into this atmosphere of generous Christian brotherhood and self-forgetfulness, he will see in it a recompense for all that he has suffered in the past. Not very long ago a white citizen of the South boastingly expressed himself in public to this effect: "I am now forty-six years of age, but have never polished my own boots, have never saddled my own horse, have never built a fire in my own room, have never hitched a horse." He was asked a short time since by a lame man to hitch his horse, but refused and told him to get a Negro to do it. Our state law requires that a voter be required to read the constitution before voting, but the last clause of the constitution is in Latin and the Negroes cannot read Latin, and so they are asked to read the Latin clause and are thus disfranchised, while the whites are permitted to read the English portion of the constitution. I do not quote these statements for the purpose of condemning the individual or the South, for though myself a member of a despised and unfortunate race, I pity from the bottom of my heart any of God's creatures whence such a statement can emanate. Evidently here is a man who, as far as mere book training is concerned, is educated, for he boasts of his knowledge of Latin, but, so far as the real purpose of education is concerned—the making of men useful, honest, and liberal—this man has never been touched. Here is a citizen in the midst of our republic, clothed in a white skin, with all the technical signs of education, but who is as little fitted for the highest purpose of life as any creature found in Central Africa. My friends, can we make our education reach down far enough to touch and help this man? Can we so control science, art, and literature as to make them to such an extent a means rather than an end; that the lowest and most unfortunate of God's creatures shall be lifted up, ennobled and glorified; shall be a freeman instead of a slave of narrow sympathies and wrong customs? Some years ago a bright young man of my race succeeded in passing a competitive examination for a cadetship at the United States naval academy at Annapolis. Says the young man, Mr. Henry Baker, in describing his stay at this institution: "I was several times attacked with stones and was forced finally to appeal to the officers, when a marine was detailed to accompany me across the campus and from the mess hall at meal times. My books were mutilated, my clothes were cut and in some instances destroyed, and all the petty annoyances which ingenuity could devise were inflicted upon me daily, and during seamanship practice aboard the *Dale* attempts were often made to do me personal injury while I would be aloft in the rigging. No one ever addressed me by name. I was called the Moke usually, the Nigger for variety. I was shunned as if I were a veritable leper and received curses and blows as the only method my persecutors had of relieving the monotony." Not once during the two years, with one exception, did any one of the more than four hundred cadets enrolled ever come to him with a word of advice, counsel, sympathy, or information, and he never held conversation with any one of them for as much as five minutes during the whole course of his experience at the academy, except on occasions when he was defending himself against their assaults. The one exception where the departure from the rule was made was in the case of a Pennsylvania boy, who stealthily brought him a piece of his birthday cake at twelve o'clock one night. The act so surprised Baker that his suspicions were aroused, but these were dispelled by the donor, who read to him a letter which he had received from his mother, from whom the cake came, in which she requested that a slice be given to the colored cadet who was without friends. I recite this incident not for the purpose merely of condemning the wrong done a member of my race; no, no, not that. I mention the case, not for the one cadet, but for the sake of the four hundred cadets, for the sake of the four hundred American families, the four hundred American communities whose civilization and Christianity these cadets represented. Here were four hundred and more picked young men representing the flower of our country, who had passed through our common schools and were preparing themselves at public expense to defend the honor of our country. And yet, with grammar, reading, and arithmetic in the public schools, and with lessons in the arts of war, the principles of physical courage at Annapolis, both systems seemed to have utterly failed to prepare a single one of these young men for real life, that he could be brave enough, Christian enough, American enough, to take this poor defenseless black boy by the hand in open daylight and let the world know that he was his friend. Education, whether of black man or white man, that gives one physical courage to stand in front of the cannon and fails to give him moral courage to stand up in defense of right and justice is a failure. With all that the Brooklyn Institute of Arts and Sciences stands for in its equipment, its endowment, its wealth and culture, its instructors, can it produce a mother that will produce a boy that will not be ashamed to have the world know that he is a friend to the most unfortunate of God's creatures? Not long ago a mother, a black mother, who lived in one of your Northern states, had heard it whispered around her community for years that the Negro was lazy, shiftless, and would not work. So when her boy grew to sufficient size, at considerable expense and great self-sacrifice, she had her boy thoroughly taught the machinist's trade. A job was secured in a neighboring shop. With dinner bucket in hand and spurred on by the prayers of the now happy mother, the boy entered the shop to begin his first day's work. What happened? Had any one of the twenty white Americans been so educated that he gave this stranger a welcome into their midst? No, not this. Every one of the twenty white men threw down his tools and deliberately walked out, swearing that he would not give a black man an opportunity to earn an honest living. Another shop was tried, with the same result, and still another and the same. Today this promising and ambitious black man is a wreck—a confirmed drunkard, with no hope, no ambition. My friends, who blasted the life of this young man? On whose hands does his blood rest? Our system of education, or want of education, is responsible. Can our public schools and colleges turn out a set of men that will throw open the doors of industry to all men everywhere regardless of color, so all shall have the same opportunity to earn a dollar that they now have to spend a dollar? I know a good many species of cowardice and prejudice, but I know none equal to this. I know not who is the worst, the ex-slaveholder who perforce compelled his slave to work without compensation, or the man who perforce compels the Negro to refrain from working for compensation. My friends, we are one in this country. The question of the highest citizenship and the complete education of all concerns nearly ten million of my own people and over sixty million of yours. We rise as you rise; when we fall you fall. When you are strong we are strong; when we are weak you are weak. There is no power that can separate our destiny. The Negro can afford to be wronged; the white man cannot afford to wrong him. Unjust laws or customs that exist in many places regarding the races injure the white man and inconvenience the Negro. No race can wrong another race simply because it has the power to do so without being permanently injured in morals. The Negro can endure the temporary inconvenience, but the injury to the white man is permanent. It is for the white man to save himself from his degradation that I plead. If a white man steals a Negro's ballot it is the white man who is permanently injured. Physical death comes to the one Negro lynched in a county, but death of the morals—death of the soul—comes to the thousands responsible for the lynching. We are a patient, humble people. We can afford to work and wait. There is plenty in this country for us to do. Away up in the atmosphere of goodness, forbearance, patience, long-suffering, and forgiveness the workers are not many or overcrowded. If others would be little we can be great. If others would be mean we can be good. If others would push us down we can help push them up. Character, not circumstances, makes the man. It is more important that we be prepared for voting than that we vote, more important that we be prepared to hold office than that we hold office, more important that we be prepared for the highest recognition than that we be recognized. Those who fought and died on the battlefield performed their duty heroically and well, but a duty remains for you and me. The mere fiat of law could not make an ignorant voter an intelligent voter; could not make one citizen respect another; these results come to the Negro, as to all races, by beginning at the bottom and working up to the highest civilization and accomplishment. In the economy of God, there can be but one standard by which an individual can succeed—there is but one for a race. This country demands that every race measure itself by the American standard. By it a race must rise or fall, succeed or fail, and in the last analysis mere sentiment counts but little. During the next half-century and more my race must continue passing through the severe American crucible.

We are to be tested in our patience, in our forbearance, our power to endure wrong, to withstand temptation, to succeed, to acquire and use skill, our ability to compete, to succeed in commerce; to disregard the superficial for the real, the appearance for the substance; to be great and yet the servant of all. This, this is the passport to all that is best in the life of our republic, and the Negro must possess it or be debarred. In working out our destiny, while the main burden and center of activity must be with us, we shall need in a large measure the help, the encouragement, the guidance that the strong can give the weak. Thus helped, we of both races in the South shall soon throw off the shackles of racial and sectional prejudice and rise above the clouds of ignorance, narrowness, and selfishness into that atmosphere, that pure sunshine, where it will be our highest ambition to serve man, our brother, regardless of race or past conditions.

W. E. Burghardt Du Bois

If the student of black American political thought in the twentieth century were to be confined to the writings of a single man, that man should be W. E. Burghardt Du Bois. Perhaps no one has expressed so fully the manifold and sometimes contradictory implications of the black man's relation to America and to himself. He is the Thomas Jefferson of black American political thought. As sociologist, poet, propagandist, and revolutionary, he pursued the riddle of the black's life within the Veil. He professed, at one time or another, Washingtonianism, racism, integration, Pan-Africanism, individualism, and Marxism.

The essays here were written during the early stages of Du Bois' career. The concern for the significance of race expressed in his 1897 essay, "The Conservation of Races," was sometimes set aside but never abandoned in his later years. "Have we in America a distinct mission as a race—a distinct sphere of action and an opportunity for race development, or is self-obliteration the highest end to which Negro blood dare aspire?" A few years

later he was giving expression to the ideas that led to the break
with Booker T. Washington, the founding of the National Association for the Advancement of Colored People, and the beginning
of Du Bois' career as the very influential editor of the NAACP's
journal, *Crisis.* During this time Du Bois redefined the problem
and set an agenda for the movement that was to dominate black
political thought and action for almost fifty years. In his explora-
tions of the awful tension between the black and white worlds,
the psychological harm of unjust segregation, Du Bois was far
more introspective than his predecessors and fully anticipated
the concerns of later generations. "This waste of double aims,
this seeking to satisfy two unreconciled ideals, has wrought sad
havoc with the courage and faith and deeds of ten thousand thousand people,—has sent them often wooing false gods and invoking false means of salvation, and at times has even seemed about
to make them ashamed of themselves." His and the NAACP's
demands for civil rights and nondiscriminatory treatment for black
Americans are well known. His educational views, while agreeing

The Conservation of Races

The American Negro has always felt an intense personal interest in
discussions as to the origins and destinies of races: primarily because
back of most discussions of race with which he is familiar, have lurked
certain assumptions as to his natural abilities, as to his political, intellectual and moral status, which he felt were wrong. He has, consequently, been led to deprecate and minimize race distinctions, to believe intensely that out of one blood God created all nations, and to
speak of human brotherhood as though it were the possibility of an
already dawning to-morrow.

Nevertheless, in our calmer moments we must acknowledge that
human beings are divided into races; that in this country the two most
extreme types of the world's races have met, and the resulting problem
as to the future relations of these types is not only of intense and living
interest to us, but forms an epoch in the history of mankind.

It is necessary, therefore, in planning our movements, in guiding

American Negro Academy Occasional Papers, No. 2, Washington, 1897.

in many ways with Washington's, depart fundamentally in their preeminent concern for the education of the "talented tenth." A very large part of the difference between the two men can be explained by the fact that while Washington's focus was on the mass, the foundation of civilization, Du Bois' was on the few, the makers and active agents of civilization. "The Negro race, like all races, is going to be saved by its exceptional men."

Additional Readings: The whole of Du Bois' *The Souls of Black Folk,* from which two essays here are taken, is well worth study; it is one of the great products of black America. The reader can follow the history of Du Bois' thought and life through his major autobiographical writings, *The Souls of Black Folk,* 1903; *Darkwater,* 1921; *Dusk of Dawn,* 1940; and the posthumous *Autobiography of W. E. B. Du Bois,* 1968. An early work of theoretical significance is his 1899 sociological study of *The Philadelphia Negro,* a portion of which is reprinted in Brotz's *Negro Social and Political Thought.* Among Du Bois' many historical works, *Black Reconstruction in America* is especially important.

our future development, that at times we rise above the pressing, but smaller questions of separate schools and cars, wage-discrimination and lynch law, to survey the whole question of race in human philosophy and to lay, on a basis of broad knowledge and careful insight, those large lines of policy and higher ideals which may form our guiding lines and boundaries in the practical difficulties of every day. For it is certain that all human striving must recognize the hard limits of natural law, and that any striving, no matter how intense and earnest, which is against the constitution of the world, is vain. The question, then, which we must seriously consider is this: What is the real meaning of Race; what has, in the past, been the law of race development, and what lessons has the past history of race development to teach the rising Negro people?

When we thus come to inquire into the essential difference of races we find it hard to come at once to any definite conclusion. Many criteria of race differences have in the past been proposed, as color, hair, cranial measurements and language. And manifestly, in each of these respects, human beings differ widely. They vary in color, for instance, from the marble-like pallor of the Scandinavian to the rich, dark brown of the Zulu, passing by the creamy Slav, the yellow Chinese, the light brown Sicilian and the brown Egyptian. Men vary, too, in the texture of hair from the obstinately straight hair of the Chinese to the obstinately tufted and frizzled hair of the Bushman. In measurement of heads, again, men vary; from the broad-headed Tartar to the medium-headed European and the narrow-headed Hottentot; or, again in language, from the highly-inflected Roman tongue to the monosyllabic Chinese. All these physical characteristics are patent enough, and if they agreed with each other it would be very easy to classify mankind. Unfortunately for scientists, however, these criteria of race are most exasperatingly intermingled. Color does not agree with texture of hair, for many of the dark races have straight hair; nor does color agree with the breadth of the head, for the yellow Tartar has a broader head than the German; nor, again, has the science of language as yet succeeded in clearing up the relative authority of these various and contradictory criteria. The final word of science, so far, is that we have at least two, perhaps three, great families of human beings—the whites and Negroes, possibly the yellow race. That other races have arisen from the intermingling of the blood of these two. This broad division of the world's races which men like Huxley and Raetzel have introduced as more nearly true than the old five-race scheme of Blumenbach, is nothing more than an acknowledgment that, so far as purely physical characteristics are concerned, the differences between men do not explain all the differences of their history. It declares, as Darwin himself said, that great as is the physical unlikeness of the various races of men their likenesses are greater, and upon this rests the whole scientific doctrine of Human Brotherhood.

Although the wonderful developments of human history teach that the grosser physical differences of color, hair and bone go but a short way toward explaining the different roles which groups of men have played in Human Progress, yet there are differences—subtle, delicate and elusive, though they may be—which have silently but definitely separated men into groups. While these subtle forces have generally followed the natural cleavage of common blood, descent and physical peculiarities, they have at other times swept across and ignored these. At all times, however, they have divided human beings into races, which, while they perhaps transcend scientific definition, nevertheless, are clearly defined to the eye of the Historian and Sociologist.

If this be true, then the history of the world is the history, not of individuals, but of groups, not of nations, but of races, and he who ignores or seeks to override the race idea in human history ignores and overrides the central thought of all history. What, then, is a race? It is a vast family of human beings, generally of common blood and language, always of common history, traditions and impulses, who are both voluntarily and involuntarily striving together for the accomplishment of certain more or less vividly conceived ideals of life.

Turning to real history, there can be no doubt, first, as to the widespread, nay, universal, prevalence of the race idea, the race spirit, the race ideal, and as to its efficiency as the vastest and most ingenious invention for human progress. We, who have been reared and trained under the individualistic philosophy of the Declaration of Independence and the laisser-faire philosophy of Adam Smith, are loath to see and loath to acknowledge this patent fact of human history. We see the Pharaohs, Caesars, Toussaints and Napoleons of history and forget the vast races of which they were but epitomized expressions. We are apt to think in our American impatience, that while it may have been true in the past that closed race groups made history, that here in conglomerate America *nous avons changer tout cela*—we have changed all that, and have no need of this ancient instrument of progress. This assumption of which the Negro people are especially fond, can not be established by a careful consideration of history.

We find upon the world's stage today eight distinctly differentiated races, in the sense in which History tells us the word must be used. They are, the Slavs of eastern Europe, the Teutons of middle Europe, the English of Great Britain and America, the Romance nations of Southern and Western Europe, the Negroes of Africa and America, the Semitic people of Western Asia and Northern Africa, the Hindoos of Central Asia and the Mongolians of Eastern Asia. There are, of course, other minor race groups, as the American Indians, the Esquimaux and the South Sea Islanders; these larger races, too, are far from homogeneous; the Slav includes the Czech, the Magyar, the Pole and the Russian; the Teuton includes the German, the Scandinavian and the Dutch; the English include the Scotch, the Irish and the conglomerate American. Under Romance nations the widely-differing Frenchman, Italian, Sicilian and Spaniard are comprehended. The term Negro is, perhaps, the most indefinite of all, combining the Mulattoes and Zamboes of America and the Egyptians, Bantus and Bushmen of Africa. Among the Hindoos are traces of widely differing nations, while the great Chinese, Tartar, Corean and Japanese families fall under the one designation—Mongolian.

The question now is: What is the real distinction between these nations? Is it the physical differences of blood, color and cranial measurements? Certainly we must all acknowledge that physical differences play a great part, and that, with wide exceptions and qualifications, these eight great races of to-day follow the cleavage of physical race distinctions; the English and Teuton represent the white variety of mankind; the Mongolian, the yellow; the Negroes, the black. Between these are many crosses and mixtures, where Mongolian and Teuton have blended into the Slav, and other mixtures have produced the Romance

· nations and the Semites. But while race differences have followed mainly physical race lines, yet no mere physical distinctions would really define or explain the deeper differences—the cohesiveness and continuity of these groups. The deeper differences are spiritual, psychical, differences—undoubtedly based on the physical, but infinitely transcending them. The forces that bind together the Teuton nations are, then, first, their race identity and common blood; secondly, and more important, a common history, common laws and religion, similar habits of thought and a conscious striving together for certain ideals of life. The whole process which has brought about these race differentiations has been a growth, and the great characteristic of this growth has been the differentiation of spiritual and mental differences between great races of mankind and the integration of physical differences.

The age of nomadic tribes of closely related individuals represents the maximum of physical differences. They were practically vast families, and there were as many groups as families. As the families came together to form cities the physical differences lessened, purity of blood was replaced by the requirement of domicile, and all who lived within the city bounds became gradually to be regarded as members of the group; *i.e.*, there was a slight and slow breaking down of physical barriers. This, however, was accompanied by an increase of the spiritual and social differences between cities. This city became husbandmen, this, merchants, another warriors, and so on. The *ideals of life* for which the different cities struggled were different. When at last cities began to coalesce into nations there was another breaking down of barriers which separated groups of men. The larger and broader differences of color, hair and physical proportions were not by any means ignored, but myriads of minor differences disappeared, and the sociological and historical races of men began to approximate the present division of races as indicated by physical researches. At the same time the spiritual and physical differences of race groups which constituted the nations became deep and decisive. The English nation stood for constitutional liberty and commercial freedom; the German nation for science and philosophy; The Romance nations stood for literature and art, and the other race groups are striving, each in its own way, to develope for civilization its particular message, its particular ideal, which shall help to guide the world nearer and nearer that perfection of human life for which we all long, that

one far off Divine event.

This has been the function of race differences up to the present time. What shall be its function in the future? Manifestly some of the great races of today—particularly the Negro race—have not as yet given to civilization the full spiritual message which they are capable of giving. I will not say that the Negro race has as yet given no message to the world, for it is still a mooted question among scientists as to just how far Egyptian civilization was Negro in its origin; if it was not wholly Negro, it was certainly very closely allied. Be that as it may, however, the fact still remains that the full, complete Negro message of the whole Negro race has not as yet been given to the world: that the messages and ideal of the yellow race have not been completed, and that the striving of the mighty Slavs has but begun. The question is, then: How shall this message be delivered; how shall these various ideals be realized? The answer is plain: By the development of these race groups, not as individuals, but as races. For the development of Japanese genius, Japanese literature and art, Japanese spirit, only Japanese, bound and welded together, Japanese inspired by one vast ideal, can work out in its fullness the wonderful message which Japan has for the nations of the earth. For the development of Negro genius, of Negro literature and art, of Negro spirit, only Negroes bound and welded together, Negroes inspired by one vast ideal, can work out in its fullness the great message we have for humanity. We cannot reverse history; we are subject to the same natural laws as other races, and if the Negro is ever to be a factor in the world's history — if among the gaily-colored banners that deck the broad ramparts of civilization is to hang one uncompromising black, then it must be placed there by black hands, fashioned by black heads and hallowed by the travail of 200,000,000 black hearts beating in one glad song of jubilee.

For this reason, the advance guard of the Negro people — the 8,000,000 people of Negro blood in the United States of America — must soon come to realize that if they are to take their just place in the van of Pan-Negroism, then their destiny is *not* absorption by the white Americans. That if in America it is to be proven for the first time in the modern world that not only Negroes are capable of evolving individual men like Toussaint, the Saviour, but are a nation stored with wonderful possibilities of culture, then their destiny is not a servile imitation of Anglo-Saxon culture, but a stalwart originality which shall unswervingly follow Negro ideals.

It may, however, be objected here that the situation of our race in America renders this attitude impossible; that our sole hope of salvation lies in our being able to lose our race identity in the commingled blood of the nation; and that any other course would merely increase the friction of races which we call race prejudice, and against which we have so long and so earnestly fought.

Here, then, is the dilemma, and it is a puzzling one, I admit. No Negro who has given earnest thought to the situation of his people in America has failed, at some time in life, to find himself at these cross-roads; has failed to ask himself at some time: What, after all, am I? Am I an American or am I a Negro? Can I be both? Or is it my duty to cease to be a Negro as soon as possible and be an American? If I strive as a Negro, am I not perpetuating the very cleft that threatens and separates Black and White America? Is not my only possible practical aim the subduction of all that is Negro in me to the American? Does my black blood place upon me any more obligation to assert my nationality than German, or Irish or Italian blood would?

It is such incessant self-questioning and the hesitation that arises from it, that is making the present period a time of vacillation and contradiction for the American Negro; combined race action is stifled, race responsibility is shirked, race enterprises languish, and the best blood, the best talent, the best energy of the Negro people cannot be marshalled to do the bidding of the race. They stand back to make room for every rascal and demagogue who chooses to cloak his selfish deviltry under the veil of race pride.

Is this right? Is it rational? Is it good policy? Have we in America a distinct mission as a race—a distinct sphere of action and an opportunity for race development, or is self-obliteration the highest end to which Negro blood dare aspire?

If we carefully consider what race prejudice really is, we find it, historically, to be nothing but the friction between different groups of people; it is the difference in aim, in feeling, in ideals of two different races; if, now, this difference exists touching territory, laws, language, or even religion, it is manifest that these people cannot live in the same territory without fatal collision; but if, on the other hand, there is substantial agreement in laws, language and religion; if there is a satisfactory adjustment of economic life, then there is no reason why, in the same country and on the same street, two or three great national ideals might not thrive and develop, that men of different races might not strive together for their race ideals as well, perhaps even better, than in isolation. Here, it seems to me, is the reading of the riddle that puzzles so many of us. We are Americans, not only by birth and by citizenship, but by our political ideals, our language, our religion. Farther than that, our Americanism does not go. At that point, we are Negroes, members of a vast historic race that from the very dawn of creation has slept, but half awakening in the dark forests of its African fatherland. We are the first fruits of this new nation, the harbinger of that black to-morrow which is yet destined to soften the whiteness of the Teutonic to-day. We are that people whose subtle sense of song has given America its only American music, its only American fairy tales, its only touch of pathos and humor amid its mad money-getting plutocracy. As such, it is our duty to conserve our physical powers, our intellectual endowments, our spiritual ideals; as a race we must strive by race organization, by race solidarity, by race unity to the realization of that broader humanity which freely recognizes differences in men, but sternly deprecates inequality in their opportunities of development.

For the accomplishment of these ends we need race organizations: Negro colleges, Negro newspapers, Negro business organizations, a Negro school of literature and art, and an intellectual clearing house, for all these products of the Negro mind, which we may call a Negro Academy. Not only is all this necessary for positive advance, it is absolutely imperative for negative defense. Let us not deceive ourselves at our situation in this country. Weighted with a heritage of moral iniquity from our past history, hard pressed in the economic world by foreign immigrants and native prejudice, hated here, despised there and pitied everywhere; our one haven of refuge is ourselves, and but one means of advance, our own belief in our great destiny, our own implicit trust in our ability and worth. There is no power under God's high heaven that can stop the advance of eight thousand thousand honest, earnest, inspired and united people. But—and here is the rub—they *must* be honest, fearlessly criticising their own faults, zealously correcting them; they must be *earnest*. No people that laughs at itself, and ridicules itself, and wishes to God it was anything but itself ever wrote its name in history; it *must* be inspired with the Divine faith of our black mothers, that out of the blood and dust of battle will march a victorious host, a mighty nation, a peculiar people, to speak to the nations of earth a Divine truth that shall make them free. And such a people must be united; not merely united for the organized theft of political spoils, not united to disgrace religion with whoremongers and ward-heelers; not united merely to protest and pass resolutions, but united to stop the ravages of consumption among the Negro people, united to keep black boys from loafing, gambling and crime; united to guard the purity of black women and to reduce that vast army of black prostitutes that is today marching to hell; and united in serious organizations, to determine by careful conference and thoughtful interchange of opinion the broad lines of policy and action for the American Negro.

This, is the reason for being which the American Negro Academy has. It aims at once to be the epitome and expression of the intellect of the black-blooded people of America, the exponent of the race ideals of one of the world's great races. As such, the Academy must, if successful, be

(a). Representative in character.

(b). Impartial in conduct.

(c). Firm in leadership.

It must be representative in character; not in that it represents all interests or all factions, but in that it seeks to comprise something of the *best* thought, the most unselfish striving and the highest ideals. There are scattered in forgotten nooks and corners throughout the land, Negroes of some considerable training, of high minds, and high motives, who are unknown to their fellows, who exert far too little influence. These the Negro Academy should strive to bring into touch with each other and to give them a common mouthpiece.

The Academy should be impartial in conduct; while it aims to exalt the people it should aim to do so by truth — not by lies, by honesty — not by flattery. It should continually impress the fact upon the Negro people that they must not expect to have things done for them — they MUST DO FOR THEMSELVES; that they have on their hands a vast work of self-reformation to do, and that a little less complaint and whining, and a little more dogged work and manly striving would do us more credit and benefit than a thousand Force or Civil Rights bills.

Finally, the American Negro Academy must point out a practical path of advance to the Negro people; there lie before every Negro today hundreds of questions of policy and right which must be settled and which each one settles now, not in accordance with any rule, but by impulse or individual preference; for instance: What should be the attitude of Negroes toward the educational qualification for voters? What should be our attitude toward separate schools? How should we meet discriminations on railways and in hotels? Such questions need not so much specific answers for each part as a general expression of policy, and nobody should be better fitted to announce such a policy than a representative honest Negro Academy.

All this, however, must come in time after careful organization and long conference. The immediate work before us should be practical and have direct bearing upon the situation of the Negro. The historical work of collecting the laws of the United States and of the various States of the Union with regard to the Negro is a work of such magnitude and importance that no body but one like this could think of undertaking it. If we could accomplish that one task we would justify our existence.

In the field of Sociology an appalling work lies before us. First, we must unflinchingly and bravely face the truth, not with apologies, but with solemn earnestness. The Negro Academy ought to sound a note of warning that would echo in every black cabin in the land: *Unless we conquer our present vices they will conquer us;* we are diseased, we are developing criminal tendencies, and an alarmingly large percentage of our men and women are sexually impure. The Negro Academy should stand and proclaim this over the housetops, crying with Garrison: *I will not equivocate, I will not retreat a single inch, and I will be heard.* The Academy should seek to gather about it the talented, unselfish men, the pure and noble-minded women, to fight an army of devils that disgraces our manhood and our womanhood. There does not stand today upon God's earth a race more capable in muscle, in intellect, in morals, than the American Negro, if he will bend his energies in the right direction; if he will

> Burst his birth's invidious bar
> And grasp the skirts of happy chance,
> And breast the blows of circumstance,
> And grapple with his evil star.

In science and morals, I have indicated two fields of work for the Academy. Finally, in practical policy, I wish to suggest the following *Academy Creed:*

1. We believe that the Negro people, as a race, have a contribution to make to civilization and humanity, which no other race can make.

2. We believe it the duty of the Americans of Negro descent, as a body, to maintain their race identity until this mission of the Negro people is accomplished, and the ideal of human brotherhood has become a practical possibility.

3. We believe that, unless modern civilization is a failure, it is entirely feasible and practicable for two races in such essential political, economic and religious harmony as the white and colored people of America, to develop side by side in peace and mutual happiness, the peculiar contribution which each has to make to the culture of their common country.

4. As a means to this end we advocate, not such social equality between these races as would disregard human likes and dislikes, but such a social equilibrium as would, throughout all the complicated relations of life, give due and just consideration to culture, ability, and moral worth, whether they be found under white or black skins.

5. We believe that the first and greatest step toward the settlement of the present friction between the races — commonly called the Negro Problem — lies in the correction of the immorality, crime and laziness among the Negroes themselves, which still remains as a heritage from slavery. We believe that only earnest and long continued efforts on our own part can cure these social ills.

6. We believe that the second great step toward a better adjustment of the relations between the races, should be a more impartial selection of ability in the economic and intellectual world, and a greater respect for personal liberty and worth, regardless of race. We believe that only earnest efforts on the part of the white people of this country will bring much needed reform in these matters.

7. On the basis of the foregoing declaration, and firmly believing in our high destiny, we, as American Negroes, are resolved to strive in

every honorable way for the realization of the best and highest aims, for the development of strong manhood and pure womanhood, and for the rearing of a race ideal in America and Africa, to the glory of God and the uplifting of the Negro people.

Of Our Spiritual Strivings

Between me and the other world there is ever an unasked question: unasked by some through feelings of delicacy; by others through the difficulty of rightly framing it. All, nevertheless, flutter round it. They approach me in a half-hesitant sort of way, eye me curiously or compassionately, and then, instead of saying directly, How does it feel to be a problem? they say, I know an excellent colored man in my town; or, I fought at Mechanicsville; or, Do not these Southern outrages make your blood boil? At these I smile, or am interested, or reduce the boiling to a simmer, as the occasion may require. To the real question, How does it feel to be a problem? I answer seldom a word.

And yet, being a problem is a strange experience, — peculiar even for one who has never been anything else, save perhaps in babyhood and in Europe. It is in the early days of rollicking boyhood that the revelation first bursts upon one, all in a day, as it were. I remember well when the shadow swept across me. I was a little thing, away up in the hills of New England, where the dark Housatonic winds between Hoosac and Tagh-kanic to the sea. In a wee wooden schoolhouse, something put it into the boys' and girls' heads to buy gorgeous visiting-cards — ten cents a package — and exchange. The exchange was merry, till one girl, a tall new-comer, refused my card, — refused it peremptorily, with a glance. Then it dawned upon me with a certain suddenness that I was different from the others; or like, mayhap, in heart and life and longing, but shut out from their world by a vast veil. I had thereafter no desire to tear down that veil, to creep through; I held all beyond it in common contempt, and lived above it in a region of blue sky and great wandering shadows. That sky was bluest when I could beat my mates at examination-time, or beat them at a foot-race, or even beat their stringy heads. Alas, with the years all this fine contempt began to fade; for the worlds I longed

From *Souls of Black Folk* by W. E. B. Du Bois, ch. 1. Published by A. C. McClurg & Co., 1903.

for, and all their dazzling opportunities, were theirs, not mine. But they should not keep these prizes, I said; some, all, I would wrest from them. Just how I would do it I could never decide: by reading law, by healing the sick, by telling the wonderful tales that swam in my head,— some way. With other black boys the strife was not so fiercely sunny: their youth shrunk into tasteless sycophancy, or into silent hatred of the pale world about them and mocking distrust of everything white; or wasted itself in a bitter cry, Why did God make me an outcast and a stranger in mine own house? The shades of the prison-house closed round about us all: walls strait and stubborn to the whitest, but relentlessly narrow, tall, and unscalable to sons of night who must plod darkly on in resignation, or beat unavailing palms against the stone, or steadily, half hopelessly, watch the streak of blue above.

After the Egyptian and Indian, the Greek and Roman, the Teuton and Mongolian, the Negro is a sort of seventh son, born with a veil, and gifted with second-sight in this American world,—a world which yields him no true self-consciousness, but only lets him see himself through the revelation of the other world. It is a peculiar sensation, this double-consciousness, this sense of always looking at one's self through the eyes of others, of measuring one's soul by the tape of a world that looks on in amused contempt and pity. One ever feels his two-ness,—an American, a Negro; two souls, two thoughts, two unreconciled strivings; two warring ideals in one dark body, whose dogged strength alone keeps it from being torn asunder.

The history of the American Negro is the history of this strife,—this longing to attain self-conscious manhood, to merge his double self into a better and truer self. In this merging he wishes neither of the older selves to be lost. He would not Africanize America, for America has too much to teach the world and Africa. He would not bleach his Negro soul in a flood of white Americanism, for he knows that Negro blood has a message for the world. He simply wishes to make it possible for a man to be both a Negro and an American, without being cursed and spit upon by his fellows, without having the doors of Opportunity closed roughly in his face.

This, then, is the end of his striving: to be a co-worker in the kingdom of culture, to escape both death and isolation, to husband and use his best powers and his latent genius. These powers of body and mind have in the past been strangely wasted, dispersed, or forgotten. The shadow of a mighty Negro past flits through the tale of Ethiopia the Shadowy and of Egypt the Sphinx. Throughout history, the powers of single black men flash here and there like falling stars, and die sometimes before the world has rightly gauged their brightness. Here in America, in the few days since Emancipation, the black man's turning hither and thither in hesitant and doubtful striving has often made his very strength to lose effectiveness, to seem like absence of power, like weakness. And yet it is not weakness,—it is the contradiction of double aims. The double-aimed struggle of the black artisan—on the one hand to escape white contempt for a nation of mere hewers of wood and drawers of water, and on the other hand to plough and nail and dig for a poverty-stricken horde—could only result in making him a poor craftsman, for he had but half a heart in either cause. By the poverty and ignorance of his people, the Negro minister or doctor was tempted toward quackery and demagogy; and by the criticism of the other world, toward ideals that made him ashamed of his lowly tasks. The would-be black *savant* was confronted by the paradox that the knowledge his people needed was a twice-told tale to his white neighbors, while the knowledge which would teach the white world was Greek to his own flesh and blood. The innate love of harmony and beauty that set the ruder souls of his people a-dancing and a-singing raised but confusion and doubt in the soul of the black artist; for the beauty revealed to him was the soul-beauty of a race which his larger audience despised, and he could not articulate the message of another people. This waste of double aims, this seeking to satisfy two unreconciled ideals, has wrought sad havoc with the courage and faith and deeds of ten thousand thousand people,—has sent them often wooing false gods and invoking false means of salvation, and at times has even seemed about to make them ashamed of themselves.

Away back in the days of bondage they thought to see in one divine event the end of all doubt and disappointment; few men ever worshipped Freedom with half such unquestioning faith as did the American Negro for two centuries. To him, so far as he thought and dreamed, slavery was indeed the sum of all villainies, the cause of all sorrow, the root of all prejudice; Emancipation was the key to a promised land of sweeter beauty than ever stretched before the eyes of wearied Israelites. In song and exhortation swelled one refrain—Liberty; in his tears and curses the God he implored had Freedom in his right hand. At last it came,—suddenly, fearfully, like a dream. With one wild carnival of blood and passion came the message in his own plaintive cadences:—

> Shout, O children!
> Shout, you're free!
> For God has bought your liberty!

Years have passed away since then,—ten, twenty, forty; forty years of national life, forty years of renewal and development, and yet the swarthy spectre sits in its accustomed seat at the Nation's feast. In vain do we cry to this our vastest social problem:—

> Take any shape but that, and my firm nerves
> Shall never tremble!

The Nation has not yet found peace from its sins; the freedman has not yet found in freedom his promised land. Whatever of good may have come in these years of change, the shadow of a deep disappointment rests upon the Negro people, — a disappointment all the more bitter because the unattained ideal was unbounded save by the simple ignorance of a lowly people.

The first decade was merely a prolongation of the vain search for freedom, the boon that seemed ever barely to elude their grasp, — like a tantalizing will-o'-the-wisp, maddening and misleading the headless host. The holocaust of war, the terrors of the Ku-Klux Klan, the lies of carpet-baggers, the disorganization of industry, and the contradictory advice of friends and foes, left the bewildered serf with no new watchword beyond the old cry for freedom. As the time flew, however, he began to grasp a new idea. The ideal of liberty demanded for its attainment powerful means, and these the Fifteenth Amendment gave him. The ballot, which before he had looked upon as a visible sign of freedom, he now regarded as the chief means of gaining and perfecting the liberty with which war had partially endowed him. And why not? Had not votes made war and emancipated millions? Had not votes enfranchised the freedmen? Was anything impossible to a power that had done all this? A million black men started with renewed zeal to vote themselves into the kingdom. So the decade flew away, the revolution of 1876 came, and left the half-free serf weary, wondering, but still inspired. Slowly but steadily, in the following years, a new vision began gradually to replace the dream of political power, — a powerful movement, the rise of another ideal to guide the unguided, another pillar of fire by night after a clouded day. It was the ideal of "book-learning"; the curiosity, born of compulsory ignorance, to know and test the power of the cabalistic letters of the white man, the longing to know. Here at last seemed to have been discovered the mountain path to Canaan; longer than the highway of Emancipation and law, steep and rugged, but straight, leading to heights high enough to overlook life.

Up the new path the advance guard toiled, slowly, heavily, doggedly; only those who have watched and guided the faltering feet, the misty minds, the dull understandings, of the dark pupils of these schools know how faithfully, how piteously, this people strove to learn. It was weary work. The cold statistician wrote down the inches of progress here and there, noted also where here and there a foot had slipped or some one had fallen. To the tired climbers, the horizon was ever dark, the mists were often cold, the Canaan was always dim and far away. If, however, the vistas disclosed as yet no goal, no resting-place, little but flattery and criticism, the journey at least gave leisure for reflection and self-examination; it changed the child of Emancipation to the youth with dawning self-consciousness, self-realization, self-respect. In those sombre forests of his striving his own soul rose before him, and he saw himself,—darkly as through a veil; and yet he saw in himself some faint revelation of his power, of his mission. He began to have a dim feeling that, to attain his place in the world, he must be himself, and not another. For the first time he sought to analyze the burden he bore upon his back, that dead-weight of social degradation partially masked behind a half-named Negro problem. He felt his poverty; without a cent, without a home, without land, tools, or savings, he had entered into competition with rich, landed, skilled neighbors. To be a poor man is hard, but to be a poor race in a land of dollars is the very bottom of hardships. He felt the weight of his ignorance,—not simply of letters, but of life, of business, of the humanities; the accumulated sloth and shirking and awkwardness of decades and centuries shackled his hands and feet. Nor was his burden all poverty and ignorance. The red stain of bastardy, which two centuries of systematic legal defilement of Negro women had stamped upon his race, meant not only the loss of ancient African chastity, but also the hereditary weight of a mass of corruption from white adulterers, threatening almost the obliteration of the Negro home.

A people thus handicapped ought not to be asked to race with the world, but rather allowed to give all its time and thought to its own social problems. But alas! while sociologists gleefully count his bastards and his prostitutes, the very soul of the toiling, sweating black man is darkened by the shadow of a vast despair. Men call the shadow prejudice, and learnedly explain it as the natural defence of culture against barbarism, learning against ignorance, purity against crime, the "higher" against the "lower" races. To which the Negro cries Amen! and swears that to so much of this strange prejudice as is founded on just homage to civilization, culture, righteousness, and progress, he humbly bows and meekly does obeisance. But before that nameless prejudice that leaps beyond all this he stands helpless, dismayed, and well-nigh speechless; before that personal disrespect and mockery, the ridicule and systematic humiliation, the distortion of fact and wanton license of fancy, the cynical ignoring of the better and the boisterous welcoming of the worse, the all-pervading desire to inculcate disdain for everything black, from Toussaint to the devil,—before this there rises a sickening despair that would disarm and discourage any nation save that black host to whom "discouragement" is an unwritten word.

But the facing of so vast a prejudice could not but bring the inevitable self-questioning, self-disparagement, and lowering of ideals which ever accompany repression and breed in an atmosphere of contempt and hate. Whisperings and portents came borne upon the four winds: Lo! we are diseased and dying, cried the dark hosts; we cannot write, our voting is vain; what need of education, since we must always cook and serve? And the Nation echoed and enforced this self-criticism, saying: Be content to be servants, and nothing more; what need of higher culture for half-men? Away with the black man's ballot, by force or fraud,—and behold the suicide of a race! Nevertheless, out of the evil came something of good,—the more careful adjustment of education to real life, the clearer perception of the Negroes' social responsibilities, and the sobering realization of the meaning of progress.

So dawned the time of *Sturm und Drang:* storm and stress to-day rocks our little boat on the mad waters of the world-sea; there is within and without the sound of conflict, the burning of body and rending of soul; inspiration strives with doubt, and faith with vain questionings. The bright ideals of the past,—physical freedom, political power, the training of brains and the training of hands,—all these in turn have waxed and waned, until even the last grows dim and overcast. Are they all wrong,—all false? No, not that, but each alone was over-simple and incomplete,—the dreams of a credulous race-childhood, or the fond imaginings of the other world which does not know and does not want to know our power. To be really true, all these ideals must be melted and welded into one. The training of the schools we need to-day more than ever,—the training of deft hands, quick eyes and ears, and above all the broader, deeper, higher culture of gifted minds and pure hearts. The power of the ballot we need in sheer self-defence,—else what shall save us from a second slavery? Freedom, too, the long-sought, we still seek, —the freedom of life and limb, the freedom to work and think, the freedom to love and aspire. Work, culture, liberty,—all these we need, not singly but together, not successively but together, each growing and aiding each, and all striving toward that vaster ideal that swims before the Negro people, the ideal of human brotherhood, gained through the unifying ideal of Race; the ideal of fostering and developing the traits and talents of the Negro, not in opposition to or contempt for other races, but rather in large conformity to the greater ideals of the American Republic, in order that some day on American soil two world-races may give each to each those characteristics both so sadly lack. We the darker ones come even now not altogether empty-handed: there are to-day no truer exponents of the pure human spirit of the Declaration of Independence than the American Negroes; there is no true American music but the wild sweet melodies of the Negro slave; the American fairy tales and folk-lore are Indian and African; and, all in all, we black men seem the sole oasis of simple faith and reverence in a dusty desert of dollars and smartness. Will America be poorer if she replace her brutal dyspeptic blundering with light-hearted but determined Negro humility? or her coarse and cruel wit with loving jovial good-humor? or her vulgar music with the soul of the Sorrow Songs?

Merely a concrete test of the underlying principles of the great republic is the Negro Problem, and the spiritual striving of the freedmen's sons is the travail of souls whose burden is almost beyond the measure of their strength, but who bear it in the name of an historic race, in the name of this the land of their fathers' fathers, and in the name of human opportunity.

Of Mr. Booker T. Washington and Others

Easily the most striking thing in the history of the American Negro since 1876 is the ascendancy of Mr. Booker T. Washington. It began at the time when war memories and ideals were rapidly passing; a day of astonishing commercial development was dawning; a sense of doubt and hesitation overtook the freedmen's sons,—then it was that his leading began. Mr. Washington came, with a simple definite programme, at the psychological moment when the nation was a little ashamed of having bestowed so much sentiment on Negroes, and was concentrating its energies on Dollars. His programme of industrial education, conciliation of the South, and submission and silence as to civil and political rights, was not wholly original; the Free Negroes from 1830 up to war-time had striven to build industrial schools, and the American Missionary Association had from the first taught various trades; and Price and others had sought a way of honorable alliance with the best of the Southerners. But Mr. Washington first indissolubly linked these things; he put enthusiasm, unlimited energy, and perfect faith into this programme, and changed it from a by-path into a veritable Way of Life. And the tale of the methods by which he did this is a fascinating study of human life.

It startled the nation to hear a Negro advocating such a programme after many decades of bitter complaint; it startled and won the applause

From *Souls of Black Folk* by W. E. B. Du Bois, ch. 3. Published by A. C. McClurg & Co., 1903.

of the South, it interested and won the admiration of the North; and after a confused murmur of protest, it silenced if it did not convert the Negroes themselves.

To gain the sympathy and cooperation of the various elements comprising the white South was Mr. Washington's first task; and this, at the time Tuskegee was founded, seemed, for a black man, well-nigh impossible. And yet ten years later it was done in the word spoken at Atlanta: "In all things purely social we can be as separate as the five fingers, and yet one as the hand in all things essential to mutual progress." This "Atlanta Compromise" is by all odds the most notable thing in Mr. Washington's career. The South interpreted it in different ways: the radicals received it as a complete surrender of the demand for civil and political equality; the conservatives, as a generously conceived working basis for mutual understanding. So both approved it, and to-day its author is certainly the most distinguished Southerner since Jefferson Davis, and the one with the largest personal following.

Next to this achievement comes Mr. Washington's work in gaining place and consideration in the North. Others less shrewd and tactful had formerly essayed to sit on these two stools and had fallen between them; but as Mr. Washington knew the heart of the South from birth and training, so by singular insight he intuitively grasped the spirit of the age which was dominating the North. And so thoroughly did he learn the speech and thought of triumphant commercialism, and the ideals of material prosperity, that the picture of a lone black boy poring over a French grammar amid the weeds and dirt of a neglected home soon seemed to him the acme of absurdities. One wonders what Socrates and St. Francis of Assisi would say to this.

And yet this very singleness of vision and thorough oneness with his age is a mark of the successful man. It is as though Nature must needs make men narrow in order to give them force. So Mr. Washington's cult has gained unquestioning followers, his work has wonderfully prospered, his friends are legion, and his enemies are confounded. To-day he stands as the one recognized spokesman of his ten million fellows, and one of the most notable figures in a nation of seventy millions. One hesitates, therefore, to criticise a life which, beginning with so little, has done so much. And yet the time is come when one may speak in all sincerity and utter courtesy of the mistakes and shortcomings of Mr. Washington's career, as well as of his triumphs, without being thought captious or envious, and without forgetting that it is easier to do ill than well in the world.

The criticism that has hitherto met Mr. Washington has not always been of this broad character. In the South especially has he had to walk warily to avoid the harshest judgments, — and naturally so, for he is dealing with the one subject of deepest sensitiveness to that section. Twice —

once when at the Chicago celebration of the Spanish-American War he alluded to the color-prejudice that is "eating away the vitals of the South," and once when he dined with President Roosevelt—has the resulting Southern criticism been violent enough to threaten seriously his popularity. In the North the feeling has several times forced itself into words, that Mr. Washington's counsels of submission overlooked certain elements of true manhood, and that his educational programme was unnecessarily narrow. Usually, however, such criticism has not found open expression, although, too, the spiritual sons of the Abolitionists have not been prepared to acknowledge that the schools founded before Tuskegee, by men of broad ideals and self-sacrificing spirit, were wholly failures or worthy of ridicule. While, then, criticism has not failed to follow Mr. Washington, yet the prevailing public opinion of the land has been but too willing to deliver the solution of a wearisome problem into his hands, and say, "If that is all you and your race ask, take it."

Among his own people, however, Mr. Washington has encountered the strongest and most lasting opposition, amounting at times to bitterness, and even to-day continuing strong and insistent even though largely silenced in outward expression by the public opinion of the nation. Some of this opposition is, of course, mere envy; the disappointment of displaced demagogues and the spite of narrow minds. But aside from this, there is among educated and thoughtful colored men in all parts of the land a feeling of deep regret, sorrow, and apprehension at the wide currency and ascendancy which some of Mr. Washington's theories have gained. These same men admire his sincerity of purpose, and are willing to forgive much to honest endeavor which is doing something worth the doing. They cooperate with Mr. Washington as far as they conscientiously can; and, indeed, it is no ordinary tribute to this man's tact and power that, steering as he must between so many diverse interests and opinions, he so largely retains the respect of all.

But the hushing of the criticism of honest opponents is a dangerous thing. It leads some of the best of the critics to unfortunate silence and paralysis of effort, and others to burst into speech so passionately and intemperately as to lose listeners. Honest and earnest criticism from those whose interests are most nearly touched,—criticism of writers by readers, of government by those governed, of leaders by those led,—this is the soul of democracy and the safeguard of modern society. If the best of the American Negroes receive by outer pressure a leader whom they had not recognized before, manifestly there is here a certain palpable gain. Yet there is also irreparable loss,—a loss of that peculiarly valuable education which a group receives when by search and criticism it finds and commissions its own leaders. The way in which this is done is at once the most elementary and the nicest problem of social growth. History is but the record of such group-leadership; and yet how infinitely changeful is its type and character! And of all types and kinds, what can be more instructive than the leadership of a group within a group?—that curious double movement where real progress may be negative and actual advance be relative retrogression. All this is the social student's inspiration and despair.

Now in the past the American Negro has had instructive experience in the choosing of group leaders, founding thus a peculiar dynasty which in the light of present conditions is worth while studying. When sticks and stones and beasts form the sole environment of a people, their attitude is largely one of determined opposition to and conquest of natural forces. But when to earth and brute is added an environment of men and ideas, then the attitude of the imprisoned group may take three main forms,—a feeling of revolt and revenge; an attempt to adjust all thought and action to the will of the greater group; or, finally, a determined effort at self-realization and self-development despite environing opinion. The influence of all of these attitudes at various times can be traced in the history of the American Negro, and in the evolution of his successive leaders.

Before 1750, while the fire of African freedom still burned in the veins of the slaves, there was in all leadership or attempted leadership but the one motive of revolt and revenge,—typified in the terrible Maroons, the Danish blacks, and Cato of Stono, and veiling all the Americas in fear of insurrection. The liberalizing tendencies of the latter half of the eighteenth century brought, along with kindlier relations between black and white, thoughts of ultimate adjustment and assimilation. Such aspiration was especially voiced in the earnest songs of Phyllis, in the martyrdom of Attucks, the fighting of Salem and Poor, the intellectual accomplishments of Banneker and Derham, and the political demands of the Cuffes.

Stern financial and social stress after the war cooled much of the previous humanitarian ardor. The disappointment and impatience of the Negroes at the persistence of slavery and serfdom voiced itself in two movements. The slaves in the South, aroused undoubtedly by vague rumors of the Haytian revolt, made three fierce attempts at insurrection,—in 1800 under Gabriel in Virginia, in 1822 under Vesey in Carolina, and in 1831 again in Virginia under the terrible Nat Turner. In the Free States, on the other hand, a new and curious attempt at self-development was made. In Philadelphia and New York color-prescription led to a withdrawal of Negro communicants from white churches and the formation of a peculiar socio-religious institution among the Negroes known as the African Church,—an organization still living and controlling in its various branches over a million of men.

Walker's wild appeal against the trend of the times showed how the world was changing after the coming of the cotton-gin. By 1830 slavery seemed hopelessly fastened on the South, and the slaves thoroughly cowed into submission. The free Negroes of the North, inspired by the mulatto immigrants from the West Indies, began to change the basis of their demands; they recognized the slavery of slaves, but insisted that they themselves were freemen, and sought assimilation and amalgamation with the nation on the same terms with other men. Thus, Forten and Purvis of Philadelphia, Shad of Wilmington, Du Bois of New Haven, Barbadoes of Boston, and others, strove singly and together as men, they said, not as slaves; as "people of color," not as "Negroes." The trend of the times, however, refused them recognition save in individual and exceptional cases, considered them as one with all the despised blacks, and they soon found themselves striving to keep even the rights they formerly had of voting and working and moving as freemen. Schemes of migration and colonization arose among them; but these they refused to entertain, and they eventually turned to the Abolition movement as a final refuge.

Here, led by Remond, Nell, Wells-Brown, and Douglass, a new period of self-assertion and self-development dawned. To be sure, ultimate freedom and assimilation was the ideal before the leaders, but the assertion of the manhood rights of the Negro by himself was the main reliance, and John Brown's raid was the extreme of its logic. After the war and emancipation, the great form of Frederick Douglass, the greatest of American Negro leaders, still led the host. Self-assertion, especially in political lines, was the main programme, and behind Douglass came Elliot, Bruce, and Langston, and the Reconstruction politicians, and, less conspicuous but of greater social significance[,] Alexander Crummell and Bishop Daniel Payne.

Then came the Revolution of 1876, the suppression of the Negro votes, the changing and shifting of ideals, and the seeking of new lights in the great night. Douglass, in his old age, still bravely stood for the ideals of his early manhood, — ultimate assimilation *through* self-assertion, and on no other terms. For a time Price arose as a new leader, destined, it seemed, not to give up, but to re-state the old ideals in a form less repugnant to the white South. But he passed away in his prime. Then came the new leader. Nearly all the former ones had become leaders by the silent suffrage of their fellows, had sought to lead their own people alone, and were usually, save Douglass, little known outside their race. But Booker T. Washington arose as essentially the leader not of one race but of two, — a compromiser between the South, the North, and the Negro. Naturally the Negroes resented, at first bitterly, signs of compromise which surrendered their civil and political rights, even though this was to be exchanged for larger chances of economic development. The rich and dominating North, however, was not only weary of the race problem, but was investing largely in Southern enterprises, and welcomed any method of peaceful cooperation. Thus, by national opinion, the Negroes began to recognize Mr. Washington's leadership; and the voice of criticism was hushed.

Mr. Washington represents in Negro thought the old attitude of adjustment and submission; but adjustment at such a peculiar time as to make his programme unique. This is an age of unusual economic development, and Mr. Washington's programme naturally takes an economic cast, becoming a gospel of Work and Money to such an extent as apparently almost completely to overshadow the higher aims of life. Moreover, this is an age when the more advanced races are coming in closer contact with the less developed races, and the race-feeling is therefore intensified; and Mr. Washington's programme practically accepts the alleged inferiority of the Negro races. Again, in our own land, the reaction from the sentiment of war time has given impetus to race-prejudice against Negroes, and Mr. Washington withdraws many of the high demands of Negroes as men and American citizens. In other periods of intensified prejudice all the Negro's tendency to self-assertion has been called forth; at this period a policy of submission is advocated. In the history of nearly all other races and peoples the doctrine preached at such crises has been that manly self-respect is worth more than lands and houses, and that a people who voluntarily surrender such respect, or cease striving for it, are not worth civilizing.

In answer to this, it has been claimed that the Negro can survive only through submission. Mr. Washington distinctly asks that black people give up, at least for the present, three things,—

First, political power,

Second, insistence on civil rights,

Third, higher education of Negro youth,—

and concentrate all their energies on industrial education, the accumulation of wealth, and the conciliation of the South. This policy has been courageously and insistently advocated for over fifteen years, and has been triumphant for perhaps ten years. As a result of this tender of the palm-branch, what has been the return? In these years there have occurred:

1. The disfranchisement of the Negro.

2. The legal creation of a distinct status of civil inferiority for the Negro.

3. The steady withdrawal of aid from institutions for the higher training of the Negro.

These movements are not, to be sure, direct results of Mr. Washington's teachings; but his propaganda has, without a shadow of doubt, helped their speedier accomplishment. The question then comes: Is it possible, and probable, that nine millions of men can make effective progress in economic lines if they are deprived of political rights, made a servile caste, and allowed only the most meagre chance for developing their exceptional men? If history and reason give any distinct answer to these questions, it is an emphatic *No.* And Mr. Washington thus faces the triple paradox of his career:

1. He is striving nobly to make Negro artisans business men and property-owners; but it is utterly impossible, under modern competitive methods, for workingmen and property-owners to defend their rights and exist without the right of suffrage.

2. He insists on thrift and self-respect, but at the same time counsels a silent submission to civic inferiority such as is bound to sap the manhood of any race in the long run.

3. He advocates common-school and industrial training, and depreciates institutions of higher learning; but neither the Negro common-schools, nor Tuskegee itself, could remain open a day were it not for teachers trained in Negro colleges, or trained by their graduates.

This triple paradox in Mr. Washington's position is the object of criticism by two classes of colored Americans. One class is spiritually descended from Toussaint the Savior, through Gabriel, Vesey, and Turner, and they represent the attitude of revolt and revenge; they hate the white South blindly and distrust the white race generally, and so far as they agree on definite action, think that the Negro's only hope lies in emigration beyond the borders of the United States. And yet, by the irony of fate, nothing has more effectually made this programme seem hopeless than the recent course of the United States toward weaker and darker peoples in the West Indies, Hawaii, and the Philippines,— for where in the world may we go and be safe from lying and brute force?

The other class of Negroes who cannot agree with Mr. Washington has hitherto said little aloud. They deprecate the sight of scattered counsels, of internal disagreement; and especially they dislike making their just criticism of a useful and earnest man an excuse for a general discharge of venom from small-minded opponents. Nevertheless, the questions involved are so fundamental and serious that it is difficult to see how men like the Grimkes, Kelly Miller, J. W. E. Bowen, and other representatives of this group, can much longer be silent. Such men feel in conscience bound to ask of this nation three things:

1. The right to vote.
2. Civic equality.
3. The education of youth according to ability.

They acknowledge Mr. Washington's invaluable service in counselling patience and courtesy in such demands; they do not ask that ignorant black men vote when ignorant whites are debarred, or that any reasonable restrictions in the suffrage should not be applied; they know that the low social level of the mass of the race is responsible for much discrimination against it, but they also know, and the nation knows, that relentless color-prejudice is more often a cause than a result of the Negro's degradation; they seek the abatement of this relic of barbarism, and not its systematic encouragement and pampering by all agencies of social power from the Associated Press to the Church of Christ. They advocate, with Mr. Washington, a broad system of Negro common schools supplemented by thorough industrial training; but they are surprised that a man of Mr. Washington's insight cannot see that no such educational system ever has rested or can rest on any other basis than that of the well-equipped college and university, and they insist that there is a demand for a few such institutions throughout the South to train the best of the Negro youth as teachers, professional men, and leaders.

This group of men honor Mr. Washington for his attitude of conciliation toward the white South; they accept the "Atlanta Compromise" in its broadest interpretation; they recognize, with him, many signs of promise, many men of high purpose and fair judgment, in this section; they know that no easy task has been laid upon a region already tottering under heavy burdens. But, nevertheless, they insist that the way to truth and right lies in straightforward honesty, not in indiscriminate flattery; in praising those of the South who do well and criticising uncompromisingly those who do ill; in taking advantage of the opportunities at hand and urging their fellows to do the same, but at the same time in remembering that only a firm adherence to their higher ideals and aspirations will ever keep those ideals within the realm of possibility. They do not expect that the free right to vote, to enjoy civic rights, and to be educated, will come in a moment; they do not expect to see the bias and prejudices of years disappear at the blast of a trumpet; but they are absolutely certain that the way for a people to gain their reasonable rights is not by voluntarily throwing them away and insisting that they do not want them; that the way for a people to gain respect is not by continually belittling and ridiculing themselves; that, on the contrary, Negroes must insist continually, in season and out of season, that voting is necessary to modern manhood, that color discrimination is barbarism, and that black boys need education as well as white boys.

In failing thus to state plainly and unequivocally the legitimate demands of their people, even at the cost of opposing an honored leader, the thinking classes of American Negroes would shirk a heavy responsibility,—a responsibility to themselves, a responsibility to the struggling masses, a responsibility to the darker races of men whose future depends so largely on this American experiment, but especially a responsibility to this nation,—this common Fatherland. It is wrong to encourage a man or a people in evil-doing; it is wrong to aid and abet a national crime simply because it is unpopular not to do so. The growing spirit of kindliness and reconciliation between the North and South after the frightful differences of a generation ago ought to be a source of deep congratulation to all, and especially to those whose mistreatment caused the war; but if that reconciliation is to be marked by the industrial slavery and civic death of those same black men, with permanent legislation into a position of inferiority, then those black men, if they are really men, are called upon by every consideration of patriotism and loyalty to oppose such a course by all civilized methods, even though such opposition involves disagreement with Mr. Booker T. Washington. We have no right to sit silently by while the inevitable seeds are sown for a harvest of disaster to our children, black and white.

First, it is the duty of black men to judge the South discriminatingly. The present generation of Southerners are not responsible for the past, and they should not be blindly hated or blamed for it. Furthermore, to no class is the indiscriminate endorsement of the recent course of the South toward Negroes more nauseating than to the best thought of the South. The South is not "solid"; it is a land in the ferment of social change, wherein forces of all kinds are fighting for supremacy; and to praise the ill the South is to-day perpetrating is just as wrong as to condemn the good. Discriminating and broad-minded criticism is what the South needs,—needs it for the sake of her own white sons and daughters, and for the insurance of robust, healthy mental and moral development.

To-day even the attitude of the Southern whites toward the blacks is not, as so many assume, in all cases the same; the ignorant Southerner hates the Negro, the workingmen fear his competition, the money-makers wish to use him as a laborer, some of the educated see a menace in his upward development, while others — usually the sons of the masters — wish to help him to rise. National opinion has enabled this last class to maintain the Negro common schools, and to protect the Negro partially in property, life, and limb. Through the pressure of the money-makers, the Negro is in danger of being reduced to semi-slavery, especially in the country districts; the workingmen, and those of the educated who fear the Negro, have united to disfranchise him, and some have urged his deportation; while the passions of the ignorant are easily aroused to lynch and abuse any black man. To praise this intricate whirl of thought and prejudice is nonsense; to inveigh indiscriminately against "the South" is unjust; but to use the same breath in praising Governor Aycock, exposing Senator Morgan, arguing with Mr. Thomas Nelson Page, and denouncing Senator Ben Tillman, is not only sane, but the imperative duty of thinking black men.

It would be unjust to Mr. Washington not to acknowledge that in several instances he has opposed movements in the South which were unjust to the Negro; he sent memorials to the Louisiana and Alabama constitutional conventions, he has spoken against lynching, and in other ways has openly or silently set his influence against sinister schemes and unfortunate happenings. Notwithstanding this, it is equally true to assert that on the whole the distinct impression left by Mr. Washington's propaganda is, first, that the South is justified in its present attitude toward the Negro because of the Negro's degradation; secondly, that the prime cause of the Negro's failure to rise more quickly is his wrong education in the past; and, thirdly, that his future rise depends primarily on his own efforts. Each of these propositions is a dangerous half-truth. The supplementary truths must never be lost sight of: first, slavery and race-prejudice are potent if not sufficient causes of the Negro's position; second, industrial and common-school training were necessarily slow in planting because they had to await the black teachers trained by higher institutions, — it being extremely doubtful if any essentially different development was possible, and certainly a Tuskegee was unthinkable before 1880; and, third, while it is a great truth to say that the Negro must strive and strive mightily to help himself, it is equally true that unless his striving be not simply seconded, but rather aroused and encouraged, by the initiative of the richer and wiser environing group, he cannot hope for great success.

In his failure to realize and impress this last point, Mr. Washington is especially to be criticised. His doctrine has tended to make the whites, North and South, shift the burden of the Negro problem to the Negro's shoulders and stand aside as critical and rather pessimistic spectators; when in fact the burden belongs to the nation, and the hands of none of us are clean if we bend not our energies to righting these great wrongs.

The South ought to be led, by candid and honest criticism, to assert her better self and do her full duty to the race she has cruelly wronged and is still wronging. The North—her co-partner in guilt—cannot salve her conscience by plastering it with gold. We cannot settle this problem by diplomacy and suaveness, by "policy" alone. If worse come to worst, can the moral fibre of this country survive the slow throttling and murder of nine millions of men?

The black men of America have a duty to perform, a duty stern and delicate, — a forward movement to oppose a part of the work of their greatest leader. So far as Mr. Washington preaches Thrift, Patience, and Industrial Training for the masses, we must hold up his hands and strive with him, rejoicing in his honors and glorying in the strength of this Joshua called of God and of man to lead the headless host. But so far as Mr. Washington apologizes for injustice, North or South, does not rightly value the privilege and duty of voting, belittles the emasculating effects of caste distinctions, and opposes the higher training and ambition of our brighter minds,—so far as he, the South, or the Nation, does this,—we must unceasingly and firmly oppose them. By every civilized and peaceful method we must strive for the rights which the world accords to men, clinging unwaveringly to those great words which the sons of the Fathers would fain forget: "We hold these truths to be self-evident: That all men are created equal; that they are endowed by their Creator with certain unalienable rights; that among these are life, liberty, and the pursuit of happiness."

The Talented Tenth

The Negro race, like all races, is going to be saved by its exceptional men. The problem of education, then, among Negroes must first of all deal with the Talented Tenth; it is the problem of developing the Best of this race that they may guide the Mass away from the contamination and death of the Worst, in their own and other races. Now the training of men is a difficult and intricate task. Its technique is a matter for educational experts, but its object is for the vision of seers. If we make money the object of man-training, we shall develop money-makers but not necessarily men; if we make technical skill the object of education, we may possess artisans but not, in nature, men. Men we shall have only as we make manhood the object of the work of the schools—intelligence, broad sympathy, knowledge of the world that was and is, and of the relation of men to it—this is the curriculum of that Higher Education which must underlie true life. On this foundation we may build bread winning, skill of hand and quickness of brain, with never a fear lest the child and man mistake the means of living for the object of life.

· · ·

Who are to-day guiding the work of the Negro people? The "exceptions" of course. And yet so sure as this Talented Tenth is pointed out, the blind worshippers of the Average cry out in alarm: "These are exceptions, look here at death, disease and crime—these are the happy rule." Of course they are the rule, because a silly nation made them

From *The Negro Problem* by Booker T. Washington et al., pp. 33–75. Published by James Pott & Co., 1903.

the rule: Because for three long centuries this people lynched Negroes who dared to be brave, raped black women who dared to be virtuous, crushed dark-hued youth who dared to be ambitious, and encouraged and made to flourish servility and lewdness and apathy. But not even this was able to crush all manhood and chastity and aspiration from black folk. A saving remnant continually survives and persists, continually aspires, continually shows itself in thrift and ability and character. Exceptional it is to be sure, but this is its chiefest promise; it shows the capability of Negro blood, the promise of black men. Do Americans ever stop to reflect that there are in this land a million men of Negro blood, well-educated, owners of homes, against the honor of whose womanhood no breath was ever raised, whose men occupy positions of trust and usefulness, and who, judged by any standard, have reached the full measure of the best type of modern European culture? Is it fair, is it decent, is it Christian to ignore these facts of the Negro problem, to belittle such aspiration, to nullify such leadership and seek to crush these people back into the mass out of which by toil and travail, they and their fathers have raised themselves?

Can the masses of the Negro people be in any possible way more quickly raised than by the effort and example of this aristocracy of talent and character? Was there ever a nation on God's fair earth civilized from the bottom upward? Never; it is, ever was and ever will be from the top downward that culture filters. The Talented Tenth rises and pulls all that are worth the saving up to their vantage ground. This is the history of human progress; and the two historic mistakes which have hindered that progress were the thinking first that no more could ever rise save the few already risen; or second, that it would better the unrisen to pull the risen down.

How then shall the leaders of a struggling people be trained and the hands of the risen few strengthened? There can be but one answer: The best and most capable of their youth must be schooled in the colleges and universities of the land. We will not quarrel as to just what the university of the Negro should teach or how it should teach it—I willingly admit that each soul and each race-soul needs its own peculiar curriculum. But this is true: A university is a human invention for the transmission of knowledge and culture from generation to generation, through the training of quick minds and pure hearts, and for this work no other human invention will suffice, not even trade and industrial schools.

All men cannot go to college but some men must; every isolated group or nation must have its yeast, must have for the talented few centers of training where men are not so mystified and befuddled by the hard and necessary toil of earning a living, as to have no aims higher than their bellies, and no God greater than Gold. This is true training, and thus in the beginning were the favored sons of the freedmen trained. Out of the colleges of the North came, after the blood of war, Ware, Cravath, Chase, Andrews, Bumstead and Spence to build the foundations of knowledge and civilization in the black South. Where ought they to have begun to build? At the bottom, of course, quibbles the mole with his eyes in the earth. Aye! truly at the bottom, at the very bottom; at the bottom of knowledge, down in the very depths of knowledge there where the roots of justice strike into the lowest soil of Truth. And so they did begin; they founded colleges, and up from the colleges shot normal schools, and out from the normal schools went teachers, and around the normal teachers clustered other teachers to teach the public schools; the college trained in Greek and Latin and mathematics, 2,000 men; and these men trained full 50,000 others in morals and manners, and they in turn taught thrift and the alphabet to nine millions of men, who to-day hold $300,000,000 of property. It was a miracle—the most wonderful peace-battle of the 19th century, and yet to-day men smile at it, and in fine superiority tell us that it was all a strange mistake; that a proper way to found a system of education is first to gather the children and buy them spelling books and hoes; afterward men may look about for teachers, if haply they may find them; or again they would teach men Work, but as for Life—why, what has Work to do with Life, they ask vacantly.

$$\bullet \quad \bullet \quad \bullet$$

Men of America, the problem is plain before you. Here is a race transplanted through the criminal foolishness of your fathers. Whether you like it or not the millions are here, and here they will remain. If you do not lift them up, they will pull you down. Education and work are the levers to uplift a people. Work alone will not do it unless inspired by the right ideals and guided by intelligence. Education must not simply teach work—it must teach Life. The Talented Tenth of the Negro race must be made leaders of thought and missionaries of culture among their people. No others can do this work and Negro colleges must train men for it. The Negro race, like all other races, is going to be saved by its exceptional men.

James Weldon Johnson

With the founding of the National Association for the Advancement of Colored People in 1909, the thought and activity of most black leaders were increasingly devoted to the achievement of civil and political rights for blacks, the elimination of government sponsored or sanctioned racial discrimination, and the reduction of race prejudice. These efforts were rewarded in the judicial victories and federal civil rights legislation of the 1950's and 1960's. These were in the main the years of lawyers and administrators and organizers rather than political thinkers. The aims seemed to be clear and unproblematic and to require little reflection. In the excerpt here James Weldon Johnson provides a typical statement of the integrationist philosophy of the NAACP.

Additional Readings: The writings of W. E. B. Du Bois are, of course, a major source of NAACP doctrine, though Du Bois was by no means always in agreement with the organization. Other good sources include the writings of Walter White, especially his autobiographical *A Man Called White,* and James Weldon Johnson's autobiographical *Along This Way.* Francis L. Broderick and August Meier's *Negro Protest Thought in the Twentieth Century* contains a good selection of relevant writings. An un-

Isolation or Integration?

. . .

By this process of elimination we have reduced choices of a way out to two. There remain, on the one hand, the continuation of our efforts to achieve integration and, on the other hand, an acknowledgment of our isolation and the determination to accept and make the best of it.

Throughout our entire intellectual history there has been a division of opinion as to which of these two divergent courses the race should follow. From early times there have been sincere thinkers among us who were brought to the conclusion that our only salvation lies in the making of the race into a self-contained economic, social, and cultural unit; in a word, in the building of an *imperium in imperio.*

All along, however, majority opinion has held that the only salvation worth achieving lies in the making of the race into a component part of the nation, with all the common rights and privileges, as well as duties,

usually informative and thoughtful discussion of the transition from the strongly assimilationist, "color blind" civil rights movement to a moderate form of race pride and Black Power can be found in James Farmer's *Freedom—When?* Whitney Young's *To Be Equal* and *Beyond Racism* are also of interest.

of citizenship. This attitude has been basic in the general policy of the race—so far as it has had a general policy—for generations, the policy of striving zealously to gain full admission to citizenship and guarding jealously each single advance made.

But this question of direction, of goal, is not a settled one. There is in us all a stronger tendency toward isolation than we may be aware of. There come times when the most persistent integrationist becomes an isolationist, when he curses the White world and consigns it to hell. This tendency toward isolation is strong because it springs from a deep-seated, natural desire—a desire for respite from the unremitting, grueling struggle; for a place in which refuge might be taken. We are again and again confronted by this question. It is ever present, though often dormant. Recently it was emphatically brought forward by the utterances of so authoritative a voice as that of Dr. Du Bois.

The question is not one to be lightly brushed aside. Those who stand for making the race into a self-sufficient unit point out that after years of effort we are still Jim-Crowed, discriminated against, segregated, and lynched; that we are still shut out from industry, barred from the main avenues of business, and cut off from free participation in national life. They point out that in some sections of the country we have not even secured equal protection of life and property under the laws. They declare that entrance of the Negro into full citizenship is as distant as it was seventy years ago. And they ask: What is the Negro to do? Give himself over to wishful thinking? Stand shooting at the stars with a popgun? Is it not rather a duty and a necessity for him to face the facts of his condition and environment, to acknowledge them as facts, and to make the best use of them that he can? These are questions which the thinkers of the race should strive to sift clearly.

To this writer it seems that one of the first results of clear thinking is a realization of the truth that the making of the race into a self-sustaining unit, the creating of an *imperium in imperio,* does not offer an easier or more feasible task than does the task of achieving full citizenship. Such an *imperium* would have to rest upon a basis of separate group economic independence, and the trend of all present-day forces is against the building of any foundation of that sort.

After thoughtful consideration, I cannot see the slightest possibility of our being able to duplicate the economic and social machinery of the country. I do not believe that any other special group could do it. The isolationists declare that because of imposed segregation we have, to a large degree, already done it. But the situation they point to is more apparent than real. Our separate schools and some of our other race institutions, many of our race enterprises, the greater part of our employment, and most of our fundamental activities are contingent upon our interrelationship with the country as a whole.

Clear thinking reveals that the outcome of voluntary isolation would be a permanent secondary status, so acknowledged by the race. Such a status would, it is true, solve some phases of the race question. It would smooth away a good part of the friction and bring about a certain protection and security. The status of slavery carried some advantages of that sort. But I do not believe we shall ever be willing to pay such a price for security and peace.

If Negro Americans could do what reasonably appears to be impossible, and as a separate unit achieve self-sufficiency built upon group economic independence, does anyone suppose that that would abolish prejudice against them and allay opposition, or that the struggle to maintain their self-sufficiency would be in any degree less bitter than the present struggle to become an integral part of the nation? Taking into account human nature as it is, would not the achievement be more likely to arouse envy and bring on even more violent hatreds and persecutions?

Certainly, the isolationists are stating a truth when they contend that we should not, ostrich-like, hide our heads in the sand, making believe that prejudice is non-existent; but in so doing they are apostles of the obvious. Calling upon the race to realize that prejudice is an actuality is a needless effort; it is placing emphasis on what has never been ques-

tioned. The danger for us does not lie in a possible failure to acknowledge prejudice as a reality, but in acknowledging it too fully. We cannot
ignore the fact that we are segregated, no matter how much we might
wish to do so; and the smallest amount of common sense forces us to
extract as much good from the situation as there is in it. Any degree
of sagacity forces us at the same time to use all our powers to abolish
imposed segregation; for it is an evil *per se* and the negation of equality
either of opportunity or of awards. We should by all means make our
schools and institutions as excellent as we can possibly make them—and
by that very act we reduce the certainty that they will forever remain
schools and institutions "for Negroes only." We should make our business
enterprises and other strictly group undertakings as successful as we
can possibly make them. We should gather all the strength and experience we can from imposed segregation. But any good we are able to
derive from the system we should consider as a means, not an end. The
strength and experience we gain from it should be applied to the objective of *entering into,* not *staying out of* the body politic.

Clear thinking shows, too, that, as bad as conditions are, they are not
as bad as they are declared to be by discouraged and pessimistic isolationists. To say that in the past two generations or more Negro Americans have not advanced a single step toward a fuller share in the
commonwealth becomes, in the light of easily ascertainable facts, an
absurdity. Only the shortest view of the situation gives color of truth
to such a statement; any reasonably long view proves it to be utterly
false.

With our choice narrowed down to these two courses, wisdom and far-
sightedness and possibility of achievement demand that we follow the
line that leads to equal rights for us, based on the common terms and
conditions under which they are accorded and guaranteed to the other
groups that go into the making up of our national family. It is not necessary for our advancement that such an outcome should suddenly erad-
icate all prejudices. It would not, of course, have the effect of suddenly
doing away with voluntary grouping in religious and secular organizations or of abolishing group enterprises—for example, Negro newspapers.
The accordance of full civil and political rights has not in the case of the
greater number of groups in the nation had that effect. Nevertheless,
it would be an immeasurable step forward, and would place us where
we had a fair start with the other American groups. More than that we
do not need to ask.

Martin Luther King, Jr.

Following his rise to national prominence during the 1964 Montgomery bus boycott, Martin Luther King, Jr. was the dominant spokesman of and to black America until his assassination in 1968. King's contribution, as he understood it, was to express a "philosophy" to guide the civil rights movement with respect to both ends and means. This philosophy was strongly assimilationist and nonpolitical (at least in the usual sense). King's influence on the general outlook of both white and black Americans was probably greater than that of any other black leader since Booker T. Washington, though he never enjoyed the undisputed leadership that was Washington's for many years. King's justification for civil disobedience is one of the major statements of contemporary American political thought. "I submit that an individual who breaks a law that conscience tells him is unjust, and who willingly accepts the penalty of imprisonment in order to arouse the conscience of the community over its injustice, is in reality expressing the highest respect for law."

The selections here contain King's thoughts on the evils of segregation, his account of the reflections that led him to espouse the philosophy of nonviolent direct action, and his principal statement of that philosophy. The reader should consider the moral demands made by the doctrine of nonviolent resistance (it is not, as King presents it, an easy or soft doctrine); the place and meaning of love in King's philosophy; King's criticism of segregation; and the political viability of King's position.

Additional Readings: King's three main works are *Stride Toward Freedom,* 1958; *Why We Can't Wait,* 1963; and *Where Do We Go From Here?*, 1967. The first describes the development and implementation of King's philosophy; the second (which contains the Letter from Birmingham Jail) describes the theory and

Pilgrimage to Nonviolence

Since the philosophy of nonviolence played such a positive role in the Montgomery Movement, it may be wise to turn to a brief discussion of some basic aspects of this philosophy.

First, it must be emphasized that nonviolent resistance is not a method for cowards; it does resist. If one uses this method because he is afraid or merely because he lacks the instruments of violence, he is not truly nonviolent. This is why Gandhi often said that if cowardice is the only alternative to violence, it is better to fight. He made this statement conscious of the fact that there is always another alternative: no individual or group need submit to any wrong, nor need they use violence to right the wrong; there is the way of nonviolence resistance. This is ultimately the way of the strong man. It is not a method of stagnant passivity. The phrase "passive resistance" often gives the false impression that this is a sort of "do-nothing method" in which the resister quietly practice of nonviolent direct action at its maturity; and the third describes the beginning of a modification of King's views under the pressure of experience and the arguments of Black Power. This last book would be especially interesting to the student concerned with recent black political movements. Also important are King's short speech accepting the Nobel Peace Prize (*New York Times,* December 11, 1964); the collection of his sermons in *Strength to Love;* and his well known "I Have a Dream" speech, given at the March on Washington, August 27, 1963. James Farmer's *Freedom—When?* is an interesting parallel account. A good introduction to the very important psychological side of the argument against segregation is provided in Kenneth Clark's *Prejudice and Your Child.*

and passively accepts evil. But nothing is further from the truth. For while the nonviolent resister is passive in the sense that he is not physically aggressive toward his opponent, his mind and emotions are always active, constantly seeking to persuade his opponent that he is wrong. The method is passive physically, but strongly active spiritually. It is not passive nonresistance to evil, it is active nonviolent resistance to evil.

A second basic fact that characterizes nonviolence is that it does not seek to defeat or humiliate the opponent, but to win his friendship and understanding. The nonviolent resister must often express his protest through noncoöperation or boycotts, but he realizes that these are not ends themselves; they are merely means to awaken a sense of moral shame in the opponent. The end is redemption and reconciliation. The aftermath of nonviolence is the creation of the beloved community, while the aftermath of violence is tragic bitterness.

A third characteristic of this method is that the attack is directed against forces of evil rather than against persons who happen to be doing the evil. It is evil that the nonviolent resister seeks to defeat, not the persons victimized by evil. If he is opposing racial injustice, the nonviolent resister has the vision to see that the basic tension is not between races. As I like to say to the people in Montgomery: "The tension in this city is not between white people and Negro people. The tension is, at bottom, between justice and injustice, between the forces of light and the forces of darkness. And if there is a victory, it will be a victory not merely for fifty thousand Negroes, but a victory for justice and the forces of light. We are out to defeat injustice and not white persons who may be unjust."

A fourth point that characterizes nonviolent resistance is a willingness to accept suffering without retaliation, to accept blows from the opponent without striking back. "Rivers of blood may have to flow before we gain our freedom, but it must be our blood," Gandhi said to his countrymen. The nonviolent resister is willing to accept violence if necessary, but never to inflict it. He does not seek to dodge jail. If going to jail is necessary, he enters it "as a bridegroom enters the bride's chamber."

One may well ask: "What is the nonviolent resister's justification for this ordeal to which he invites men, for this mass political application of the ancient doctrine of turning the other cheek?" The answer is found in the realization that unearned suffering is redemptive. Suffering, the nonviolent resister realizes, has tremendous educational and transforming possibilities. "Things of fundamental importance to people are not secured by reason alone, but have to be purchased with their suffering," said Gandhi. He continues: "Suffering is infinitely more powerful than the law of the jungle for converting the opponent and opening his ears which are otherwise shut to the voice of reason."

A fifth point concerning nonviolent resistance is that it avoids not only external physical violence but also internal violence of spirit. The nonviolent resister not only refuses to shoot his opponent but he also refuses to hate him. At the center of nonviolence stands the principle of love. The nonviolent resister would contend that in the struggle for human dignity, the oppressed people of the world must not succumb to the temptation of becoming bitter or indulging in hate campaigns. To retaliate in kind would do nothing but intensify the existence of hate in the universe. Along the way of life, someone must have sense enough and morality enough to cut off the chain of hate. This can only be done by projecting the ethic of love to the center of our lives.

In speaking of love at this point, we are not referring to some sentimental or affectionate emotion. It would be nonsense to urge men to love their oppressors in an affectionate sense. Love in this connection means understanding, redemptive good will. Here the Greek language comes to our aid. There are three words for love in the Greek New Testament. First, there is *eros*. In Platonic philosophy *eros* meant the yearning of the soul for the realm of the divine. It has come now to mean a sort of aesthetic or romantic love. Second, there is *philia* which means intimate affection between personal friends. *Philia* denotes a sort of reciprocal love; the person loves because he is loved. When we speak of loving those who oppose us, we refer to neither *eros* nor *philia*; we speak of a love which is expressed in the Greek word *agape*. *Agape* means understanding, redeeming good will for all men. It is an overflowing love which is purely spontaneous, unmotivated, groundless, and creative. It is not set in motion by any quality or function of its object. It is the love of God operating in the human heart.

Agape is disinterested love. It is a love in which the individual seeks not his own good, but the good of his neighbor (I Cor. 10:24). *Agape* does not begin by discriminating between worthy and unworthy people, or any qualities people possess. It begins by loving others *for their sakes.* It is an entirely "neighbor-regarding concern for others," which discovers the neighbor in every man it meets. Therefore, *agape* makes no distinction between friend and enemy; it is directed toward both. If one loves an individual merely on account of his friendliness, he loves him for the sake of the benefits to be gained from the friendship, rather than for the friend's own sake. Consequently, the best way to assure oneself that Love is disinterested is to have love for the enemy-neighbor from whom you can expect no good in return, but only hostility and persecution.

Another basic point about *agape* is that it springs from the *need* of the other person — his need for belonging to the best in the human family. The Samaritan who helped the Jew on the Jericho Road was "good" because he responded to the human need that he was presented with. God's love is eternal and fails not because man needs his love. St. Paul assures us that the loving act of redemption was done "while we were yet sinners" — that is, at the point of our greatest need for love. Since the white man's personality is greatly distorted by segregation, and his soul is greatly scarred, he needs the love of the Negro. The Negro must love the white man, because the white man needs his love to remove his tensions, insecurities, and fears.

Agape is not a weak, passive love. It is love in action. *Agape* is love seeking to preserve and create community. It is insistence on community even when one seeks to break it. *Agape* is a willingness to sacrifice in the interest of mutuality. *Agape* is a willingness to go to any length to restore community. It doesn't stop at the first mile, but it goes the second mile to restore community. It is a willingness to forgive, not seven times, but seventy times seven to restore community. The cross is the eternal expression of the length to which God will go in order to restore broken community. The resurrection is a symbol of God's triumph over all the forces that seek to block community. The Holy Spirit is the continuing community creating reality that moves through history. He who works against community is working against the whole of creation. Therefore, if I respond to hate with a reciprocal hate I do nothing but intensify the cleavage in broken community. I can only close the gap in broken community by meeting hate with love. If I meet hate with hate, I become depersonalized, because creation is so designed that my personality can only be fulfilled in the context of community. Booker T. Washington was right: "Let no man pull you so low as to make you hate him." When he pulls you that low he brings you to the point of working against community; he drags you to the point of defying creation, and thereby becoming depersonalized.

In the final analysis, *agape* means a recognition of the fact that all life is interrelated. All humanity is involved in a single process, and all men are brothers. To the degree that I harm my brother, no matter what he is doing to me, to that extent I am harming myself. For example, white men often refuse federal aid to education in order to avoid giving the Negro his rights; but because all men are brothers they cannot deny Negro children without harming their own. They end, all efforts to the contrary, by hurting themselves. Why is this? Because men are brothers. If you harm me, you harm yourself.

Love, *agape*, is the only cement that can hold this broken community together. When I am commanded to love, I am commanded to restore community, to resist injustice, and to meet the needs of my brothers.

A sixth basic fact about nonviolent resistance is that it is based on the conviction that the universe is on the side of justice. Consequently, the believer in nonviolence has deep faith in the future. This faith is another reason why the nonviolent resister can accept suffering without retaliation. For he knows that in his struggle for justice he has cosmic companionship. It is true that there are devout believers in nonviolence who find it difficult to believe in a personal God. But even these persons believe in the existence of some creative force that works for universal wholeness. Whether we call it an unconscious process, an impersonal Brahman, or a Personal Being of matchless power and infinite love, there is a creative force in this universe that works to bring the disconnected aspects of reality into a harmonious whole.

Letter from Birmingham Jail*

April 16, 1963

My Dear Fellow Clergymen:

While confined here in the Birmingham city jail, I came across your recent statement calling my present activities "unwise and untimely." Seldom do I pause to answer criticism of my work and ideas. If I sought to answer all the criticisms that cross my desk, my secretaries would have little time for anything other than such correspondence in the course of the day, and I would have no time for constructive work. But since I feel that you are men of genuine good will and that your criticisms are sincerely set forth, I want to try to answer your statement in what I hope will be patient and reasonable terms.

I think I should indicate why I am here in Birmingham, since you have been influenced by the view which argues against "outsiders coming in." I have the honor of serving as president of the Southern Christian Leadership Conference, an organization operating in every southern state, with headquarters in Atlanta, Georgia. We have some eighty-five affiliated organizations across the South, and one of them is the Alabama Christian Movement for Human Rights. Frequently we share staff, educational and financial resources with our affiliates. Several months ago the affiliate here in Birmingham asked us to be on call to engage in a nonviolent direct-action program if such were deemed necessary. We readily consented, and when the hour came we lived up to our promise. So I, along with several members of my staff, am here because I was invited here. I am here because I have organizational ties here.

But more basically, I am in Birmingham because injustice is here. Just as the prophets of the eighth century B.C. left their villages and carried their "thus saith the Lord" far beyond the boundaries of their home towns, and just as the Apostle Paul left his village of Tarsus and carried the gospel of Jesus Christ to the far corners of the Greco-Roman

---

"Letter from Birmingham Jail"—April 16, 1963—in *Why We Can't Wait* by Martin Luther King, Jr. Copyright © 1958 by Martin Luther King, Jr. Reprinted by permission of Harper & Row, Publishers.

*AUTHOR'S NOTE: This response to a published statement by eight fellow clergymen from Alabama (Bishop C. C. J. Carpenter, Bishop Joseph A. Durick, Rabbi Hilton L. Grafman, Bishop Paul Hardin, Bishop Holan B. Harmon, the Reverend George M. Murray, the Reverend Edward V. Ramage and the Reverend Earl Stallings) was composed under somewhat constricting circumstances. Begun on the margins of the newspaper in which the statement appeared while I was in jail, the letter was continued on scraps of writing paper supplied by a friendly Negro trusty, and concluded on a pad my attorneys were eventually permitted to leave me. Although the text remains in substance unaltered, I have indulged in the author's prerogative of polishing it for publication.

world, so am I compelled to carry the gospel of freedom beyond my own home town. Like Paul, I must constantly respond to the Macedonian call for aid.

Moreover, I am cognizant of the interrelatedness of all communities and states. I cannot sit idly by in Atlanta and not be concerned about what happens in Birmingham. Injustice anywhere is a threat to justice everywhere. We are caught in an inescapable network of mutuality, tied in a single garment of destiny. Whatever affects one directly, affects all indirectly. Never again can we afford to live with the narrow, provincial "outside agitator" idea. Anyone who lives inside the United States can never be considered an outsider anywhere within its bounds.

You deplore the demonstrations taking place in Birmingham. But your statement, I am sorry to say, fails to express a similar concern for the conditions that brought about the demonstrations. I am sure that none of you would want to rest content with the superficial kind of social analysis that deals merely with effects and does not grapple with underlying causes. It is unfortunate that demonstrations are taking place in Birmingham, but it is even more unfortunate that the city's white power structure left the Negro community with no alternative.

In any nonviolent campaign there are four basic steps: collection of the facts to determine whether injustices exist; negotiation; self-purification; and direct action. We have gone through all these steps in Birmingham. There can be no gainsaying the fact that racial injustice engulfs this community. Birmingham is probably the most thoroughly segregated city in the United States. Its ugly record of brutality is widely known. Negroes have experienced grossly unjust treatment in the courts. There have been more unsolved bombings of Negro homes and churches in Birmingham than in any other city in the nation. These are the hard, brutal facts of the case. On the basis of these conditions, Negro leaders sought to negotiate with the city fathers. But the latter consistently refused to engage in good-faith negotiation.

Then, last September, came the opportunity to talk with leaders of Birmingham's economic community. In the course of the negotiations, certain promises were made by the merchants—for example, to remove the stores' humiliating racial signs. On the basis of these promises, the Reverend Fred Shuttlesworth and the leaders of the Alabama Christian Movement for Human Rights agreed to a moratorium on all demonstrations. As the weeks and months went by, we realized that we were the victims of a broken promise. A few signs, briefly removed, returned; the others remained.

As in so many past experiences, our hopes had been blasted, and the shadow of deep disappointment settled upon us. We had no alternative except to prepare for direct action, whereby we would present our very bodies as a means of laying our case before the conscience of the local and the national community. Mindful of the difficulties involved, we decided to undertake a process of self-purification. We began a series of workshops on nonviolence, and we repeatedly asked ourselves: "Are you able to accept blows without retaliating?" "Are you able to endure the ordeal of jail?" We decided to schedule our direct-action program for the Easter season, realizing that except for Christmas, this is the main shopping period of the year. Knowing that a strong economic-withdrawal program would be the by-product of direct action, we felt that this would be the best time to bring pressure to bear on the merchants for the needed change.

Then it occurred to us that Birmingham's mayoral election was coming up in March, and we speedily decided to postpone action until after election day. When we discovered that the Commissioner of Public Safety, Eugene "Bull" Connor, had piled up enough votes to be in the run-off, we decided again to postpone action until the day after the run-off so that the demonstrations could not be used to cloud the issues. Like many others, we waited to see Mr. Connor defeated, and to this end we endured postponement after postponement. Having aided in this community need, we felt that our direct-action program could be delayed no longer.

You may well ask: "Why direct action? Why sit-ins, marches and so forth? Isn't negotiation a better path?" You are quite right in calling for negotiation. Indeed, this is the very purpose of direct action. Nonviolent direct action seeks to create such a crisis and foster such a tension that a community which has constantly refused to negotiate is forced to confront the issue. It seeks so to dramatize the issue that it can no longer be ignored. My citing the creation of tension as part of the work of the nonviolent-resister may sound rather shocking. But I must confess that I am not afraid of the word "tension." I have earnestly opposed violent tension, but there is a type of constructive, nonviolent tension which is necessary for growth. Just as Socrates felt that it was necessary to create a tension in the mind so that individuals could rise from the bondage of myths and half-truths to the unfettered realm of creative analysis and objective appraisal, so must we see the need for nonviolent gadflies to create the kind of tension in society that will help men rise from the dark depths of prejudice and racism to the majestic heights of understanding and brotherhood.

The purpose of our direct-action program is to create a situation so crisis-packed that it will inevitably open the door to negotiation. I therefore concur with you in your call for negotiation. Too long has our beloved Southland been bogged down in a tragic effort to live in monologue rather than dialogue.

One of the basic points in your statement is that the action that I and my associates have taken in Birmingham is untimely. Some have asked: "Why didn't you give the new city administration time to act?" The only answer that I can give to this query is that the new Birmingham administration must be prodded about as much as the outgoing one, before it will act. We are sadly mistaken if we feel that the election of Albert Boutwell as mayor will bring the millennium to Birmingham. While Mr. Boutwell is a much more gentle person than Mr. Connor, they are both segregationists, dedicated to maintenance of the status quo. I have hope that Mr. Boutwell will be reasonable enough to see the futility of massive resistance to desegregation. But he will not see this without pressure from devotees of civil rights. My friends, I must say to you that we have not made a single gain in civil rights without determined legal and nonviolent pressure. Lamentably, it is an historical fact that privileged groups seldom give up their privileges voluntarily. Individuals may see the moral light and voluntarily give up their unjust posture; but, as Reinhold Niebuhr has reminded us, groups tend to be more immoral than individuals.

We know through painful experience that freedom is never voluntarily given by the oppressor; it must be demanded by the oppressed. Frankly, I have yet to engage in a direct-action campaign that was "well timed" in the view of those who have not suffered unduly from the disease of segregation. For years now I have heard the word "Wait!" It rings in the ear of every Negro with piercing familiarity. This "Wait" has almost always meant "Never." We must come to see, with one of our distinguished jurists, that "justice too long delayed is justice denied."

We have waited for more than 340 years for our constitutional and God-given rights. The nations of Asia and Africa are moving with jet-like speed toward gaining political independence, but we still creep at horse-and-buggy pace toward gaining a cup of coffee at a lunch counter. Perhaps it is easy for those who have never felt the stinging darts of segregation to say, "Wait." But when you have seen vicious mobs lynch your mothers and fathers at will and drown your sisters and brothers at whim; when you have seen hate-filled policemen curse, kick and even kill your black brothers and sisters; when you see the vast majority of your twenty million Negro brothers smothering in an airtight cage of poverty in the midst of an affluent society; when you suddenly find your tongue twisted and your speech stammering as you seek to explain to your six-year-old daughter why she can't go to the public amusement park that has just been advertised on television, and see tears welling up in her eyes when she is told that Funtown is closed to colored children, and see ominous clouds of inferiority beginning to form in her little mental sky, and see her beginning to distort her personality by developing an unconscious bitterness toward white people; when you have to concoct an answer for a five-year-old son who is asking: "Daddy, why do white people treat colored people so mean?"; when you take a cross-country drive and find it necessary to sleep night after night in the uncomfortable corners of your automobile because no motel will accept you; when you are humiliated day in and day out by nagging signs reading "white" and "colored"; when your first name becomes "nigger," your middle name becomes "boy" (however old you are) and your last name becomes "John," and your wife and mother are never given the respected title "Mrs."; when you are harried by day and haunted by night by the fact that you are a Negro, living constantly at tiptoe stance, never quite knowing what to expect next, and are plagued with inner fears and outer resentments; when you are forever fighting a degenerating sense of "nobodiness"—then you will understand why we find it difficult to wait. There comes a time when the cup of endurance runs over, and men are no longer willing to be plunged into the abyss of despair. I hope, sirs, you can understand our legitimate and unavoidable impatience.

You express a great deal of anxiety over our willingness to break laws. This is certainly a legitimate concern. Since we so diligently urge people to obey the Supreme Court's decision of 1954 outlawing segregation in the public schools, at first glance it may seem rather paradoxical for us consciously to break laws. One may well ask: "How can you advocate breaking some laws and obeying others?" The answer lies in the fact that there are two types of laws: just and unjust. I would be the first to advocate obeying just laws. One has not only a legal but a moral responsibility to obey just laws. Conversely, one has a moral responsibility to disobey unjust laws. I would agree with St. Augustine that "an unjust law is no law at all."

Now, what is the difference between the two? How does one determine whether a law is just or unjust? A just law is a man-made code that squares with the moral law or the law of God. An unjust law is a code that is out of harmony with the moral law. To put it in the terms of St. Thomas Aquinas: An unjust law is a human law that is not rooted in eternal law and natural law. Any law that uplifts human personality is just. Any law that degrades human personality is unjust. All segregation statutes are unjust because segregation distorts the soul and damages the personality. It gives the segregator a false sense of superiority and the segregated a false sense of inferiority. Segregation, to use the terminology of the Jewish philosopher Martin Buber, substitutes an "I—it" relationship for an "I—thou" relationship and ends up relegating persons to the status of things. Hence segregation is not only politically, economically and sociologically unsound, it is morally wrong and sinful.

Paul Tillich has said that sin is separation. Is not segregation an existential expression of man's tragic separation, his awful estrangement, his terrible sinfulness? Thus it is that I can urge men to obey the 1954 decision of the Supreme Court, for it is morally right; and I can urge them to disobey segregation ordinances, for they are morally wrong.

Let us consider a more concrete example of just and unjust laws. An unjust law is a code that a numerical or power majority group compels a minority group to obey but does not make binding on itself. This is *difference* made legal. By the same token, a just law is a code that a majority compels a minority to follow and that it is willing to follow itself. This is *sameness* made legal.

Let me give another explanation. A law is unjust if it is inflicted on a minority that, as a result of being denied the right to vote, had no part in enacting or devising the law. Who can say that the legislature of Alabama which set up that state's segregation laws was democratically elected? Throughout Alabama all sorts of devious methods are used to prevent Negroes from becoming registered voters, and there are some counties in which, even though Negroes constitute a majority of the population, not a single Negro is registered. Can any law enacted under such circumstances be considered democratically structured?

Sometimes a law is just on its face and unjust in its application. For instance, I have been arrested on a charge of parading without a permit. Now, there is nothing wrong in having an ordinance which requires a permit for a parade. But such an ordinance becomes unjust when it is used to maintain segregation and to deny citizens the First-Amendment privilege of peaceful assembly and protest.

I hope you are able to see the distinction I am trying to point out. In no sense do I advocate evading or defying the law, as would the rabid segregationist. That would lead to anarchy. One who breaks an unjust law must do so openly, lovingly, and with a willingness to accept the penalty. I submit that an individual who breaks a law that conscience tells him is unjust, and who willingly accepts the penalty of imprisonment in order to arouse the conscience of the community over its injustice, is in reality expressing the highest respect for law.

Of course, there is nothing new about this kind of civil disobedience. It was evidenced sublimely in the refusal of Shadrach, Meshach and Abednego to obey the laws of Nebuchadnezzar, on the ground that a higher moral law was at stake. It was practiced superbly by the early Christians, who were willing to face hungry lions and the excruciating pain of chopping blocks rather than submit to certain unjust laws of the Roman Empire. To a degree, academic freedom is a reality today because Socrates practiced civil disobedience. In our own nation, the Boston Tea Party represented a massive act of civil disobedience.

We should never forget that everything Adolf Hitler did in Germany was "legal" and everything the Hungarian freedom fighters did in Hungary was "illegal." It was "illegal" to aid and comfort a Jew in Hitler's Germany. Even so, I am sure that, had I lived in Germany at the time, I would have aided and comforted my Jewish brothers. If today I lived in a Communist country where certain principles dear to the Christian faith are suppressed, I would openly advocate disobeying that country's antireligious laws.

I must make two honest confessions to you, my Christian and Jewish brothers. First, I must confess that over the past few years I have been gravely disappointed with the white moderate. I have almost reached the regrettable conclusion that the Negro's great stumbling block in his stride toward freedom is not the White Citizen's Counciler or the Ku Klux Klanner, but the white moderate, who is more devoted to "order" than to justice; who prefers a negative peace which is the absence of tension to a positive peace which is the presence of justice; who constantly says: "I agree with you in the goal you seek, but I cannot agree with your methods of direct action"; who paternalistically believes he can set the timetable for another man's freedom; who lives by a mythical concept of time and who constantly advises the Negro to wait for a "more convenient season." Shallow understanding from people of good will is more frustrating than absolute misunderstanding from people of ill will. Lukewarm acceptance is much more bewildering than outright rejection.

I had hoped that the white moderate would understand that law and order exist for the purpose of establishing justice and that when they fail in this purpose they become the dangerously structured dams that block the flow of social progress. I had hoped that the white moderate would understand that the present tension in the South is a necessary phase of the transition from an obnoxious negative peace, in which the Negro passively accepted his unjust plight, to a substantive and positive peace, in which all men will respect the dignity and worth of human personality. Actually, we who engage in nonviolent direct action are not the creators of tension. We merely bring to the surface the hidden tension that is already alive. We bring it out in the open, where it can be seen and dealt with. Like a boil that can never be cured so long as it is covered up but must be opened with all its ugliness to the natural medicines of air and light, injustice must be exposed, with all the tension its exposure creates, to the light of human conscience and the air of national opinion before it can be cured.

In your statement you assert that our actions, even though peaceful, must be condemned because they precipitate violence. But is this a logical assertion? Isn't this like condemning a robbed man because his possession of money precipitated the evil act of robbery? Isn't this like condemning Socrates because his unswerving commitment to truth and his philosophical inquiries precipitated the act by the misguided populace in which they made him drink hemlock? Isn't this like condemning Jesus because his unique God-consciousness and never-ceasing devotion to God's will precipitated the evil act of crucifixion? We must come to see that, as the federal courts have consistently affirmed, it is wrong to urge an individual to cease his efforts to gain his basic constitutional rights because the quest may precipitate violence. Society must protect the robbed and punish the robber.

I had also hoped that the white moderate would reject the myth concerning time in relation to the struggle for freedom. I have just received a letter from a white brother in Texas. He writes: "All Christians know that the colored people will receive equal rights eventually, but it is possible that you are in too great a religious hurry. It has taken Christianity almost two thousand years to accomplish what it has. The teachings of Christ take time to come to earth." Such an attitude stems from a tragic misconception of time, from the strangely irrational notion that there is something in the very flow of time that will inevitably cure all ills. Actually, time itself is neutral, it can be used either destructively or constructively. More and more I feel that the people of ill will have used time much more effectively than have the people of good will. We will have to repent in this generation not merely for the hateful words and actions of the bad people but for the appalling silence of the good people. Human progress never rolls in on wheels of inevitability; it comes through the tireless efforts of men willing to be co-workers with God, and without this hard work, time itself becomes an ally of the forces of social stagnation. We must use time creatively, in the knowledge that the time is always ripe to do right. Now is the time to make real the promise of democracy and transform our pending national elegy into a creative psalm of brotherhood. Now is the time to lift our national policy from the quicksand of racial injustice to the solid rock of human dignity.

You speak of our activity in Birmingham as extreme. At first I was rather disappointed that fellow clergymen would see my nonviolent efforts as those of an extremist. I began thinking about the fact that I stand in the middle of two opposing forces in the Negro community. One is a force of complacency, made up in part of Negroes who, as a result of long years of oppression, are so drained of self-respect and a sense of "somebodiness" that they have adjusted to segregation; and in part of a few middle-class Negroes who, because of a degree of academic and economic security and because in some ways they profit by segregation, have become insensitive to the problems of the masses. The other force is one of bitterness and hatred, and it comes perilously close to advocating violence. It is expressed in the various black nationalist groups that are springing up across the nation, the largest and best-known being Elijah Muhammad's Muslim movement. Nourished by the Negro's frustration over the continued existence of racial discrimination, this movement is made up of people who have lost faith in America, who have absolutely repudiated Christianity, and who have concluded that the white man is an incorrigible "devil."

I have tried to stand between these two forces, saying that we need emulate neither the "do-nothingism" of the complacent nor the hatred and despair of the black nationalist. For there is the more excellent way of love and nonviolent protest. I am grateful to God that, through the influence of the Negro church, the way of nonviolence became an integral part of our struggle.

If this philosophy had not emerged, by now many streets of the South would, I am convinced, be flowing with blood. And I am further convinced that if our white brothers dismiss as "rabble-rousers" and "outside agitators" those of us who employ nonviolent direct action, and if they refuse to support our nonviolent efforts, millions of Negroes will, out of frustration and despair, seek solace and security in black-nationalist ideologies—a development that would inevitably lead to a frightening racial nightmare.

Oppressed people cannot remain oppressed forever. The yearning for freedom eventually manifests itself, and that is what has happened to the American Negro. Something within has reminded him of his birthright of freedom, and something without has reminded him that it can be gained. Consciously or unconsciously, he has been caught up by the *Zeitgeist,* and with his black brothers of Africa and his brown and yellow brothers of Asia, South America and the Caribbean, the United States Negro is moving with a sense of great urgency toward the promised land of racial justice. If one recognizes this vital urge that has engulfed the Negro community, one should readily understand why public demonstrations are taking place. The Negro has many pent-up resentments and latent frustrations, and he must release them. So let him march; let him make prayer pilgrimages to the city hall; let him go on freedom rides— and try to understand why he must do so. If his repressed emotions are not released in nonviolent ways, they will seek expression through violence; this is not a threat but a fact of history. So I have not said to my people: "Get rid of your discontent." Rather, I have tried to say that this normal and healthy discontent can be channeled into the creative outlet of nonviolent direct action. And now this approach is being termed extremist.

But though I was initially disappointed at being categorized as an extremist, as I continued to think about the matter I gradually gained a measure of satisfaction from the label. Was not Jesus an extremist for love: "Love your enemies, bless them that curse you, do good to them that hate you, and pray for them which despitefully use you, and persecute you." Was not Amos an extremist for justice: "Let justice roll down like waters and righteousness like an ever-flowing stream." Was not Paul an extremist for the Christian gospel: "I bear in my body the marks of the Lord Jesus." Was not Martin Luther an extremist: "Here I stand; I cannot do otherwise, so help me God." And John Bunyan: "I will stay in jail to the end of my days before I make a butchery of my conscience." And Abraham Lincoln: "This nation cannot survive half slave and half free." And Thomas Jefferson: "We hold these truths to be self-evident, that all men are created equal . . ." So the question is not whether we will be extremists, but what kind of extremists we will be. Will we be extremists for hate or for love? Will we be extremists for the preservation of injustice or for the extension of justice? In that dramatic scene on Calvary's hill three men were crucified. We must never forget that all three were crucified for the same crime — the crime of extremism. Two were extremists for immorality, and thus fell below their environment. The other, Jesus Christ, was an extremist for love, truth and goodness, and thereby rose above his environment. Perhaps the South, the nation and the world are in dire need of creative extremists.

I had hoped that the white moderate would see this need. Perhaps I was too optimistic; perhaps I expected too much. I suppose I should have realized that few members of the oppressor race can understand the deep groans and passionate yearnings of the oppressed race, and still fewer have the vision to see that injustice must be rooted out by strong, persistent and determined action. I am thankful, however, that some of our white brothers in the South have grasped the meaning of this social revolution and committed themselves to it. They are still all too few in quantity, but they are big in quality. Some — such as Ralph McGill, Lillian Smith, Harry Golden, James McBride Dabbs, Ann Braden and Sarah Patton Boyle — have written about our struggle in eloquent and prophetic terms. Others have marched with us down nameless streets of the South. They have languished in filthy, roach-infested jails, suffering the abuse and brutality of policemen who view them as "dirty nigger-lovers." Unlike so many of their moderate brothers and sisters, they have recognized the urgency of the moment and sensed the need for powerful "action" antidotes to combat the disease of segregation.

Let me take note of my other major disappointment. I have been so greatly disappointed with the white church and its leadership. Of course, there are some notable exceptions. I am not unmindful of the fact that each of you has taken some significant stands on this issue. I commend you, Reverend Stallings, for your Christian stand on this past Sunday, in welcoming Negroes to your worship service on a nonsegregated basis.

I commend the Catholic leaders of this state for integrating Spring Hill College several years ago.

But despite these notable exceptions, I must honestly reiterate that I have been disappointed with the church. I do not say this as one of those negative critics who can always find something wrong with the church. I say this as a minister of the gospel, who loves the church; who was nurtured in its bosom; who has been sustained by its spiritual blessings and who will remain true to it as long as the cord of life shall lengthen.

When I was suddenly catapulted into the leadership of the bus protest in Montgomery, Alabama, a few years ago, I felt we would be supported by the white church. I felt that the white ministers, priests and rabbis of the South would be among our strongest allies. Instead, some have been outright opponents, refusing to understand the freedom movement and misrepresenting its leaders; all too many others have been more cautious than courageous and have remained silent behind the anesthetizing security of stained-glass windows.

In spite of my shattered dreams, I came to Birmingham with the hope that the white religious leadership of this community would see the justice of our cause and, with deep moral concern, would serve as the channel through which our just grievances could reach the power structure. I had hoped that each of you would understand. But again I have been disappointed.

I have heard numerous southern religious leaders admonish their worshipers to comply with a desegregation decision because it is the law, but I have longed to hear white ministers declare: "Follow this decree because integration is morally right and because the Negro is your brother." In the midst of blatant injustices inflicted upon the Negro, I have watched white churchmen stand on the sideline and mouth pious irrelevancies and sanctimonious trivialities. In the midst of a mighty struggle to rid our nation of racial and economic injustice, I have heard many ministers say: "Those are social issues, with which the gospel has no real concern." And I have watched many churches commit themselves to a completely otherworldly religion which makes a strange, un-Biblical distinction between body and soul, between the sacred and the secular.

I have traveled the length and breadth of Alabama, Mississippi and all the other southern states. On sweltering summer days and crisp autumn mornings I have looked at the South's beautiful churches with their lofty spires pointing heavenward. I have beheld the impressive outlines of her massive religious-education buildings. Over and over I have found myself asking: "What kind of people worship here? Who is their God? Where were their voices when the lips of Governor Barnett dripped with words of interposition and nullification? Where were they when Governor Wallace gave a clarion call for defiance and hatred?

Where were their voices of support when bruised and weary Negro men and women decided to rise from the dark dungeons of complacency to the bright hills of creative protest?"

Yes, these questions are still in my mind. In deep disappointment I have wept over the laxity of the church. But be assured that my tears have been tears of love. There can be no deep disappointment where there is not deep love. Yes, I love the church. How could I do otherwise? I am in the rather unique position of being the son, the grandson and the great-grandson of preachers. Yes, I see the church as the body of Christ. But, oh! How we have blemished and scarred that body through social neglect and through fear of being nonconformists.

There was a time when the church was very powerful—in the time when the early Christians rejoiced at being deemed worthy to suffer for what they believed. In those days the church was not merely a thermometer that recorded the ideas and principles of popular opinion; it was a thermostat that transformed the mores of society. Whenever the early Christians entered a town, the people in power became disturbed and immediately sought to convict the Christians for being "disturbers of the peace" and "outside agitators." But the Christians pressed on, in the conviction that they were "a colony of heaven," called to obey God rather than man. Small in number, they were big in commitment. They were too God-intoxicated to be "astronomically intimidated." By their effort and example they brought an end to such ancient evils as infanticide and gladiatorial contests.

Things are different now. So often the contemporary church is a weak, ineffectual voice with an uncertain sound. So often it is an archdefender of the status quo. Far from being disturbed by the presence of the church, the power structure of the average community is consoled by the church's silent—and often even vocal—sanction of things as they are.

But the judgment of God is upon the church as never before. If today's church does not recapture the sacrificial spirit of the early church, it will lose its authenticity, forfeit the loyalty of millions, and be dismissed as an irrelevant social club with no meaning for the twentieth century. Every day I meet young people whose disappointment with the church has turned into outright disgust.

Perhaps I have once again been too optimistic. Is organized religion too inextricably bound to the status quo to save our nation and the world? Perhaps I must turn my faith to the inner spiritual church, the church within the church, as the true *ekklesia* and the hope of the world. But again I am thankful to God that some noble souls from the ranks of organized religion have broken loose from the paralyzing chains of conformity and joined us as active partners in the struggle for freedom. They have left their secure congregations and walked the streets of Albany,

Georgia, with us. They have gone down the highways of the South on tortuous rides for freedom. Yes, they have gone to jail with us. Some have been dismissed from their churches, have lost the support of their bishops and fellow ministers. But they have acted in the faith that right defeated is stronger than evil triumphant. Their witness has been the spiritual salt that has preserved the true meaning of the gospel in these troubled times. They have carved a tunnel of hope through the dark mountain of disappointment.

I hope the church as a whole will meet the challenge of this decisive hour. But even if the church does not come to the aid of justice, I have no despair about the future. I have no fear about the outcome of our struggle in Birmingham, even if our motives are at present misunderstood. We will reach the goal of freedom in Birmingham and all over the nation, because the goal of America is freedom. Abused and scorned though we may be, our destiny is tied up with America's destiny. Before the pilgrims landed at Plymouth, we were here. Before the pen of Jefferson etched the majestic words of the Declaration of Independence across the pages of history, we were here. For more than two centuries our forebears labored in this country without wages; they made cotton king; they built the homes of their masters while suffering gross injustice and shameful humiliation—and yet out of a bottomless vitality they continued to thrive and develop. If the inexpressible cruelties of slavery could not stop us, the opposition we now face will surely fail. We will win our freedom because the sacred heritage of our nation and the eternal will of God are embodied in our echoing demands.

Before closing I feel impelled to mention one other point in your statement that has troubled me profoundly. You warmly commended the Birmingham police force for keeping "order" and "preventing violence." I doubt that you would have so warmly commended the police force if you had seen its dogs sinking their teeth into unarmed, nonviolent Negroes. I doubt that you would so quickly commend the policemen if you were to observe their ugly and inhumane treatment of Negroes here in the city jail; if you were to watch them push and curse old Negro women and young Negro girls; if you were to see them slap and kick old Negro men and young boys; if you were to observe them, as they did on two occasions, refuse to give us food because we wanted to sing our grace together. I cannot join you in your praise of the Birmingham police department.

It is true that the police have exercised a degree of discipline in handling the demonstrators. In this sense they have conducted themselves rather "nonviolently" in public. But for what purpose? To preserve the evil system of segregation. Over the past few years I have consistently preached that nonviolence demands that the means we use must be as pure as the ends we seek. I have tried to make clear that it is wrong to use immoral means to attain moral ends. But now I must affirm that it is just as wrong, or perhaps even more so, to use moral means to preserve immoral ends. Perhaps Mr. Connor and his policemen have been rather nonviolent in public, as was Chief Pritchett in Albany, Georgia, but they have used the moral means of nonviolence to maintain the immoral end of racial injustice. As T. S. Eliot has said: "The last temptation is the greatest treason: To do the right deed for the wrong reason."

I wish you had commended the Negro sit-inners and demonstrators of Birmingham for their sublime courage, their willingness to suffer and their amazing discipline in the midst of great provocation. One day the South will recognize its real heroes. They will be the James Merediths, with the noble sense of purpose that enables them to face jeering and hostile mobs, and with the agonizing loneliness that characterizes the life of the pioneer. They will be old, oppressed, battered Negro women, symbolized in a seventy-two-year-old woman in Montgomery, Alabama, who rose up with a sense of dignity and with her people decided not to ride segregated buses, and who responded with ungrammatical profundity to one who inquired about her weariness: "My feets is tired, but my soul is at rest." They will be the young high school and college students, the young ministers of the gospel and a host of their elders, courageously and nonviolently sitting in at lunch counters and willingly going to jail for conscience' sake. One day the South will know that when these disinherited children of God sat down at lunch counters, they were in reality standing up for what is best in the American dream and for the most sacred values in our Judaeo-Christian heritage, thereby bringing our nation back to those great wells of democracy which were dug deep by the founding fathers in their formulation of the Constitution and the Declaration of Independence.

Never before have I written so long a letter. I'm afraid it is much too long to take your precious time. I can assure you that it would have been much shorter if I had been writing from a comfortable desk, but what else can one do when he is alone in a narrow jail cell, other than write long letters, think long thoughts and pray long prayers?

If I have said anything in this letter that overstates the truth and indicates an unreasonable impatience, I beg you to forgive me. If I have said anything that understates the truth and indicates my having a patience that allows me to settle for anything less than brotherhood, I beg God to forgive me.

I hope this letter finds you strong in the faith. I also hope that circumstances will soon make it possible for me to meet each of you, not as an integrationist or a civil-rights leader but as a fellow clergyman and a Christian brother. Let us all hope that the dark clouds of racial prejudice will soon pass away and the deep fog of misunderstanding will be lifted from our fear-drenched communities, and in some not too distant tomorrow the radiant stars of love and brotherhood will shine over our great nation with all their scintillating beauty.

Yours for the cause of Peace and Brotherhood,

MARTIN LUTHER KING, JR.

Joseph H. Jackson

Joseph H. Jackson is minister of the Olivet Baptist Church in Chicago and president of the National Baptist Convention, Inc., one of the largest Negro organizations in the United States. He has long been a spokesman of "conservative" elements of black leadership. He is an American patriot, and it is his understanding of the American ideal that guides him, even while he is criticizing America. "As patriotic Americans we are devoted to our nation's course, and are wedded to its ideals and principles. . . . We draw a clear distinction between that which is germane to the nation's life and that which is foreign, hostile, and antagonistic to the soul of our nation." In the address here he gives thoughtful expression to the idea that the Negro's aim is to be fully a part of America, not to reject it or separate from it, and that he should adopt means consistent with that end. Jackson emphasizes the need for political action and for strenuous efforts towards black self-improvement in business, education, and elsewhere. Clearly he has strong links to the tradition of Booker T. Washington. Yet even more interesting to the present-day reader, perhaps, are the similarities to black nationalist and Black Power arguments. Many leaders who scorned Jackson's ideas as Uncle Tomism have themselves adopted some of these same ideas under the name of Black Power. There are still major differences between Jackson's views and

Annual Address, 1964

. . .

PARTICIPATING IN THE STRUGGLE OF AMERICA

As Christians we are a part of our nation and a part of the struggle of America. America was brought into being to satisfy and to answer the human longing for freedom. There was the urge in man to be related to other men as men without a modifier or any kind of limitation or restriction. There was an awareness of a human kinship deeper than race, more profound than nationality, and more inclusive than any accepted religious creed. In addition to the quest for a new geographical spot there was a search for a new human relationship, a new freedom, and new opportunities. These basic urges inspired the early colonies to brave the dangers of a rough and unknown sea, and seek a land in which they

Annual Address of President J. H. Jackson, delivered at the eighty-fourth Annual Session of the National Baptist Convention, U.S.A., Inc., September 10, 1964, Cobo Hall-Arena, Detroit, Michigan. (Abridged.)

those of Black Power leaders, but the issue is not so clear-cut as it once seemed.

Additional Readings: Jackson's thoughts are given expression mainly in his annual speeches to the National Baptist Convention, which are printed in pamphlet form, and in several books. See *Unholy Shadows and Freedom's Holy Light,* and also *The Eternal Flame* and *Many But One.*

could live as free men and aspire to the highest possible goals of life without the enslavement of the past or being the victims of the determinism of enforced circumstances. They wanted a chance to explore and to search out the meaning of life for themselves, and an opportunity to worship God according to the dictates of their conscience.

They soon became convinced that there was no such land, no such Utopia, but all they would find would be an opportunity to make such a land and such a country. They were convinced it could be made out of the desires that now possessed their souls and out of the thirst for liberty that dominated their lives.

America was born in a struggle and as a struggle for freedom, and for the opportunity to develop the highest resources of mankind. The Declaration of Independence and the Federal Constitution were the results of our fathers' attempts to put on paper the ideals that inspired the birth of the nation, and those principles by which and on which the nation was erected and sustained. There have been errors, mistakes, and gross sins committed against this American venture, but this high venture has not been repudiated or negated. The Massachusetts theocracy became oppressive and hostile toward freedom. Some human beings were slain in the episode of the great Witch Hunt. Slavery took its toll, denying to thousands the human dignity that God had bestowed upon them; and as a result of the defense of this cruel institution, the nation was divided into two armed camps, and a cruel civil war saw Americans take the lives of Americans, and brothers shedding their brothers' blood. But from the dust and dirt of this tragic event the American ideals sprang up again with new vigor and vitality, and continued its upward march on the rough highway of human history. This American venture is powerful but not perfect; ever growing but not grown; and still becoming, but is not yet complete. The kind hand of destiny and the benevolent providence of Almighty God have placed the American Negro along with other races and nationalities in this flowing stream of the nation's life for which we are justly proud. As patriotic Americans we are devoted to our nation's cause, and are wedded to its ideals and principles. By precept and example, by instinct and intuition, we now know the difference between that which is truly American and that which is not. We draw a clear distinction between that which is germane to the nation's life and that which is foreign, hostile, and antagonistic to the soul of our nation. To the former we pledge our total allegiance and commit every ounce of energy, our strength, all of our powers, and even our very lives. But against the latter we stand with uncompromising determination, and will not rest until all the enemies of our nation have been subdued and conquered. This is the true meaning of the civil rights struggle.

THE CIVIL RIGHTS STRUGGLE

Much time and space is given in the public press to the problem of civil rights. It has engaged the minds of our congressmen, and has occasioned many days of debate and deliberation. In the name of civil rights thousands have marched through the streets of our cities, boycotts have been staged, picket lines have been thrown around places of businesses, institutions of learning; and in every nook and corner of the country voices have been heard in the defense of and in the interest of civil rights.

What is this struggle for civil rights? I answer, it is an effort of American citizens to get full equality of opportunity. It is the resolution and the determination that there shall be in these United States one class of citizens and that is first class citizens. This is a struggle to adopt in practice as well as theory the concept of man on which the Declaration of Independence is based, and to fully implement the Federal Constitution, one of the greatest documents for human freedom since the writing of the Magna Carta. The civil rights struggle is a struggle for full freedom, justice, and equality before the law. It is a struggle to bring from paper the lofty ideals of America, and to apply them in practice to the lives and actions of all Americans. In reality it is America's struggle to be herself, to fulfill the highest promises of her being, and to build a social order after the pattern and dreams of our founding fathers and in the light of the wisdom of the ages.

The civil rights struggle then is not a struggle to negate the high and lofty philosophy of American freedom. It is not an attempt to convert the nation into an armed camp or to substitute panic and anarchy in the place of law and order. It is in no wise an attempt to negate or to amend downward the highest laws of this land proclaiming freedom and justice for all.

WHY THEN THE STRUGGLE?

The answer is there is a group in the United States that believes that when the constitution speaks of the rights of American citizens it meant only men whose skins were white. This group believes in segregation as a means of protecting the best interests of the nation and of keeping the races separate and pure. But as we look at the degrees of pigmentation among all the races in these United States, I ask my segregationist friends, don't you think it is rather late now to talk about the purity of the race; for the blood of white segregationists is in the veins of many whom they would ostracize, and their kinship is a biological fact. Many segregationists fear that granting equality of opportunity to people of color will in some way jeopardize their liberties, encroach upon their freedom, and threaten their rank, position, and security. But such fear is unfounded if the doctrine of American democracy is true. For no free man has any grounds to fear the spread of the privileges of true freedom to all men, for the greater the number of free men the more secure is freedom and less is the power and danger of oppression. Abraham Lincoln sensed this fact when he said: "By giving freedom to the slaves we insure freedom to the free." The presence of one bound man pollutes the whole stream of human society; and the rattle of one chain of oppression creates a discord that breaks the harmony in every democratic system, and disturbs the mind and poisons the heart of every man with fear and dread, so that the would-be master finds himself mentally and morally the dweller in the hovels of slaves, the servant of a cause that is hostile to democracy, and becomes himself, the victim of the baser emotions of his own nature.

This struggle for civil rights has remained for a hundred years because there are persons among us who are still the victims of the psychology of chattel slavery and are yet blinded to the verdict of history and indifferent to the logic of life, and in deep rebellion against the voice of God.

Some believe that their very future and the future well-being of their families depend on keeping alive the cursed demon of segregation. In the language of one segregationist: "Yes, we believe in segregation, and we will not be changed. We will not be frightened or forced. We will oppose you with every ounce of strength that we have. We will fight you from breakfast until noon. We will eat our noon-day meal and then return to the field of battle and fight you until sunset. If opportunity permits we will catch a bite to eat in the twilight and return to our post and fight until the morning comes." With such determination, with such faith in the way of segregation, with such commitment to the evils of discrimination, and with such opponents of democracy and freedom, it is no surprise that the struggle for civil rights has remained so long and still remains one of the grave struggles of the land and country.

The second reason why the struggle for civil rights has continued is that the segregated does not and cannot accept segregation as a way of life. The bound men have read with care the great promises of our Federal Constitution, and they have heard clearly the pronouncements of statesmen, and have followed the logic of every philosopher of freedom, and they now know that segregation and racial discrimination have no logical or legitimate place in the American character and constitution. The segregated is just as determined to destroy the awful demand of racial segregation as segregationists are to keep it alive.

This struggle will continue because of the inner nature of the segregated themselves. There has been implanted in the hearts and minds of all men the hope, the love, and expectation of freedom, and this inner conviction compels us, and the freedom of soul constrains us so that we cannot rest in chains or be at peace in a house of bondage, or compromise with the dungeons of discrimination and accept as our lot the cruel and oppressive hand of those heartless masters who allow pigmentation of skin to blind them to the inner principles of truth and to the revealed purposes of God. The struggle goes on because two determinations meet: one; to enslave, and the other; to be free, and here can be no compromise, and from the task of solving the problem of freedom there must be no retreat.

SOME SUGGESTIONS TO THE AMERICAN NEGRO

But we as a people must keep ever before us the true meaning of our struggle so that we will never be used as tools in the hands of those who love not the nation's cause but seek the nation's hurt and not our help. Hence there are some things that we must do.

1. In our struggle for civil rights we must remain always in the main

stream of American democracy. Our cause must never be divorced from the American cause, and our struggle must not be separated from the American struggle. We must stick to law and order, for as I have said in the past I say now, there are no problems in American life that cannot be solved through commitment to the highest laws of our land and in obedience to the American philosophy and way of life. In spite of criticisms and not-with-standing threats and open attacks, I have not retreated from this position and never will as long as America is the America of the Federal Constitution and a land of due process of law. We cannot win our battle through force and unreasonable intimidation. As a minority group we cannot win outside of the protection and power of the just laws of this land. Read history with open eyes and attentive minds, and we will discover that no minority group has and can win in a struggle by the direct confrontation of the majority and by employing the same type of pressures and powers that the majority possess in abundance. The hope of the minority struggle is with the just laws of the land and the moral and constructive forces that are germane to this nation's life and character.

While we must be determined to achieve the best, we must not be guided by a spirit of revenge, blind emotions, and uncontrolled temper. When we act by these baser emotions we find ourselves contradicting ourselves. We will deny freedom of speech to those who differ with us, and will seek to do the things that will embarrass others however costly it may be to us and to them. When we are guided by revenge we do not choose our program of action wisely. There are some groups who are thus motivated, will go in, sit in, or lie in, in places that have objected to their presence. These same groups when they are dissatisfied in places that have accepted them, will give up their achieved rights and walk out in protest and revenge. Our actions must be guided both by logic and by law.

2. The methods that we employ in the present struggle must not lead us into open opposition to the laws of the land. In some cases the technique of direct action and demonstrations have led to mob violence and to vandalism. At least some who have desired to practice these negative methods have used the technique of so-called direct action.

· · ·

3. Negroes must become registered voters and fight their battles in the polling booth. In the coming campaign we must not allow our prejudices, our hatred for individuals, to lead us into emotional outbursts and disrespect. The candidates contending for the presidency of the United States deserve, and should enjoy, the respect from every American citizen. It is beneath the dignity of this fair land of ours to seek to howl down, and to boo from platforms any candidate whom we do not favor. We must

make choice of the candidate whom we think will serve the best inter-est of this nation and the nation's cause, and then take our ballot and help to elect our choice. As I told this convention in 1956, I tell you again, the ballot is our most important weapon. We must not neglect it, for-feit or sell it, but use it for the protection of the nation, the promotion of freedom, the promotion of every citizen, and for the glory of the United States of America. What I said in 1956 I still say now.

4. Negroes must still make their own leaders. We must not expect the public press, radio, and television to do this job for us. These news media are too busy with other responsibilities to be assigned the task of choos-ing Negro leaders to represent the race in these days of stress and strain. Negroes must not forget that we have many fields in which leaders are necessary and important, and we should accept and follow the leaders in their respective field; that is, when they are right. We have political leaders, many of whom are worthy of our confidence and our respect. We shall follow them and show our appreciation for them. We have some dedicated civil rights leaders. We should respect them and follow them in their chosen field when they are right. We have religious leaders. We should respect and follow them when they are committed to the task of human betterment, human uplift, and the work of re-making the social order in the name of justice, righteousness, and peace.

We have worthy business leaders who can show us the way to improve our economic status, and to develop our available economic resources. Let us follow them. We have educators who are making their contribu-tion in the field of thought and of mental growth. Let us honor them and respect them, and let us not discourage Negro educators by advocat-ing directly or indirectly, that they are by nature inferior to educators in other racial groups.

We have athletes and comedians. Let us still applaud our athletes when they achieve on the field of competition, and let us join with others and freely laugh at the jokes that our comedians give. But we must not confuse these various fields. There must not develop any dictatorship of any one field, and athletes and comedians must not make the mistake of assuming the role of political, religious, and cultural leaders. We as a race must see to it that each man serves in his field, and we must not allow the white community to pick our leaders or to tell us what Negro we should follow.

5. Let us be courageous enough not only to oppose the wrong and the un-American actions in our nation, but we must also appreciate and re-joice in the achievements of our nation. There are some recent achieve-ments which give us reason for hope, grounds for trust, and basis for rejoicing.

Ten years ago the Supreme Court of the United States rose above its old concept of separate but equal, and declared that segregation had no place in America's system of public education. This year, after a long, hard, and laborious fight, the Congress of the United States passed the strongest civil rights bill in its history, and the president signed into law a document that said that segregation has no place in American life and destiny. The call is to all of us to accept these facts and build on them. We must not ignore the constructive laws of our land, we must not organize, condone, or support mobs that parade in the name of freedom. We must not turn aside from decency and the constructive American standards in our quest for freedom. In our haste let us not be haughty. In our determination we must not become detrimental, and in our demonstrations we cannot afford to damn the nation of which we are a vital part.

6. DIRECT ACTION IN THE POSITIVE

We have heard much in recent months about direct action in terms of boycotts, pickets, sit-ins, and demonstrations of various kinds. In each case the purpose as stated is a lofty one; namely, the winning of civil rights and the achievement of the equality of opportunity. I repeat, these are worthy ends and desirable goals, but this kind of direct action is orientated against others, and for the most part, must be classified in the negative since they have been designed to stop, arrest, or hinder certain orderly procedures in the interest of civil rights. In some cases however, these actions have been against practices and laws considered to be both evil and unjust.

Today, I call for another type of direct action; that is, direct action in the positive which is orientated towards the Negro's ability, talent, genius, and capacity. Let us take our economic resources, however insignificant and small, and organize and harness them, not to stop the economic growth of others, but to develop our own and to help our own community. If our patronage withdrawn from any store or business enterprise will weaken said enterprise, why not organize these resources and channel them into producing enterprises that we ourselves can direct and control. In the act of boycotting, our best economic talents are not called into play, and we ourselves are less productive and seek to render others the same. Why not build for ourselves instead of boycotting what others have produced? We must not be guilty of possessing the minds and actions of a blind Sampson who pulled a massive building down upon himself as well as his enemies, and died with them in a final act of revenge. No act of revenge will lift a race from thralldom, and any direct actions that reduce the economic strength and life of the community is sure to punish the poor as well as the rich. Direct actions that encourage and create more tensions, ill will, hostility, and hate, will tend to make more difficult the mental, moral, and spiritual changes essential to new growth and creativity in human relations. Remember that when we seek to change certain acquired notions and habits of men we are seeking to change that which is very vital in human nature. When we labor to change segregationists and racists who believe they are right, we are facing the task of re-conditioning human emotions and building within, new patterns of thought, and changing human nature itself. In addition to that type of direct action which is negative and aimed at the correction of others, we need the type of direct action also that starts with ourselves which tends to produce a higher type of life within us as well as within others, and which aims to build a better community in which the available moral forces may be used to create new attitudes and new dispositions where human beings will regard others as they regard themselves. Why should we expect direct actions against others to bear immediate fruit, and then procrastinate and postpone the direct actions that will make us better business men, better statesmen, better thinkers, and better men and women with better homes and better fellowship NOW? Now must not only be applied to the needs for changes and attitudes of segregationists, it must also be applied to us as a people and as a race when we aspire for the best and seek the more constructive and creative methods of life. We can be better now. We can acquire a better education now, we can organize our capital now and receive our share in this economy of free enterprise now. In spite of all that we have attained as a people we have not exhausted our possibilities, and the past does not define the limits of our potential. Are we not as well equipped to respond to the call of the right, the just, the good, the highest, and the best as are the white segregationists against whom we fight? Has not the great God put in our souls the thirst for truth and righteousness? Are we not endowed as co-workers with the great creative spirit of the universe? Then we need not wait until all is well before we harness our resources and venture upon new ways of life and creativity.

We must not play ourselves too cheap or postpone the day of greater things when the hour of fulfillment is already at hand. To the leaders of school boycotts who have called children to remain out of school in order to help correct the evils and errors of an imperfect system of education, are you willing now to use your influence to lead young people to desert the ranks of drop-outs and struggle now to make the best out of the education that is now available? The call to stay out of school does not appeal to the highest in students but to the ordinary and the easy. It requires less initiative to stay out of school than it does to attend school. It requires less mental alertness to refuse to study than it does to study.

Is not some education better than no education? Of course we should get all the education possible and go as far up the ladder of intellectual attainments as our powers will allow us. We must strive for the very best opportunities, the best possible schools, and the best possible teachers, but if these are not available to us then let us make the best use of what we do have. Remember that the future is with the person who knows, thinks, understands, and who has character and soul, and who can produce, invest, create and live in harmony with the highest and the best. Of course we adults must continue to correct all the evils which make education more difficult. We must strive for quality education and seek to make available all the resources possible for the education of the young, but our young people must keep their feet in the upward path of learning and their minds stayed on the quest for truth.

The progress of the race lies not in continued street demonstrations, and the liberation of an oppressed people shall not come by acts of revenge and retaliation but by the constructive use of all available opportunities and a creative expansion of the circumstances of the past into stepping stones to higher things.

. . .

Malcolm X

After enthusiastically serving the various devils that American society offers to the degraded black, Malcolm X came under the influence of the teachings of Elijah Muhammad, lifted himself out of his degradation, and took up the work of fighting the white devils. He served for several years as Muhammad's chief lieutenant, building the organization, preaching the doctrine, and acting as the vehicle of direct confrontation with the white world. Following a break with Elijah Muhammad in 1964, Malcolm entered into an extremely fruitful if often chaotic period during which he was principally concerned with thinking through his own position. He was assassinated in February, 1965, before that task had been accomplished, and in the speeches of his last year we find a set of vigorous, challenging, and sometimes contradictory reflections.

Although various claims have been made that Malcolm "really" decided on this or that basic doctrine during his final months, as

145

far as the evidence shows he was still open, still uncertain, still thinking. This openness can be seen in his discussion of almost all of the issues he takes up: the black's relation with America, the meaning of revolution, integration, the question of violence and political action. In the speech reprinted here Malcolm pursued a very common theme of his last year, the ballot or the bullet, a theme that itself reflects his own uncertainty or (Malcolm might have contended) the contradictions in the situation of the black man in America. Whatever their cause, the uncertainties or contradictions of Malcolm's arguments are anything but passive or weak. Malcolm was always active, probing, exploring. Despite the claims of those who have tried to make him a prophet, the heritage of Malcolm X is not doctrines but *questions.*

Additional Readings: The chief source of Malcolm's thought

The Ballot or the Bullet

Mr. Moderator, Brother Lomax, brothers and sisters, friends and enemies: I just can't believe everyone in here is a friend and I don't want to leave anybody out. The question tonight, as I understand it, is "The Negro Revolt, and Where Do We Go From Here?" or "What Next?" In my little humble way of understanding it, it points toward either the ballot or the bullet.

Before we try and explain what is meant by the ballot or the bullet, I would like to clarify something concerning myself. I'm still a Muslim, my religion is still Islam. That's my personal belief. Just as Adam Clayton Powell is a Christian minister who heads the Abyssinian Baptist Church in New York, but at the same time takes part in the political struggles to try and bring about rights to the black people in this country; and Dr. Martin Luther King is a Christian minister down in Atlanta, Georgia, who heads another organization fighting for the civil rights of black

From *Malcolm X Speaks.* Copyright © 1965 by Merit Publishers and Betty Shabazz. Reprinted by permission of Merit Publishers.

during the period that followed the break with Elijah Muhammad is the collection edited by George Breitman, *Malcolm X Speaks,* from which the speech, "The Ballot or the Bullet," is taken. Other speeches from this period will be found in Archie Epps (ed.), *The Speeches of Malcolm X at Harvard* and *Malcolm X on Afro-American History;* but these do not add significantly to *Malcolm X Speaks. The Autobiography of Malcolm X* provides an extraordinary account of life in the black slums, of this man's escape from that life, of his work among the Muslims and his break with Elijah Muhammad, and of his experiences and thoughts following the break. It is an autobiography that deserves to be read and compared with those of Douglass, Washington, Du Bois, and King, although Malcolm's life and thought were, to a much greater extent than theirs, unfinished.

people in this country; and Rev. Galamison, I guess you've heard of him, is another Christian minister in New York who has been deeply involved in the school boycotts to eliminate segregated education; well, I myself am a minister, not a Christian minister, but a Muslim minister; and I believe in action on all fronts by whatever means necessary.

Although I'm still a Muslim, I'm not here tonight to discuss my religion. I'm not here to try and change your religion. I'm not here to argue or discuss anything that we differ about, because it's time for us to submerge our differences and realize that it is best for us to first see that we have the same problem, a common problem—a problem that will make you catch hell whether you're a Baptist, or a Methodist, or a Muslim, or a nationalist. Whether you're educated or illiterate, whether you live on the boulevard or in the alley, you're going to catch hell just like I am. We're all in the same boat and we all are going to catch the same hell from the same man. He just happens to be a white man. All of us have suffered here, in this country, political oppression at the hands of the white man, economic exploitation at the hands of the white man, and social degradation at the hands of the white man.

Now in speaking like this, it doesn't mean that we're anti-white, but it does mean we're anti-exploitation, we're anti-degradation, we're anti-oppression. And if the white man doesn't want us to be anti-him, let him stop oppressing and exploiting and degrading us. Whether we are Christians or Muslims or nationalists or agnostics or atheists, we must first learn to forget our differences. If we have differences, let us differ in the closet; when we come out in front, let us not have anything to argue about until we get finished arguing with the man. If the late President Kennedy could get together with Khrushchev and exchange some wheat, we certainly have more in common with each other than Kennedy and Khrushchev had with each other.

If we don't do something real soon, I think you'll have to agree that we're going to be forced either to use the ballot or the bullet. It's one or the other in 1964. It isn't that time is running out—time has run out! 1964 threatens to be the most explosive year America has ever witnessed. The most explosive year. Why? It's also a political year. It's the year when all of the white politicians will be back in the so-called Negro community jiving you and me for some votes. The year when all of the white political crooks will be right back in your and my community with their false promises, building up our hopes for a letdown, with their trickery and their treachery, with their false promises which they don't intend to keep. As they nourish these dissatisfactions, it can only lead to one thing, an explosion; and now we have the type of black man on the scene in America today—I'm sorry, Brother Lomax—who just doesn't intend to turn the other cheek any longer.

Don't let anybody tell you anything about the odds are against you. If they draft you, they send you to Korea and make you face 800 million Chinese. If you can be brave over there, you can be brave right here. These odds aren't as great as those odds. And if you fight here, you will at least know what you're fighting for.

I'm not a politician, not even a student of politics; in fact, I'm not a student of much of anything. I'm not a Democrat, I'm not a Republican, and I don't even consider myself an American. If you and I were Americans, there'd be no problem. Those Hunkies that just got off the boat, they're already Americans; Polacks are already Americans; the Italian refugees are already Americans. Everything that came out of Europe, every blue-eyed thing, is already an American. And as long as you and I have been over here, we aren't Americans yet.

Well, I am one who doesn't believe in deluding myself. I'm not going to sit at your table and watch you eat, with nothing on my plate, and call myself a diner. Sitting at the table doesn't make you a diner, unless you eat some of what's on that plate. Being here in America doesn't make you an American. Being born here in America doesn't make you an American. Why, if birth made you American, you wouldn't need any legislation, you wouldn't need any amendments to the Constitution, you wouldn't be faced with civil-rights filibustering in Washington, D.C., right now. They don't have to pass civil-rights legislation to make a Polack an American.

No, I'm not an American. I'm one of the 22 million black people who are the victims of Americanism. One of the 22 million black people who are the victims of democracy, nothing but disguised hypocrisy. So, I'm not standing here speaking to you as an American, or a patriot, or a flag-saluter, or a flag-waver—no, not I. I'm speaking as a victim of this American system. And I see America through the eyes of the victim. I don't see any American dream; I see an American nightmare.

These 22 million victims are waking up. Their eyes are coming open. They're beginning to see what they used to only look at. They're becoming politically mature. They are realizing that there are new political trends from coast to coast. As they see these new political trends, it's possible for them to see that every time there's an election the races are so close that they have to have a recount. They had to recount in Massachusetts to see who was going to be governor, it was so close. It was the same way in Rhode Island, in Minnesota, and in many other parts of the country. And the same with Kennedy and Nixon when they ran for president. It was so close they had to count all over again. Well, what does this mean? It means that when white people are evenly divided, and black people have a bloc of votes of their own, it is left up to them to determine who's going to sit in the White House and who's going to be in the dog house.

It was the black man's vote that put the present administration in Washington, D.C. Your vote, your dumb vote, your ignorant vote, your wasted vote put in an administration in Washington, D.C., that has seen fit to pass every kind of legislation imaginable, saving you until last, then filibustering on top of that. And your and my leaders have the audacity to run around clapping their hands and talk about how much progress we're making. And what a good president we have. If he wasn't good in Texas, he sure can't be good in Washington, D.C. Because Texas is a lynch state. It is in the same breath as Mississippi, no different; only they lynch you in Texas with a Texas accent and lynch you in Mississippi with a Mississippi accent. And these Negro leaders have the audacity to go and have some coffee in the White House with a Texan, a Southern cracker—that's all he is—and then come out and tell you and me that he's going to be better for us because, since he's from the South, he knows how to deal with the Southerners. What kind of logic is that? Let Eastland be president, he's from the South too. He should be better able to deal with them than Johnson.

In this present administration they have in the House of Representatives 257 Democrats to only 177 Republicans. They control two-thirds of the House vote. Why can't they pass something that will help you and me? In the Senate, there are 67 senators who are of the Democratic Party. Only 33 of them are Republicans. Why, the Democrats have got the government sewed up, and you're the one who sewed it up for them. And what have they given you for it? Four years in office, and just now getting around to some civil-rights legislation. Just now, after everything else is gone, out of the way, they're going to sit down now and play with you all summer long—the same old giant con game that they call filibuster. All those are in cahoots together. Don't you ever think they're not in cahoots together, for the man that is heading the civil-rights filibuster is a man from Georgia named Richard Russell. When Johnson became president, the first man he asked for when he got back to Washington, D.C., was "Dicky"—that's how tight they are. That's his boy, that's his pal, that's his buddy. But they're playing that old con game. One of them makes believe he's for you, and he's got it fixed where the other one is so tight against you, he never has to keep his promise.

So it's time in 1964 to wake up. And when you see them coming up with that kind of conspiracy, let them know your eyes are open. And let them know you got something else that's wide open too. It's got to be the ballot or the bullet. The ballot or the bullet. If you're afraid to use an expression like that, you should get on out of the country, you should get back in the cotton patch, you should get back in the alley. They get all the Negro vote, and after they get it, the Negro gets nothing in return. All they did when they got to Washington was give a few big Negroes big jobs. Those big Negroes didn't need big jobs, they already had jobs. That's camouflage, that's trickery, that's treachery, window-dressing. I'm not trying to knock out the Democrats for the Republicans, we'll get to them in a minute. But it is true—you put the Democrats first and the Democrats put you last.

Look at it the way it is. What alibis do they use, since they control Congress and the Senate? What alibi do they use when you and I ask, "Well, when are you going to keep your promise?" They blame the Dixiecrats. What is a Dixiecrat? A Democrat. A Dixiecrat is nothing but a Democrat in disguise. The titular head of the Democrats is also the head of the Dixiecrats, because the Dixiecrats are a part of the Democratic Party. The Democrats have never kicked the Dixiecrats out of the party. The Dixiecrats bolted themselves once, but the Democrats didn't put them out. Imagine, these lowdown Southern segregationists put the Northern Democrats down. But the Northern Democrats have never put the Dixiecrats down. No, look at that thing the way it is. They have got a con game going on, a political con game, and you and I are in the middle. It's time for you and me to wake up and start looking at it like it is, and trying to understand it like it is; and then we can deal with it like it is.

The Dixiecrats in Washington, D.C., control the key committees that run the government. The only reason the Dixiecrats control these committees is because they have seniority. The only reason they have seniority is because they come from states where Negroes can't vote. This is not even a government that's based on democracy. It is not a government that is made up of representatives of the people. Half of the people in the South can't even vote. Eastland is not even supposed to be in Washington. Half of the senators and congressmen who occupy these key positions in Washington, D.C., are there illegally, are there unconstitutionally.

I was in Washington, D.C., a week ago Thursday, when they were debating whether or not they should let the bill come onto the floor. And in the back of the room where the Senate meets, there's a huge map of the United States, and on that map it shows the location of Negroes throughout the country. And it shows that the Southern section of the country, the states that are most heavily concentrated with Negroes, are the ones that have senators and congressmen standing up filibustering and doing all other kinds of trickery to keep the Negro from being able to vote. This is pitiful. But it's not pitiful for us any longer; it's actually pitiful for the white man, because soon now, as the Negro awakens a little more and sees the vise that he's in, sees the bag that he's in, sees the real game that he's in, then the Negro's going to develop a new tactic.

These senators and congressmen actually violate the constitutional amendments that guarantee the people of that particular state or county the right to vote. And the Constitution itself has within it the machinery to expel any representative from a state where the voting rights of the people are violated. You don't even need new legislation. Any person in Congress right now, who is there from a state or a district where the voting rights of the people are violated, that particular person should be expelled from Congress. And when you expel him, you've removed one of the obstacles in the path of any real meaningful legislation in this country. In fact, when you expel them, you don't need new legislation, because they will be replaced by black representatives from counties and districts where the black man is in the majority, not in the minority.

If the black man in these Southern states had his full voting rights, the key Dixiecrats in Washington, D.C., which means the key Democrats in Washington, D.C., would lose their seats. The Democratic Party itself would lose its power. It would cease to be powerful as a party. When you see the amount of power that would be lost by the Democratic Party if it were to lose the Dixiecrat wing, or branch, or element, you can see where it's against the interests of the Democrats to give voting rights to Negroes in states where the Democrats have been in complete power and authority ever since the Civil War. You just can't belong to that party without analyzing it.

I say again, I'm not anti-Democrat, I'm not anti-Republican, I'm not anti-anything. I'm just questioning their sincerity, and some of the strategy that they've been using on our people by promising them promises that they don't intend to keep. When you keep the Democrats in power, you're keeping the Dixiecrats in power. I doubt that my good Brother Lomax will deny that. A vote for a Democrat is a vote for a Dixiecrat. That's why, in 1964, it's time now for you and me to become more politically mature and realize what the ballot is for; what we're supposed to get when we cast a ballot; and that if we don't cast a ballot, it's going to end up in a situation where we're going to have to cast a bullet. It's either a ballot or a bullet.

In the North, they do it a different way. They have a system that's known as gerrymandering, whatever that means. It means when Negroes become too heavily concentrated in a certain area, and begin to gain too much political power, the white man comes along and changes the district lines. You may say, "Why do you keep saying white man?" Because it's the white man who does it. I haven't ever seen any Negro changing any lines. They don't let him get near the line. It's the white man who does this. And usually, it's the white man who grins at you the most, and pats you on the back, and is supposed to be your friend. He may be friendly, but he's not your friend.

So, what I'm trying to impress upon you, in essence, is this: You and I in America are faced not with a segregationist conspiracy, we're faced with a government conspiracy. Everyone who's filibustering is a senátor—that's the government. Everyone who's finagling in Washington, D.C., is a congressman—that's the government. You don't have anybody putting blocks in your path but people who are a part of the government. The same government that you go abroad to fight for and die for is the government that is in a conspiracy to deprive you of your voting rights, deprive you of your economic opportunities, deprive you of decent housing, deprive you of decent education. You don't need to go to the employer alone, it is the government itself, the government of America, that is responsible for the oppression and exploitation and degradation of black people in this country. And you should drop it in their lap. This government has failed the Negro. This so-called democracy has failed the Negro. And all these white liberals have definitely failed the Negro.

So, where do we go from here? First, we need some friends. We need some new allies. The entire civil-rights struggle needs a new interpretation, a broader interpretation. We need to look at this civil-rights thing from another angle—from the inside as well as from the outside. To those of us whose philosophy is black nationalism, the only way you can get involved in the civil-rights struggle is give it a new interpretation. That old interpretation excluded us. It kept us out. So, we're giving a new interpretation to the civil-rights struggle, an interpretation that will enable us to come into it, take part in it. And these handkerchief-heads who have been dillydallying and pussyfooting and compromising— we don't intend to let them pussyfoot and dillydally and compromise any longer.

How can you thank a man for giving you what's already yours? How then can you thank him for giving you only part of what's already yours? You haven't even made progress, if what's being given to you, you should have had already. That's not progress. And I love my Brother Lomax, the way he pointed out we're right back where we were in 1954. We're not even as far up as we were in 1954. We're behind where we were in 1954. There's more segregation now than there was in 1954. There's more racial animosity, more racial hatred, more racial violence today in 1964, than there was in 1954. Where is the progress?

And now you're facing a situation where the young Negro's coming up. They don't want to hear that "turn-the-other-cheek" stuff, no. In Jacksonville, those were teenagers, they were throwing Molotov cocktails. Negroes have never done that before. But it shows you there's a new deal coming in. There's new thinking coming in. There's new strategy coming in. It'll be Molotov cocktails this month, hand grenades next month, and something else next month. It'll be ballots, or it'll be bullets. It'll be liberty, or it will be death. The only difference about this kind of death—it'll be reciprocal. You know what is meant by "reciprocal"? That's one of Brother Lomax's words, I stole it from him. I don't usually deal with those big words because I don't usually deal with big people. I deal with small people. I find you can get a whole lot of small people and whip hell out of a whole lot of big people. They haven't got anything to lose, and they've got everything to gain. And they'll let you know in a minute: "It takes two to tango; when I go, you go."

The black nationalists, those whose philosophy is black nationalism, in bringing about this new interpretation of the entire meaning of civil rights, look upon it as meaning, as Brother Lomax has pointed out, equality of opportunity. Well, we're justified in seeking civil rights, if it means equality of opportunity, because all we're doing there is trying to collect for our investment. Our mothers and fathers invested sweat and blood. Three hundred and ten years we worked in this country without a dime in return—I mean without a *dime* in return. You let the white man walk around here talking about how rich this country is, but you never stop to think how it got rich so quick. It got rich because you made it rich.

You take the people who are in this audience right now. They're poor,

we're all poor as individuals. Our weekly salary individually amounts
to hardly anything. But if you take the salary of everyone in here collec-
tively it'll fill up a whole lot of baskets. It's a lot of wealth. If you can
collect the wages of just these people right here for a year, you'll be
rich—richer than rich. When you look at it like that, think how rich
Uncle Sam had to become, not with this handful, but millions of black
people. Your and my mother and father, who didn't work an eight-hour
shift, but worked from "can't see" in the morning until "can't see" at
night, and worked for nothing, making the white man rich, making Uncle
Sam rich.

This is our investment. This is our contribution—our blood. Not only
did we give of our free labor, we gave of our blood. Every time he had
a call to arms, we were the first ones in uniform. We died on every
battlefield the white man had. We have made a greater sacrifice than
anybody who's standing up in America today. We have made a greater
contribution and have collected less. Civil rights, for those of us whose
philosophy is black nationalism, means: "Give it to us now. Don't wait
for next year. Give it to us yesterday, and that's not fast enough."

I might stop right here to point out one thing. Whenever you're going
after something that belongs to you, anyone who's depriving you of the
right to have it is a criminal. Understand that. Whenever you are going
after something that is yours, you are within your legal rights to lay claim
to it. And anyone who puts forth any effort to deprive you of that which
is yours, is breaking the law, is a criminal. And this was pointed out by
the Supreme Court decision. It outlawed segregation. Which means
segregation is against the law. Which means a segregationist is breaking
the law. A segregationist is a criminal. You can't label him as anything
other than that. And when you demonstrate against segregation, the law
is on your side. The Supreme Court is on your side.

Now, who is it that opposes you in carrying out the law? The police
department itself. With police dogs and clubs. Whenever you demonstrate against segregation, whether it is segregated education, segregated
housing, or anything else, the law is on your side, and anyone who stands
in the way is not the law any longer. They are breaking the law, they are
not representatives of the law. Any time you demonstrate against segregation and a man has the audacity to put a police dog on you, kill that
dog, kill him, I'm telling you, kill that dog. I say it, if they put me in jail
tomorrow, kill—that—dog. Then you'll put a stop to it. Now, if these
white people in here don't want to see that kind of action, get down and
tell the mayor to tell the police department to pull the dogs in. That's
all you have to do. If you don't do it, someone else will.

If you don't take this kind of stand, your little children will grow up
and look at you and think "shame." If you don't take an uncompromising

stand—I don't mean go out and get violent; but at the same time you should never be nonviolent unless you run into some nonviolence. I'm nonviolent with those who are nonviolent with me. But when you drop that violence on me, then you've made me go insane, and I'm not responsible for what I do. And that's the way every Negro should get. Any time you know you're within the law, within your legal rights, within your moral rights, in accord with justice, then die for what you believe in. But don't die alone. Let your dying be reciprocal. This is what is meant by equality. What's good for the goose is good for the gander.

When we begin to get in this area, we need new friends, we need new allies. We need to expand the civil-rights struggle to a higher level—to the level of human rights. Whenever you are in a civil-rights struggle, whether you know it or not, you are confining yourself to the jurisdiction of Uncle Sam. No one from the outside world can speak out in your behalf as long as your struggle is a civil-rights struggle. Civil rights comes within the domestic affairs of this country. All of our African brothers and our Asian brothers and our Latin-American brothers cannot open their mouths and interfere in the domestic affairs of the United States. And as long as it's civil rights, this comes under the jurisdiction of Uncle Sam.

But the United Nations has what's known as the charter of human rights, it has a committee that deals in human rights. You may wonder why all of the atrocities that have been committed in Africa and in Hungary and in Asia and in Latin America are brought before the UN, and the Negro problem is never brought before the UN. This is part of the conspiracy. This old, tricky, blue-eyed liberal who is supposed to be your and my friend, supposed to be in our corner, supposed to be subsidizing our struggle, and supposed to be acting in the capacity of an adviser, never tells you anything about human rights. They keep you wrapped up in civil rights. And you spend so much time barking up the civil-rights tree, you don't even know there's a human-rights tree on the same floor.

When you expand the civil-rights struggle to the level of human rights, you can then take the case of the black man in this country before the nations in the UN. You can take it before the General Assembly. You can take Uncle Sam before a world court. But the only level you can do it on is the level of human rights. Civil rights keeps you under his restrictions, under his jurisdiction. Civil rights keeps you in his pocket. Civil rights means you're asking Uncle Sam to treat you right. Human rights are something you were born with. Human rights are your God-given rights. Human rights are the rights that are recognized by all nations of this earth. And any time any one violates your human rights, you can take them to the world court. Uncle Sam's hands are dripping with blood, dripping with the blood of the black man in this country. He's the earth's number-one hypocrite. He has the audacity—yes, he has—imagine him posing as the leader of the free world. The free world!—and you over here singing "We Shall Overcome." Expand the civil-rights struggle to the level of human rights, take it into the United Nations, where our African brothers can throw their weight on our side, where our Asian brothers can throw their weight on our side, where our Latin-American brothers can throw their weight on our side, and where 800 million Chinamen are sitting there waiting to throw their weight on our side.

Let the world know how bloody his hands are. Let the world know the hypocrisy that's practiced over here. Let it be the ballot or the bullet. Let him know that it must be the ballot or the bullet.

When you take your case to Washington, D.C., you're taking it to the criminal who's responsible; it's like running from the wolf to the fox. They're all in cahoots together. They all work political chicanery and make you look like a chump before the eyes of the world. Here you are walking around in America, getting ready to be drafted and sent abroad, like a tin soldier, and when you get over there, people ask you what are you fighting for, and you have to stick your tongue in your cheek. No, take Uncle Sam to court, take him before the world.

By ballot I only mean freedom. Don't you know—I disagree with Lomax on this issue—that the ballot is more important than the dollar? Can I prove it? Yes. Look in the UN. There are poor nations in the UN; yet those poor nations can get together with their voting power and keep the rich nations from making a move. They have one nation—one vote, everyone has an equal vote. And when those brothers from Asia, and Africa and the darker parts of this earth get together, their voting power is sufficient to hold Sam in check. Or Russia in check. Or some other section of the earth in check. So, the ballot is most important.

Right now, in this country, if you and I, 22 million African-Americans —that's what we are—Africans who are in America. You're nothing but Africans. Nothing but Africans. In fact, you'd get farther calling yourself African instead of Negro. Africans don't catch hell. You're the only one catching hell. They don't have to pass civil-rights bills for Africans. An African can go anywhere he wants right now. All you've got to do is tie your head up. That's right, go anywhere you want. Just stop being a Negro. Change your name to Hoogagagooba. That'll show you how silly the white man is. You're dealing with a silly man. A friend of mine who's very dark put a turban on his head and went into a restaurant in Atlanta before they called themselves desegregated. He went into a white restaurant, he sat down, they served him, and he said, "What would happen if a Negro came in here?" And there he's sitting, black as night, but because he had his head wrapped up the waitress looked back at him and says, "Why, there wouldn't no nigger dare come in here."

So, you're dealing with a man whose bias and prejudice are making him lose his mind, his intelligence, every day. He's frightened. He looks around and sees what's taking place on this earth, and he sees that the pendulum of time is swinging in your direction. The dark people are waking up. They're losing their fear of the white man. No place where he's fighting right now is he winning. Everywhere he's fighting, he's fighting someone your and my complexion. And they're beating him. He can't win any more. He's won his last battle. He failed to win the Korean War. He couldn't win it. He had to sign a truce. That's a loss. Any time Uncle Sam, with all his machinery for warfare, is held to a draw by some rice-eaters, he's lost the battle. He had to sign a truce. America's not supposed to sign a truce. She's supposed to be bad. But she's not bad any more. She's bad as long as she can use her hydrogen bomb, but she can't use hers for fear Russia might use hers. Russia can't use hers, for fear that Sam might use his. So, both of them are weaponless. They can't use the weapon because each's weapon nullifies the other's. So the only place where action can take place is on the ground. And the white man can't win another war fighting on the ground. Those days are over. The black man knows it, the brown man knows it, the red man knows it, and the yellow man knows it. So they engage him in guerrilla warfare. That's not his style. You've got to have heart to be a guerrilla warrior, and he hasn't got any heart. I'm telling you now.

I just want to give you a little briefing on guerrilla warfare because, before you know it, before you know it — It takes heart to be a guerrilla warrior because you're on your own. In conventional warfare you have tanks and a whole lot of other people with you to back you up, planes over your head and all that kind of stuff. But a guerrilla is on his own. All you have is a rifle, some sneakers and a bowl of rice, and that's all you need — and a lot of heart. The Japanese on some of those islands in the Pacific, when the American soldiers landed, one Japanese sometimes could hold the whole army off. He'd just wait until the sun went down, and when the sun went down they were all equal. He would take his little blade and slip from bush to bush, and from American to American. The white soldiers couldn't cope with that. Whenever you see a white soldier that fought in the Pacific, he has the shakes, he has a nervous condition, because they scared him to death.

The same thing happened to the French up in French Indochina. People who just a few years previously were rice farmers got together and ran the heavily-mechanized French army out of Indochina. You don't need it — modern warfare today won't work. This is the day of the guerrilla. They did the same thing in Algeria. Algerians, who were nothing but Bedouins, took a rifle and sneaked off to the hills, and de Gaulle and all of his highfalutin' war machinery couldn't defeat those guerrillas. Nowhere on this earth does the white man win in a guerrilla warfare. It's not his speed. Just as guerrilla warfare is prevailing in Asia and in parts of Africa and in parts of Latin America, you've got to be mighty naive, or you've got to play the black man cheap, if you don't think some day he's going to wake up and find that it's got to be the ballot or the bullet.

I would like to say, in closing, a few things concerning the Muslim Mosque, Inc., which we established recently in New York City. It's true we're Muslims and our religion is Islam, but we don't mix our religion with our politics and our economics and our social and civil activities— not any more. We keep our religion in our mosque. After our religious services are over, then as Muslims we become involved in political action, economic action and social and civic action. We become involved with anybody, anywhere, any time and in any manner that's designed to eliminate the evils, the political, economic and social evils that are afflicting the people of our community.

The political philosophy of black nationalism means that the black man should control the politics and the politicians in his own community; no more. The black man in the black community has to be re-educated into the science of politics so he will know what politics is supposed to bring him in return. Don't be throwing out any ballots. A ballot is like a bullet. You don't throw your ballots until you see a target, and if that target is not within your reach, keep your ballot in your pocket. The political philosophy of black nationalism is being taught in the Christian church. It's being taught in the NAACP. It's being taught in CORE meetings. It's being taught in SNCC [Student Nonviolent Coordinating Committee] meetings. It's being taught in Muslim meetings. It's being taught where nothing but atheists and agnostics come together. It's being taught everywhere. Black people are fed up with the dillydallying, pussyfooting, compromising approach that we've been using toward getting our freedom. We want freedom *now*, but we're not going to get it saying "We Shall Overcome." We've got to fight until we overcome.

The economic philosophy of black nationalism is pure and simple. It only means that we should control the economy of our community. Why should white people be running all the stores in our community? Why should white people be running the banks of our community? Why should the economy of our community be in the hands of the white man? Why? If a black man can't move his store into a white community, you tell me why a white man should move his store into a black community. The philosophy of black nationalism involves a re-education program in the black community in regards to economics. Our people have to be made to see that any time you take your dollar out of your community and spend it in a community where you don't live, the community where you live will get poorer and poorer, and the community where you spend your money will get richer and richer. Then you wonder why where you live is always a ghetto or a slum area. And where you and I are concerned, not only do we lose it when we spend it out of the community, but the white man has got all our stores in the community tied up; so that though we spend it in the community, at sundown the man who runs the store takes it over across town somewhere. He's got us in a vise.

So the economic philosophy of black nationalism means in every church, in every civic organization, in every fraternal order, it's time now for our people to become conscious of the importance of controlling the economy of our community. If we own the stores, if we operate the businesses, if we try and establish some industry in our own community, then we're developing to the position where we are creating employment for our own kind. Once you gain control of the economy of your own community, then you don't have to picket and boycott and beg some cracker downtown for a job in his business.

The social philosophy of black nationalism only means that we have to get together and remove the evils, the vices, alcoholism, drug addiction, and other evils that are destroying the moral fiber of our community. We ourselves have to lift the level of our community, the standard of our community to a higher level, make our own society beautiful so that we will be satisfied in our own social circles and won't be running around here trying to knock our way into a social circle where we're not wanted.

So I say, in spreading a gospel such as black nationalism, it is not designed to make the black man re-evaluate the white man—you know him already—but to make the black man re-evaluate himself. Don't change the white man's mind—you can't change his mind, and that whole thing about appealing to the moral conscience of America—America's conscience is bankrupt. She lost all conscience a long time ago. Uncle Sam has no conscience. They don't know what morals are. They don't try and eliminate an evil because it's evil, or because it's illegal, or because it's immoral; they eliminate it only when it threatens their existence. So you're wasting your time appealing to the moral conscience of a bankrupt man like Uncle Sam. If he had a conscience, he'd straighten this thing out with no more pressure being put upon him. So it is not necessary to change the white man's mind. We have to change our own mind. You can't change his mind about us. We've got to change our own minds about each other. We have to see each other with new eyes. We have to see each other as brothers and sisters. We have to come together with warmth so we can develop unity and harmony that's necessary to get this problem solved ourselves. How can we do this? How can we avoid jealousy? How can we avoid the suspicion and the divisions that exist in the community? I'll tell you how.

I have watched how Billy Graham comes into a city, spreading what he calls the gospel of Christ, which is only white nationalism. That's what he is. Billy Graham is a white nationalist; I'm a black nationalist. But since it's the natural tendency for leaders to be jealous and look upon a powerful figure like Graham with suspicion and envy, how is it possible for him to come into a city and get all the cooperation of the church leaders? Don't think because they're church leaders that they don't have weaknesses that make them envious and jealous—no, everybody's got it. It's not an accident that when they want to choose a cardinal [as Pope] over there in Rome, they get in a closet so you can't hear them cussing and fighting and carrying on.

Billy Graham comes in preaching the gospel of Christ, he evangelizes the gospel, he stirs everybody up, but he never tries to start a church. If he came in trying to start a church, all the churches would be against him. So, he just comes in talking about Christ and tells everybody who gets Christ to go to any church where Christ is; and in this way the church cooperates with him. So we're going to take a page from his book.

Our gospel is black nationalism. We're not trying to threaten the existence of any organization, but we're spreading the gospel of black nationalism. Anywhere there's a church that is also preaching and practicing the gospel of black nationalism, join that church. If the NAACP is preaching and practicing the gospel of black nationalism, join the NAACP. If CORE is spreading and practicing the gospel of black nationalism, join CORE. Join any organization that has a gospel that's for the uplift of the black man. And when you get into it and see them pussyfooting or compromising, pull out of it because that's not black nationalism. We'll find another one.

And in this manner, the organizations will increase in number and in quantity and in quality, and by August, it is then our intention to have a black nationalist convention which will consist of delegates from all over the country who are interested in the political, economic and social philosophy of black nationalism. After these delegates convene, we will hold a seminar, we will hold discussions, we will listen to everyone. We want to hear new ideas and new solutions and new answers. And at that time, if we see fit then to form a black nationalist party, we'll form a black nationalist party. If it's necessary to form a black nationalist army, we'll form a black nationalist army. It'll be the ballot or the bullet. It'll be liberty or it'll be death.

It's time for you and me to stop sitting in this country, letting some cracker senators, Northern crackers and Southern crackers, sit there in

Washington, D.C., and come to a conclusion in their mind that you and I are supposed to have civil rights. There's no white man going to tell me anything about *my* rights. Brothers and sisters, always remember, if it doesn't take senators and congressmen and presidential proclamations to give freedom to the white man, it is not necessary for legislation or proclamation or Supreme Court decisions to give freedom to the black man. You let that white man know, if this is a country of freedom, let it be a country of freedom; and if it's not a country of freedom, change it.

We will work with anybody, anywhere, at any time, who is genuinely interested in tackling the problem head-on, nonviolently as long as the enemy is nonviolent, but violent when the enemy gets violent. We'll work with you on the voter-registration drive, we'll work with you on rent strikes, we'll work with you on school boycotts—I don't believe in any kind of integration; I'm not even worried about it because I know you're not going to get it anyway; you're not going to get it because you're afraid to die; you've got to be ready to die if you try and force yourself on the white man, because he'll get just as violent as those crackers in Mississippi, right here in Cleveland. But we will still work with you on the school boycotts because we're against a segregated school system. A segregated school system produces children who, when they graduate, graduate with crippled minds. But this does not mean that a school is segregated because it's all black. A segregated school means a school that is controlled by people who have no real interest in it whatsoever.

Let me explain what I mean. A segregated district or community is a community in which people live, but outsiders control the politics and the economy of that community. They never refer to the white section as a segregated community. It's the all-Negro section that's a segregated community. Why? The white man controls his own school, his own bank, his own economy, his own politics, his own everything, his own community—but he also controls yours. When you're under someone else's control, you're segregated. They'll always give you the lowest or the worst that there is to offer, but it doesn't mean you're segregated just because you have your own. You've got to *control* your own. Just like the white man has control of his, you need to control yours.

You know the best way to get rid of segregation? The white man is more afraid of separation than he is of integration. Segregation means that he puts you away from him, but not far enough for you to be out of his jurisdiction; separation means you're gone. And the white man will integrate faster than he'll let you separate. So we will work with you against the segregated school system because it's criminal, because it is absolutely destructive, in every way imaginable, to the minds of the children who have to be exposed to that type of crippling education.

Last but not least, I must say this concerning the great controversy over rifles and shotguns. The only thing that I've ever said is that in areas where the government has proven itself either unwilling or unable to defend the lives and the property of Negroes, it's time for Negroes to defend themselves. Article number two of the constitutional amendments provides you and me the right to own a rifle or a shotgun. It is constitutionally legal to own a shotgun or a rifle. This doesn't mean you're going to get a rifle and form battalions and go out looking for white folks, although you'd be within your rights—I mean, you'd be justified; but that would be illegal and we don't do anything illegal. If the white man doesn't want the black man buying rifles and shotguns, then let the government do its job. That's all. And don't let the white man come to you and ask you what you think about what Malcolm says— why, you old Uncle Tom. He would never ask you if he thought you were going to say, "Amen!" No, he is making a Tom out of you.

So, this doesn't mean forming rifle clubs and going out looking for people, but it is time, in 1964, if you are a man, to let that man know. If he's not going to do his job in running the government and providing you and me with the protection that our taxes are supposed to be for, since he spends all those billions for his defense budget, he certainly can't begrudge you and me spending $12 or $15 for a single-shot, or double-action. I hope you understand. Don't go out shooting people, but any time, brothers and sisters, and especially the men in this audience— some of you wearing Congressional Medals of Honor, with shoulders this wide, chests this big, muscles that big—any time you and I sit around and read where they bomb a church and murder in cold blood, not some grownups, but four little girls while they were praying to the same god the white man taught them to pray to, and you and I see the government go down and can't find who did it.

Why, this man—he can find Eichmann hiding down in Argentina somewhere. Let two or three American soldiers, who are minding somebody else's business way over in South Vietnam, get killed, and he'll send battleships, sticking his nose in their business. He wanted to send troops down to Cuba and make them have what he calls free elections— this old cracker who doesn't have free elections in his own country. No, if you never see me another time in your life, if I die in the morning, I'll die saying one thing: the ballot or the bullet, the ballot or the bullet.

If a Negro in 1964 has to sit around and wait for some cracker senator to filibuster when it comes to the rights of black people, why, you and I should hang our heads in shame. You talk about a march on Washington in 1963, you haven't seen anything. There's some more going down in '64. And this time they're not going like they went last year. They're not going singing "We Shall Overcome." They're not going with white friends. They're not going with placards already painted for them. They're not going with round-trip tickets. They're going with one-way tickets.

And if they don't want that non-nonviolent army going down there, tell them to bring the filibuster to a halt. The black nationalists aren't going to wait. Lyndon B. Johnson is the head of the Democratic Party. If he's for civil rights, let him go into the Senate next week and declare himself. Let him go in there right now and declare himself. Let him go in there and denounce the Southern branch of his party. Let him go in there right now and take a moral stand—right now, not later. Tell him, don't wait until election time. If he waits too long, brothers and sisters, he will be responsible for letting a condition develop in this country which will create a climate that will bring seeds up out of the ground with vegetation on the end of them looking like something these people never dreamed of. In 1964, it's the ballot or the bullet. Thank you.

Stokely Carmichael and Charles V. Hamilton

Stokely Carmichael and Charles V. Hamilton have gone their separate ways since collaborating in writing *Black Power,* the best single explanation since Malcolm X of this much-discussed movement, and the different ways are foreshadowed in this book. This is not merely a case, however, of the different tendencies of the radical leader and the establishment political scientist: it symbolizes a deep tension in the whole Black Power movement. Revolutionary rejection of America and conventional ethnic politics—as American as apple pie—can both be found here. The reader should consider the significance of the shift from "black nationalism," the term used by Malcolm X, to "Black Power," and of the peculiar kind of ambiguity in the latter. Generally speaking,

Carmichael and Hamilton's discussion is on the moderate side, and much of its interest lies in its competent discussion of the ends and means of American black politics. Nevertheless, the radical or revolutionary element is also present; and the attempt to contain and reconcile these different elements is a major source of interest and instruction. "Before a group can enter the open society, it must first close ranks." Carmichael and Hamilton explain their objection to "integration," as it has been understood, and urge the need for maintaining and recovering black cultural integrity, without, however, exploring very far the content or specific value of that culture.

One of the chief results of the Black Power movement has been to complicate the usual dividing lines between radical and conservative. For example the links from Carmichael and Hamilton to Malcolm X and the separatists are obvious; but there are also major links to the school of thought represented by Joseph M.

Black Power: Its Need and Substance

"To carve out a place for itself in the politico-social order," V. O. Key, Jr. wrote in *Politics, Parties and Pressure Groups*, "a new group may have to fight for reorientation of many of the values of the old order" (p. 57). This is especially true when that group is composed of black people in the American society—a society that has for centuries deliberately and systematically excluded them from political participation. Black people in the United States must raise hard questions, questions which challenge the very nature of the society itself: its long-standing values, beliefs and institutions.

To do this, we must first redefine ourselves. Our basic need is to reclaim our history and our identity from what must be called cultural terrorism, from the depredation of self-justifying white guilt. We shall

Jackson. As viewed by the Black Power movement, it is the "integrationists" and the members of the civil rights movement who are the "conservatives"; and many race-oriented, self-help, non-integrationist men now seem much more "radical."

Additional Readings: Both Carmichael and Hamilton have written and spoken about Black Power on numerous occasions, but these are generally inferior elaborations or summaries of *Black Power*. Readers may, however, wish to consult Carmichael's "Towards Black Liberation" (*The Massachusetts Review,* Autumn, 1966) for his own early statement of the Black Power position. Many of the themes are anticipated not only by Malcolm X but, in different ways, by Booker T. Washington and the early Du Bois. Much of the current writing on Black Power is not very substantial, but Floyd B. Barbour's *Black Power Revolt* contains many thoughtful and provocative essays. Nathan Wright, Jr.'s moderate *Black Power and Urban Unrest* is of some interest.

---

have to struggle for the right to create our own terms through which to define ourselves and our relationship to the society, and to have these terms recognized. This is the first necessity of a free people, and the first right that any oppressor must suspend.

In *Politics Among Nations,* Hans Morgenthau defined political power as "the psychological control over the minds of men" (p. 29). This control includes the attempt by the oppressor to have *his* definitions, *his* historical descriptions, *accepted* by the oppressed. This was true in Africa no less than in the United States. To black Africans, the word "Uhuru" means "freedom," but they had to fight the white colonizers for the right to use the term. The recorded history of this country's dealings with red and black men offers other examples. In the wars between the white settlers and the "Indians," a battle won by the Cavalry was described as a "victory." The "Indians'" triumphs, however, were "massacres." (The American colonists were not unaware of the need to define their acts in their own terms. They labeled their fight against England a "revolution"; the English attempted to demean it by calling it "insubordination" or "riotous.")

The historical period following Reconstruction in the South after the Civil War has been called by many historians the period of Redemption, implying that the bigoted southern slave societies were "redeemed" from the hands of "reckless and irresponsible" black rulers. Professor John Hope Franklin's *Reconstruction* or Dr. W. E. B. Dubois' *Black Reconstruction* should be sufficient to dispel inaccurate historical notions, but the larger society persists in its own self-serving accounts. Thus black people came to be depicted as "lazy," "apathetic," "dumb," "shiftless," "good-timers." Just as red men had to be recorded as "savages" to justify the white man's theft of their land, so black men had to be vilified in order to justify their continued oppression. Those who have the right to define are the masters of the situation. Lewis Carroll understood this:

> "When I use a word," Humpty Dumpty said in a rather scornful tone, "it means just what I choose it to mean—neither more nor less."
>
> "The question is," said Alice, "whether you *can* make words mean so many different things."
>
> "The question is," said Humpty Dumpty, "which is to be master—that's all."*

Today, the American educational system continues to reinforce the entrenched values of the society through the use of words. Few people in this country question that this is "the land of the free and the home of the brave." They have had these words drummed into them from childhood. Few people question that this is the "Great Society" or that this country is fighting "Communist aggression" around the world. We mouth these things over and over, and they become truisms not to be questioned. In a similar way, black people have been saddled with epithets.

"Integration" is another current example of a word which has been defined according to the way white Americans see it. To many of them, it means black men wanting to marry white daughters; it means "race mixing"—implying bed or dance partners. To black people, it has meant a way to improve their lives—economically and politically. But the predominant white definition has stuck in the minds of too many people.

Black people must redefine themselves, and only *they* can do that. Throughout this country, vast segments of the black communities are beginning to recognize the need to assert their own definitions, to reclaim their history, their culture; to create their own sense of community and togetherness. There is a growing resentment of the word "Negro," for example, because this term is the invention of our oppressor; it is *his* image of us that he describes. Many blacks are now calling themselves African-Americans, Afro-Americans or black people because that is *our* image of ourselves. When we begin to define our own image, the stereotypes—that is, lies—that our oppressor has developed will begin in the white community and end there. The black community will have a positive image of itself that *it* has created. This means we will no longer

---

*Lewis Carroll, *Through the Looking Glass.* New York: Doubleday Books, Inc., p. 196.

call ourselves lazy, apathetic, dumb, good-timers, shiftless, etc. Those are words used by white America to define us. If we accept these adjectives, as some of us have in the past, then we see ourselves only in a negative way, precisely the way white America wants us to see ourselves. Our incentive is broken and our will to fight is surrendered. From now on we shall view ourselves as African-Americans and as black people who are in fact energetic, determined, intelligent, beautiful and peace-loving.

There is a terminology and ethos peculiar to the black community of which black people are beginning to be no longer ashamed. Black communities are the only large segments of this society where people refer to each other as brother—soul-brother, soul-sister. Some people may look upon this as *ersatz*, as make-believe, but it is not that. It is real. It is a growing sense of community. It is a growing realization that black Americans have a common bond not only among themselves, but with their African brothers. In *Black Man's Burden*, John O. Killens described his trip to ten African countries as follows:

Everywhere I went people called me brother. . . . "Welcome, American brother." It was a good feeling for me, to be in Africa. To walk in a land for the first time in your entire life knowing within yourself that your color would not be held against you. No black man ever knows this in America [p. 160].

More and more black Americans are developing this feeling. They are becoming aware that they have a history which pre-dates their forced introduction to this country. African-American history means a long history beginning on the continent of Africa, a history not taught in the standard textbooks of this country. It is absolutely essential that black people know this history, that they know their roots, that they develop an awareness of their cultural heritage. Too long have they been kept in submission by being told that they had no culture, no manifest heritage, before they landed on the slave auction blocks in this country. If black people are to know themselves as a vibrant, valiant people, they must know their roots. And they will soon learn that the Hollywood image of man-eating cannibals waiting for, and waiting on, the Great White Hunter is a lie.

With redefinition will come a clearer notion of the role black Americans can play in this world. This role will emerge clearly out of the unique, common experiences of Afro-Asians. Killens concludes:

I believe furthermore that the American Negro can be the bridge between the West and Africa-Asia. We black Americans can serve as a bridge to mutual understanding. The one thing we black Americans have in common with the other colored peoples of the world is that we have all felt the cruel and ruthless heel of white supremacy. We have all been "niggerized" on one level or another. And all of us are determined to "deniggerize" the earth. To rid the world of "niggers" is the Black Man's Burden, human reconstruction is the grand objective [p. 176].

Only when black people fully develop this sense of community, of themselves, can they begin to deal effectively with the problems of racism in *this* country. This is what we mean by a new consciousness; this is the vital first step.

The next step is what we shall call the process of political modernization — a process which must take place if the society is to be rid of racism. "Political modernization" includes many things, but we mean by it three major concepts: (1) questioning old values and institutions of the society; (2) searching for new and different forms of political structure to solve political and economic problems; and (3) broadening the base of political participation to include more people in the decision-making process. These notions (we shall take up each in turn) are central to our thinking throughout this book and to contemporary American history as a whole. As David Apter wrote in *The Politics of Modernization,* ". . . the struggle to modernize is what has given meaning to our generation. It tests our cherished institutions and our beliefs. . . . So compelling a force has it become that we are forced to ask new questions of our own institutions. Each country, whether modernized or modernizing, stands in both judgment and fear of the results. Our own society is no exception" (p. 2).

The values of this society support a racist system; we find it incongruous to ask black people to adopt and support most of those values. We also reject the assumption that the basic institutions of this society must be preserved. The goal of black people must *not* be to assimilate into middle-class America, for that class — as a whole — is without a viable conscience as regards humanity. The values of the middle class permit the perpetuation of the ravages of the black community. The values of that class are based on material aggrandizement, not the expansion of humanity. The values of that class ultimately support cloistered little closed societies tucked away neatly in tree-lined suburbia. The values of that class do *not* lead to the creation of an open society. That class *mouths* its preference for a free, competitive society, while at the same time forcefully and even viciously denying to black people as a group the opportunity to compete.

We are not unmindful of other descriptions of the social utility of the middle class. Banfield and Wilson, in *City Politics,* concluded:

The departure of the middle class from the central city is important in other ways. . . . The middle class supplies a social and political leavening in the life of a city. Middle-class people demand good schools and integrity in government. They support churches, lodges, parent-teacher associations, scout troops, better-housing committees, art galleries, and operas. It is the middle class, in short, that asserts a conception of the public interest. Now its activity is increasingly concentrated in the suburbs [p. 14].

But this same middle class manifests a sense of superior group position in regard to race. This class wants "good government" *for themselves;* it wants good schools *for its children.* At the same time, many of its members sneak into the black community by day, exploit it, and take the money home to their middle-class communities at night to support their operas and art galleries and comfortable homes. When not actually robbing, they will fight off the handful of more affluent black people who seek to move in; when they approve or even seek token integration, it applies only to black people like themselves — as "white" as possible. *This class is the backbone of institutional racism in this country.*

Thus we reject the goal of assimilation into middle-class America because the values of that class are in themselves anti-humanist and because that class as a social force perpetuates racism. We must face the fact that, in the past, what we have called the movement has not really questioned the middle-class values and institutions of this country. If anything, it has accepted those values and institutions without fully realizing their racist nature. Reorientation means an emphasis on the dignity of man, not on the sanctity of property. It means the creation of a society where human misery and poverty are repugnant to that society, not an indication of laziness or lack of initiative. The creation of new values means the establishment of a society based, as Killens expresses it in *Black Man's Burden,* on "free people," not "free enterprise" (p. 167). To do this means to modernize — *indeed, to civilize* — this country.

Supporting the old values are old political and economic structures; these must also be "modernized." We should at this point distinguish between "structures" and "system." By system, we have in mind the entire American complex of basic institutions, values, beliefs, etc. By structures, we mean the specific institutions (political parties, interest groups, bureaucratic administrations) which exist to conduct the business of that system. Obviously, the first is broader than the second. Also, the second assumes the legitimacy of the first. Our view is that, given the illegitimacy of the system, we cannot then proceed to transform that system with existing structures.

The two major political parties in this country have become non-viable

entities for the legitimate representation of the real needs of masses—
especially blacks—in this country. Walter Lippmann raised the same
point in his syndicated column of December 8, 1966. He pointed out
that the party system in the United States developed before our society
became as technologically complex as it is now. He says that the ways
in which men live and define themselves are changing radically. Old
ideological issues, once the subject of passionate controversy, Lippmann
argues, are of little interest today. He asks whether the great urban
complexes—which are rapidly becoming the centers of black population
in the U.S.—can be run with the same systems and ideas that derive from
a time when America was a country of small villages and farms. While
not addressing himself directly to the question of race, Lippmann raises
a major question about our political institutions; and the crisis of race
in America may be its major symptom.

Black people have seen the city planning commissions, the urban
renewal commissions, the boards of education and the police departments fail to speak to their needs in a meaningful way. We must devise
new structures, new institutions to replace those forms or to make them
responsive. There is nothing sacred or inevitable about old institutions;
the focus must be on people, not forms.

Existing structures and established ways of doing things have a way
of perpetuating themselves and for this reason, the modernizing process
will be difficult. Therefore, timidity in calling into question the boards
of education or the police departments will not do. They must be chal-
lenged forcefully and clearly. If this means the creation of parallel
community institutions, then that must be the solution. If this means that
black parents must gain control over the operation of the schools in the
black community, then that must be the solution. The search for new
forms means the search for institutions that will, for once, make decisions
in the interest of black people. It means, for example, a building inspec-
tion department that neither winks at violations of building codes by
absentee slumlords nor imposes meaningless fines which permit them to
continue their exploitation of the black community.

Essential to the modernization of structures is a broadened base of
political participation. More and more people must become politically
sensitive and active (we have already seen this happening in some areas
of the South). People must no longer be tied, by small incentives or handouts, to a corrupting and corruptible white machine. Black people will
choose their own leaders and hold those leaders responsible to *them*.
A broadened base means an end to the condition described by James
Wilson in *Negro Politics*, whereby "Negroes tended to be the objects
rather than the subjects of civic action. Things are often done for, or
about, or to, or because of Negroes, but they are less frequently done

by Negroes" (p. 133). Broadening the base of political participation, then, has as much to do with the quality of black participation as with the quantity. We are fully aware that the black vote, especially in the North, has been pulled out of white pockets and "delivered" whenever it was in the interest of white politicians to do so. That vote must no longer be controllable by those who have neither the interests nor the demonstrated concern of black people in mind.

As the base broadens, as more and more black people become activated, they will perceive more clearly the special disadvantages heaped upon them as a group. They will perceive that the larger society is growing more affluent while the black society is retrogressing, as daily life and mounting statistics clearly show (see Chapters I and VIII). V. O. Key describes what often happens next, in *Politics, Parties and Pressure Groups:* "A factor of great significance in the setting off of political movements is an abrupt change for the worse in the status of one group relative to that of other groups in society. . . . A rapid change for the worse . . . in the relative status of any group . . . is likely to precipitate political action" (p. 24). Black people will become increasingly active as they notice that their retrogressive status exists in large measure because of values and institutions arraigned against them. They will begin to stress and strain and call the entire system into question. Political modernization will be in motion. We believe that it is now in motion. One form of that motion is Black Power.

The adoption of the concept of Black Power is one of the most legitimate and healthy developments in American politics and race relations in our time. The concept of Black Power speaks to all the needs mentioned in this chapter. It is a call for black people in this country to unite, to recognize their heritage, to build a sense of community. It is a call for black people to begin to define their own goals, to lead their own organizations and to support those organizations. It is a call to reject the racist institutions and values of this society.

The concept of Black Power rests on a fundamental premise: *Before a group can enter the open society, it must first close ranks.* By this we mean that group solidarity is necessary before a group can operate effectively from a bargaining position of strength in a pluralistic society. Traditionally, each new ethnic group in this society has found the route to social and political viability through the organization of its own institutions with which to represent its needs within the larger society. Studies in voting behavior specifically, and political behavior generally, have made it clear that politically the American pot has not melted. Italians vote for Rubino over O'Brien; Irish for Murphy over Goldberg, etc. This phenomenon may seem distasteful to some, but it has been and remains today a central fact of the American political system. There are other examples of ways in which groups in the society have remembered their roots and used this effectively in the political arena. Theodore Sorensen describes the politics of foreign aid during the Kennedy Administration in his book *Kennedy:*

No powerful constituencies or interest groups backed foreign aid. The Marshall Plan at least had appealed to Americans who traced their roots to the Western European nations aided. But there were few voters who identified with India, Colombia or Tanganyika [p. 351].

The extent to which black Americans can and do "trace their roots" to Africa, to that extent will they be able to be more effective on the political scene.

A white reporter set forth this point in other terms when he made the following observation about white Mississippi's manipulation of the anti-poverty program:

The war on poverty has been predicated on the notion that there is such a thing as a community which can be defined geographically and mobilized for a collective effort to help the poor. This theory has no relationship to reality in the deep South. In every Mississippi county there are two communities. Despite all the pious platitudes of the moderates on both sides, these two communities habitually see their interests in terms of conflict rather than cooperation. Only when the Negro community can muster enough political, economic and professional strength to compete on somewhat equal terms, will Negroes believe in the possibility of true cooperation and whites accept its necessity. En route to integration, the Negro community needs to develop a greater independence — a chance to run its own affairs and not cave in whenever "the man" barks — or so it seems to me, and to most of the knowledgeable people with whom I talked in Mississippi. To OEO, this judgment may sound like black nationalism. . . .°

The point is obvious: black people must lead and run their own organizations. Only black people can convey the revolutionary idea — and it is a revolutionary idea — that black people are able to do things themselves. Only they can help create in the community an aroused and continuing black consciousness that will provide the basis for political strength. In the past, white allies have often furthered white supremacy without the whites involved realizing it, or even wanting to do so. Black people must come together and do things for themselves. They must achieve self-identity and self-determination in order to have their daily needs met.

Black Power means, for example, that in Lowndes County, Alabama,

---

°Christopher Jencks, "Accommodating Whites: A New Look at Mississippi," *The New Republic* (April 16, 1966).

a black sheriff can end police brutality. A black tax assessor and tax collector and county board of revenue can lay, collect, and channel tax monies for the building of better roads and schools serving black people. In such areas as Lowndes, where black people have a majority, they will attempt to use power to exercise control. This is what they seek: control. When black people lack a majority, Black Power means proper representation and sharing of control. It means the creation of power bases, of strength, from which black people can press to change local or nation-wide patterns of oppression—instead of from weakness.

It does not mean *merely* putting black faces into office. Black visibility is not Black Power. Most of the black politicians around the country today are not examples of Black Power. The power must be that of a community, and emanate from there. The black politicians must start from there. The black politicians must stop being representatives of "downtown" machines, whatever the cost might be in terms of lost patronage and holiday handouts.

Black Power recognizes—it must recognize—the ethnic basis of American politics as well as the power-oriented nature of American politics. Black Power therefore calls for black people to consolidate behind their own, so that they can bargain from a position of strength. But while we endorse the *procedure* of group solidarity and identity for the purpose of attaining certain goals in the body politic, this does not mean that black people should strive for the same kind of rewards (i.e., end results) obtained by the white society. The ultimate values and goals are not domination or exploitation of other groups, but rather an effective share in the total power of the society.

Nevertheless, some observers have labeled those who advocate Black Power as racists; they have said that the call for self-identification and self-determination is "racism in reverse" or "black supremacy." This is a deliberate and absurd lie. There is no analogy—by any stretch of definition or imagination—between the advocates of Black Power and white racists. Racism is not merely exclusion on the basis of race but exclusion for the purpose of subjugating or maintaining subjugation. The goal of the racists is to keep black people on the bottom, arbitrarily and dictatorially, as they have done in this country for over three hundred years. The goal of black self-determination and black self-identity—Black Power—is full participation in the decision-making processes affecting the lives of black people, and recognition of the virtues in themselves as black people. The black people of this country have not lynched whites, bombed their churches, murdered their children and manipulated laws and institutions to maintain oppression. White racists have. Congressional laws, one after the other, have not been necessary to stop black people from oppressing others and denying others the full enjoyment of their rights. White racists have made such laws necessary. The goal of Black Power is positive and functional to a free and viable society. No white racist can make this claim.

A great deal of public attention and press space was devoted to the hysterical accusation of "black racism" when the call for Black Power was first sounded. A national committee of influential black churchmen affiliated with the National Council of Churches, despite their obvious respectability and responsibility, had to resort to a paid advertisement to articulate their position, while anyone yapping "black racism" made front-page news. In their statement, published in the *New York Times* of July 31, 1966, the churchmen said:

> We, an informal group of Negro churchmen in America, are deeply disturbed about the crisis brought upon our country by historic distortions of important human realities in the controversy about "black power." What we see shining through the variety of rhetoric is not anything new but the same old problem of power and race which has faced our beloved country since 1619.
>
> . . . The conscience of black men is corrupted because having no power to implement the demands of conscience, the concern for justice in the absence of justice becomes a chaotic self-surrender. Powerlessness breeds a race of beggars. We are faced with a situation where powerless conscience meets conscienceless power, threatening the very foundations of our Nation.
>
> We deplore the overt violence of riots, but we feel it is more important to focus on the real sources of these eruptions. These sources may be abetted inside the Ghetto, but their basic cause lies in the silent and covert violence which white middle class America inflicts upon the victims of the inner city.
>
> . . . In short, the failure of American leaders to use American power to create equal opportunity *in life* as well as *law,* this is the real problem and not the anguished cry for black power.
>
> . . . Without the capacity to participate with power, i.e., to have some organized political and economic strength to really influence people with whom one interacts, integration is not meaningful.
>
> . . . America has asked its Negro citizens to fight for opportunity as *individuals,* whereas at certain points in our history what we have needed most has been opportunity for the *whole group,* not just for selected and approved Negroes.
>
> . . . We must not apologize for the existence of this form of group power, for we have been oppressed as a group and not as individuals. We will not find our way out of that oppression until both we and America accept the need for Negro Americans, as well as for Jews, Italians, Poles, and white Anglo-Saxon Protestants, among others, to have and to wield group power.

It is a commentary on the fundamentally racist nature of this society that the concept of group strength for black people must be articulated — not to mention defended. No other group would submit to being led by others. Italians do not run the Anti-Defamation League of B'nai B'rith. Irish do not chair Christopher Columbus Societies. Yet when black people call for black-run and all-black organizations, they are immediately classed in a category with the Ku Klux Klan. This is interesting and ironic, but by no means surprising: the society does not expect black people to be able to take care of their business, and there are many who prefer it precisely that way.

In the end, we cannot and shall not offer any guarantees that Black Power, if achieved, would be non-racist. No one can predict human behavior. Social change always has unanticipated consequences. If black racism is what the larger society fears, we cannot help them. We can only state what we hope will be the result, given the fact that the present situation is unacceptable and that we have no real alternative but to work for Black Power. The final truth is that the white society is not entitled to reassurances, even if it were possible to offer them.

We have outlined the meaning and goals of Black Power; we have also discussed one major thing which it is not. There are others of greater importance. The advocates of Black Power reject the old slogans and meaningless rhetoric of previous years in the civil rights struggle. The language of yesterday is indeed irrelevant: progress, non-violence, integration, fear of "white backlash," coalition. Let us look at the rhetoric and see why these terms must be set aside or redefined.

One of the tragedies of the struggle against racism is that up to this point there has been no national organization which could speak to the growing militancy of young black people in the urban ghettos and the black-belt South. There has been only a "civil rights" movement, whose tone of voice was adapted to an audience of middle-class whites. It served as a sort of buffer zone between that audience and angry young blacks. It claimed to speak for the needs of a community, but it did not speak in the tone of that community. None of its so-called leaders could go into a rioting community and be listened to. In a sense, the blame must be shared—along with the mass media—by those leaders for what happened in Watts, Harlem, Chicago, Cleveland and other places. Each time the black people in those cities saw Dr. Martin Luther King get slapped they became angry. When they saw little black girls bombed to death *in a church* and civil rights workers ambushed and murdered, they were angrier; and when nothing happened, they were steaming mad. We had nothing to offer that they could see, except to go out and be beaten again. We helped to build their frustration.

We had only the old language of love and suffering. And in most places—that is, from the liberals and middle class—we got back the old language of patience and progress. The civil rights leaders were saying to the country: "Look, you guys are supposed to be nice guys, and we are only going to do what we are supposed to do. Why do you beat us up? Why don't you give us what we ask? Why don't you straighten yourselves out?" For the masses of black people, this language resulted in virtually nothing. In fact, their objective day-to-day condition worsened. The unemployment rate among black people increased while that among whites declined. Housing conditions in the black communities deteriorated. Schools in the black ghettos continued to plod along on outmoded techniques, inadequate curricula, and with all too many tired and indifferent teachers. Meanwhile, the President picked up the refrain of "We Shall Overcome" while the Congress passed civil rights law after civil rights law, only to have them effectively nullified by deliberately weak enforcement. "Progress is being made," we were told.

Such language, along with admonitions to remain non-violent and fear the white backlash, convinced some that that course was the *only* course to follow. It misled some into believing that a black minority could bow its head and get whipped into a meaningful position of power. The very notion is absurd. The white society devised the language, adopted the rules and had the black community narcotized into believing that that language and those rules were, in fact, relevant. The black community was told time and again how *other* immigrants finally won *acceptance:* that is, by following the Protestant Ethic of Work and Achievement. They worked hard; therefore, they achieved. We were not told that it was by building Irish Power, Italian Power, Polish Power or Jewish Power that these groups got themselves together and operated from positions of strength. We were not told that "the American dream" wasn't designed for black people. That while today, to whites, the dream may *seem* to include black people, it cannot do so by the very nature of this nation's political and economic system, which imposes institutional racism on the black masses if not upon every individual black. A notable comment on that "dream" was made by Dr. Percy Julian, the black scientist and director of the Julian Research Institute in Chicago, a man for whom the dream seems to have come true. While not subscribing to "black power" as he understood it, Dr. Julian clearly understood the basis for it: "The false concept of basic Negro inferiority is one of the curses that still lingers. It is a problem created by the white man. Our children just no longer are going to accept the patience we were taught by our generation. We were taught a pretty little lie—excel and the whole world lies open before you. *I obeyed the injunction and found it to be wishful thinking.*" (Authors' italics)*

A key phrase in our buffer-zone days was non-violence. For years it has been thought that black people would not literally fight for their

---

The New York Times (April 30, 1967), p. 30.

lives. Why this has been so is not entirely clear; neither the larger society nor black people are noted for passivity. The notion apparently stems from the years of marches and demonstrations and sit-ins where black people did not strike back and the violence always came from white mobs. There are many who still sincerely believe in that approach. From our viewpoint, rampaging white mobs and white night-riders must be made to understand that their days of free head-whipping are over. Black people should and must fight back. Nothing more quickly repels someone bent on destroying you than the unequivocal message: "O.K., fool, make your move, and run the same risk I run—of dying."

When the concept of Black Power is set forth, many people immediately conjure up notions of violence. The country's reaction to the Deacons for Defense and Justice, which originated in Louisiana, is instructive. Here is a group which realized that the "law" and law enforcement agencies would not protect people, so they had to do it themselves. If a nation fails to protect its citizens, then that nation cannot condemn those who take up the task themselves. The Deacons and all other blacks who resort to self-defense represent a simple answer to a simple question: what man would not defend his family and home from attack?

But this frightened some white people, because they knew that black people would now fight back. They knew that this was precisely what *they* would have long since done if *they* were subjected to the injustices and oppression heaped on blacks. Those of us who advocate Black Power are quite clear in our own minds that a "non-violent" approach to civil rights is an approach black people cannot afford and a luxury white people do not deserve. It is crystal clear to us—and it must become so with the white society—*that there can be no social order without social justice.* White people must be made to understand that they must stop messing with black people, or the blacks *will* fight back!

Next, we must deal with the term "integration." According to its advocates, social justice will be accomplished by "integrating the Negro into the mainstream institutions of the society from which he has been traditionally excluded." This concept is based on the assumption that there is nothing of value in the black community and that little of value could be created among black people. The thing to do is siphon off the "acceptable" black people into the surrounding middle-class white community.

The goals of integrationists are middle-class goals, articulated primarily by a small group of Negroes with middle-class aspirations or status. Their kind of integration has meant that a few blacks "make it," leaving the black community, sapping it of leadership potential and know-how. As we noted in Chapter I, those token Negroes—absorbed into a white mass—are of no value to the remaining black masses. They become meaningless show-pieces for a conscience-soothed white society. Such people will state that they would prefer to be treated "only as individuals, not as Negroes"; that they "are not and should not be preoccupied with race." This is a totally unrealistic position. In the first place, black people have not suffered as individuals but as members of a group; therefore, their liberation lies in group action. This is why SNCC — and the concept of Black Power — affirms that helping *individual* black people to solve their problems on an *individual* basis does little to alleviate the mass of black people. Secondly, while color blindness *may* be a sound goal ultimately, we must realize that race is an overwhelming fact of life in this historical period. There is no black man in this country who can live "simply as a man." His blackness is an ever-present fact of this racist society, whether he recognizes it or not. It is unlikely that this or the next generation will witness the time when race will no longer be relevant in the conduct of public affairs and in public policy decision-making. To realize this and to attempt to deal with it does not make one a racist or overly preoccupied with race; it puts one in the forefront of a significant *struggle*. If there is no intense struggle today, there will be no meaningful results tomorrow.

"Integration" as a goal today speaks to the problem of blackness not only in an unrealistic way but also in a despicable way. It is based on complete acceptance of the fact that in order to have a decent house or education, black people must move into a white neighborhood or send their children to a white school. This reinforces, among both black and white, the idea that "white" is automatically superior and "black" is by definition inferior. For this reason, "integration" is a subterfuge for the maintenance of white supremacy. It allows the nation to focus on a handful of Southern black children who get into white schools at a great price, and to ignore the ninety-four percent who are left in unimproved all-black schools. Such situations will not change until black people become equal in a way that means something, and integration ceases to be a one-way street. Then integration does not mean draining skills and energies from the black ghetto into white neighborhoods. To sprinkle black children among white pupils in outlying schools is at best a stop-gap measure. The goal is not to take black children out of the black community and expose them to white middle-class values; the goal is to build and strengthen the black community.

"Integration" also means that black people must give up their identity, deny their heritage. We recall the conclusion of Killian and Grigg: "At the present time, integration as a solution to the race problem demands that the Negro foreswear his identity as a Negro." The fact is that integration, as traditionally articulated, would abolish the black community. The fact is that what must be abolished is not the black community, but the dependent colonial status that has been inflicted upon it.

The racial and cultural personality of the black community must be preserved and that community must win its freedom while preserving its cultural integrity. Integrity includes a pride — in the sense of self-acceptance, not chauvinism — in being black, in the historical attainments and contributions of black people. No person can be healthy, complete and mature if he must deny a part of himself; this is what "integration" has required thus far. This is the essential difference between integration as it is currently practiced and the concept of Black Power.

The idea of cultural integrity is so obvious that it seems almost simple-minded to spell things out at this length. Yet millions of Americans resist such truths when they are applied to black people. Again, that resistance is a comment on the fundamental racism in the society. Irish Catholics took care of their own first without a lot of apology for doing so, without any dubious language from timid leadership about guarding against "backlash." Everyone understood it to be a perfectly legitimate procedure. Of course, there would be "backlash." Organization begets counterorganization, but this was no reason to defer.

The so-called white backlash against black people is something else: the embedded traditions of institutional racism being brought into the open and calling forth overt manifestations of individual racism. In the summer of 1966, when the protest marches into Cicero, Illinois, began, the black people knew they were not allowed to live in Cicero and the white people knew it. When blacks began to demand the right to live in homes in that town, the whites simply reminded them of the status quo. Some people called this "backlash." It was, in fact, racism defending itself. In the black community, this is called "White folks showing their color." It is ludicrous to blame black people for what is simply an overt manifestation of white racism. Dr. Martin Luther King stated clearly that the protest marches were not the cause of the racism but merely exposed a long-term cancerous condition in the society.

Eldridge Cleaver

Imprisoned for what he describes as "insurrectionary" rape, Eldridge Cleaver put his enforced leisure and discipline to good use. Guided by the example and writings of Malcolm X and by his own rugged intelligence, Cleaver set out to give order and direction to his life and to think through the implications of the black man's situation in America. The first fruit of these reflections was his book of essays, *Soul on Ice,* in which he ranges from his private life and thoughts to an elaborate psychological typology of male-female, black-white relations. When he was released from prison on parole, Cleaver became active in the Black Panther Party and served as a staff writer for *Ramparts,* from which the essay here is taken. Cleaver's understanding of the ambiguous and provisional character of the present Black Power movement is unusually perceptive. He argues that "there is a deep land hunger in the heart of Afro-America"; that the black people in America must be understood as a colonial people; and that Black Power, while not a solution, is a preparation for a solution of the land question. Black Power is "an embryonic sovereignty" through which black people can distinguish between themselves and their enemies.

Cleaver's life and thought parallel and extend, in many ways, those of Malcolm X. Perhaps none of Malcolm's heirs have described so well the legacy he left. "I have, so to speak, washed my hands in the blood of the martyr, Malcolm X, whose retreat from the precipice of madness created new room for others to turn about in, and I am now caught up in that tiny space, attempting a maneuver of my own. Having renounced the teachings of Elijah Muhammed, I find that a rebirth does not follow automati-

The Land Question

The first thing that has to be realized is that it is a reality when people say that there's a "black colony" and a "white mother country." Only if this distinction is borne clearly in mind is it possible to understand that there are two different sets of political dynamics now functioning in America.

From the very beginning, Afro-America has had a land hang-up. The slaves were kidnapped on their own soil, transported thousands of miles across the ocean and set down in a strange land. From sunup to sundown, they worked the land: plowing, sowing and reaping crops for somebody else, for a profit they would never see or taste themselves. This is why, even today, one of the most provocative insults that can be tossed at a black is to call him a farm boy, to infer that he is in any way attached to an agrarian situation. In terms of seeking status in America, blacks — principally the black bourgeoisie — have come to measure their own value according to the number of degrees they are away from the soil.

From *Ramparts*, May, 1968. Copyright © by *Ramparts*, 1968. Reprinted by permission of *Ramparts*.

cally, of its own accord, that a void is left in one's vision, and this void seeks constantly to obliterate itself by pulling one back to one's former outlook." (*Soul on Ice,* page 66.)

Additional Readings: *Soul on Ice* contains much provocative material, especially on the question of the distinctive characteristics of the black and white psyches and their relationships. Recent essays and speeches are collected in *Eldridge Cleaver: Post-Prison Writings and Speeches,* edited by Robert Scheer. This volume contains an interview with Nat Hentoff, first published in *Playboy* magazine, which is perhaps the best general discussion by Cleaver of his views. Floyd McKissick's, *Three-Fifths of a Man* is relevant to Cleaver's discussion here of the land question.

Considered subhuman by the founders of America, black people have always been viewed by white Americans as un-American, as not really belonging here. Thus, it is not surprising that the average black man in America is schizoid on the question of his relationship to the nation as a whole, and there is a side of him that feels only the vaguest, most halting, tentative and even fleeting kinship with America. The feeling of alienation and dissociation is real, and black people would have long ago readily identified themselves with another sovereignty had a viable one existed.

THE MOTHER COUNTRY'S SOLUTION

Integration was the solution to the land question offered by the mother country—i.e., by the white liberals, white radicals and black bourgeoisie, working hand in glove with the Imperialists.

This is not to imply that white liberals, radicals and the black bourgeoisie were actively involved in a conscious conspiracy with the Imperialists. Particularly in the case of white radicals, the last thing they want to do is to help the Imperialists remain in power. Rather, we speak here of a coalescence of interests and goals. The domestic conflict over segregation was creating for the Imperialists problems on the international plane, particularly in their dealings with the new black African governments. Therefore, when the federal government "joined" the civil rights movement, the Imperialists in control of the government actually strengthened their own position and increased their power. Internationally, U.S. imperialism improved its image, making the con game it plays on the world—its pose as the champion of human freedom —easier. When President Johnson, the arch-hypocrite warmonger of the twentieth century, stood before the nation and shouted "We Shall Overcome," white liberals, radicals and the black bourgeoisie experienced a collective orgasm. What Johnson really wanted was peace and quiet at home and an integrated army to defend "democracy" abroad.

White radicals, liberals and the black bourgeoisie acted from completely different motivations, but the logic of the situation threw them into a coalition with the Imperialists, and the game that was run on them was so successful that they became some of the most ardent workers for LBJ in the election of 1964. Their motivation was to implement the American dream and the conception of America as a huge melting pot. All that remained to be done, in their view, was to integrate the black ingredient into the American stew and thus usher in the millennium of black/white solidarity wherein the white working class of the mother country would join hands with the black workers from the colony and together they would march forward to the Garden of Eden.

March forward they did, not to Eden but to Detroit and armed urban guerrilla warfare. The basic flaw in the analysis and outlook of the white liberals, radicals and the black bourgeoisie was that the concept of the American melting pot completely ignored the distinction and the contradiction between the white mother country and the black colony. And the solution of Integration, based on this false outlook, was doomed from the beginning to yield only a deceptive and disillusioning result. *Black people are a stolen people held in a colonial status on stolen land, and any analysis which does not acknowledge the colonial status of black people cannot hope to deal with the real problem.*

As an ideological tenet, Integration embodies the dream of the mother country which sees America as a huge melting pot. It seeks to pull the black colonial subjects into America and citizenize them. The mother country's euphemism of "second class citizenship" is a smokescreen that seeks to obscure the colonial status of black people in America.

Viewed on the international plane, Integration represents an attempt by the white mother country to forestall the drive for national liberation by its colonial subjects in precisely the same manner as France sought to hold onto its colonial spoils by defining its holdings as "overseas provinces," or as Britain tried to do with its Commonwealth, or as Portugal tried to do with its "overseas provinces." France, England and Portugal have all failed in attempts to keep their colonial possessions by trying to get the colonial subjects themselves to stop short of taking complete sovereignty in their drive for a better life. And America is also doomed to failure in this respect.

Until Detroit, America absolutely refused to even consider the true nature of the domestic crisis. But Detroit forced a confrontation with the facts through sheer military necessity: President Johnson was forced to place the problem in the hands of the Pentagon so that a war of suppression could be properly carried out by the same entity charged with carrying out the war of suppression against the national liberation struggle in Vietnam. But even after Detroit, after the shooting stopped, the minions of the power structure returned to their old, hackneyed rhetoric, as though Integration were still the operating slogan in the black colony.

EARLY BLACK SOLUTIONS: MARCUS GARVEY & ELIJAH MUHAMMED

Nevertheless, there is a deep land hunger in the heart of Afro-America. It has always been there, just as much so as in any other people. Even to waste time asserting this factor is to yield to racism, to argue with the racist assertion that blacks just aren't like other people. Suffice it to say that Afro-Americans are just as land hungry as were the Mau Maus, the Chinese people, the Cuban people; just as much so as all the people of the world today who are grappling with the tyrant of colonialism, trying to get possession of some land of their own.

When he projected his program for black people some 50 years ago, Marcus Garvey tapped black land hunger by claiming the continent of Africa for black people and reasserting black identification with an ancestral homeland. This marked an historic shift in the psyche of black people. It got them over a crucial hump in their struggle up from the white light of Slavery into knowledge of themselves and their past.

However, the practical prospect of Garvey actually physically transporting blacks to Africa turned most black people off because of a world situation and balance of power that made such a solution impossible. And as Garvey's fleet of ships, the Black Star line—which was supposed to provide transportation for blacks back to Africa—sank in the quicksand set at his feet by the white racist power structure and the bootlickers of his era, Afro-America's land hunger became more acute, more desperate.

Learning from Garvey's failure, Elijah Muhammed knew that he had to deal with Afro-America's land hunger, but he also knew that it would be tactically wise for him to be a little more abstract, in order to more closely approximate the true historical relationship of Afro-Americans to the land beneath their feet. He therefore was very careful never to identify any specific geographical location when he issued his call for land for Afro-America. "We must have some land! Some land of our own, or else!"—is the way Elijah Muhammed posed the land question to his people. And it is a fact that black Americans could relate to that particular formulation.

However, there is something inadequate, something lacking in that particular slogan because in practice it impeded rather than enhanced movement. In the first place, it is merely a protest slogan; there is nothing revolutionary about it, because it is asking the oppressor to make a gift to black people. The oppressor is not about to give niggers a damn thing. Black people know this from bitter experience. In a land where the racist pigs of the power structure are doing every dirty thing they can to cut off welfare payments, where they refuse medical care to sick people, where they deliberately deprive black people of education and where they leave black babies to die from lack of milk, no black person in his right mind is going to stand around waiting for those same pigs to give up some of this land, say five or six states!

A REVOLUTIONARY SOLUTION: BLACK POWER

But black people waited. They awaited a revolutionary formulation that would be suited to their relationship to America. Stokely Carmichael provided this formulation with his thesis of Black Power. The ingeniousness of this slogan derives precisely from a clear understanding of Afro-American history and a clear perception of the relationship of black people to the land.

Black Power as a slogan does not attempt to answer the land question. It does not deny the existence of that question, but rather very frankly states that at the present moment the land question cannot be dealt with, that black people must put first things first, that there are a few things that must be done before we can deal with the land question. We must first get some power so that we will be in a position to *force* a settlement of the land question. After black people put themselves, through revolutionary struggle, into a position from which they are able to inflict a political consequence upon America, to hit them where it hurts, then the land question can be brought out.

At a rally in Roxbury, the black colonial enclave of Boston, Stokely Carmichael told an enthusiastic throng of 4000 blacks: "We are poor, we have no money, but we don't have to pay for the land—we already own

it; we paid for it with 400 years of our sweat, our blood, and our suffering. . . . We need a revolution so we can live like proud human beings.
Our revolution is for land and until we take the land we are gonna stay
poor. If you're poor and if you're black, you've got no rights. We want
a redistribution of wealth in this country. We don't want any handouts."

It can be said that Stokely Carmichael has made a contribution of
historic proportions to the national liberation struggle of Afro-America
by hurling forth the thesis of Black Power. The necessity upon Afro-
America is to move, now, to begin functioning as a nation, to assume its
sovereignty, to demand that that sovereignty be recognized by other
nations of the world. Stokely Carmichael was received in Havana as a
representative of a people, of a nation, and, in principle, the assembled
revolutionaries were recognizing the sovereignty of Afro-America. This
lesson was first driven home by Malcolm X's trips to Africa, where he
was received by heads of state as an ambassador of Afro-America.

Black Power must be viewed as a projection of sovereignty, an embryonic sovereignty that black people can focus on and through which
they can make distinctions between themselves and others, between
themselves and their enemies—in short, between the white mother
country of America and the black colony dispersed throughout the continent on absentee-owned land, making Afro-America a decentralized
colony. Black Power says to black people that it is possible for them to
build a national organization on somebody else's land.

BLACK LIBERATION & THE BLACK MAN'S LAND

The parallel between the situation of the Jews at the time of the coming of Theodor Herzl and the present situation of black people in America is fascinating. The Jews had no homeland and were dispersed around
the world, cooped up in the ghettos of Europe. Functionally, a return
to Israel seemed as impractical as obtaining a homeland for Afro-America seems now.

The gravitational center of the Jewish population at that time was in
Eastern Europe. With the outbreak of massive pogroms in that area
near the end of the nineteenth century, the Jewish people were prepared psychologically to take desperate and unprecedented action. They
saw themselves faced with an immediate disastrous situation. Genocide
was staring them in the face, and this common threat galvanized them
into common action.

Psychologically, black people in America have precisely the same outlook as the Jews had then, and they are therefore prepared to take common action for the solution to a common problem. Oppressed because of

the color of their skin, black people are reacting on that basis. A nationalist consciousness has at last awakened among the black masses of Afro-America. One would have to search far and wide in the annals of history to find a case where such a tide of nationalism did not continue to sweep the people forward into nationhood—by any means necessary. Given the confusion in America over the distinction between the white mother country and the black colony, and the rapidly developing national consciousness of Afro-America, it is easy to see that unless these titanic forces are harnessed and channeled into creative outlets, such as some of those proposed by black revolutionaries, America is headed for a catastrophe of unprecedented proportions.

The facts of history show that the Jews were able to do precisely the same thing that Afro-America must now do. When Theodor Herzl founded the National Jewish Congress, he virtually founded a government in exile for a people in exile. They would build their organization, their government, and then later on they would get some land and set the government and the people down on the land, like placing one's hat on top of one's head. The Jews did it. It worked. Now Afro-Americans must do the same thing.

In fact, when Malcolm X moved to found the Organization of Afro-American Unity, this is precisely what he was doing—founding a government in exile for a people in exile. Stokely Carmichael and Rap Brown are now speaking in the name of that sovereignty, in the name of a nation. "I am not bound by the laws or the morals of America!" Rap Brown stated in Newark, New Jersey. And in California, the Black Panther Party for Self Defense has begun calling for U.N. membership for Afro-America.

Another proposal of the Black Panthers that is winning more and more support in the black colony is the call for a U.N.-supervised plebiscite in black communities across the nation. The purpose of the plebiscite is to answer the question once and for all as to just what the masses of black people want. Do the masses of black people consider themselves a nation? Do they want U.N. membership? The viability of this proposal consists in the fact that it does not call for a response beyond the means of black people. All that they are asked to do is answer yes or no—about all that they can do in America.

The mere widespread agitation for such a plebiscite will create a major crisis for U.S. imperialism. Internationally, America's enemies can be counted upon, in some cases, to endorse the proposal. In other cases, countries which are not willing to go all the way with the idea of a plebiscite will at least give an equivocal response.

Domestically, America will be placed in the peculiar position of arguing to black people that they do not need U.N. membership because they are American citizens. The blacks in the ghettos will respond with, Oh yeah? Well, if I'm an American citizen, why am I treated like a dog? The entire problem will be decisively internationalized and raised to a higher level of debate. The forces of reaction will be placed squarely on the defensive, and it will be obvious to all that fundamental changes in the status of black people in America can no longer be postponed or avoided.

So we are now engaged openly in a war for the national liberation of Afro-America from colonial bondage to the white mother country. In our epoch, guerrilla warfare is the vehicle for national liberation all around the world. That it would soon come to America could have been predicted. The spirit has always been there. Only the racist underestimation of the humanity of black people has blinded America to the potential for revolutionary violence of Afro-America. Nat Turner, Gabriel Prosser and Denmark Vesey, black men who led the most successful slave rebellions in the U.S., are the spiritual fathers of today's urban guerrillas.

Robert Williams and Malcolm X stand as two titans, even prophetic figures, who heralded the coming of the gun, the day of the gun, and the resort to armed struggle by Afro-America. The fate of these two prophetic figures is of paramount interest: Robert Williams actually picked up the gun against the racist cops of North Carolina, while Malcolm X did not actually pick up the gun but spread the word to an audience that Robert Williams never reached. Malcolm X caused the power structure more public concern that Williams ever did, but in the cloak and dagger world of the CIA and the FBI, Williams has made just as much impact as Malcolm, because Williams hurled a challenge at both the white mother country and the black colony: let the issue be settled by war; let the black colony take up arms against the mother country!

Today Malcolm X is dead and Robert Williams is still alive. Now in China, the guest of the Prophet of the Gun, Mao Tse-tung, Williams is coming into his own because his people have at last risen to his level of consciousness and are now ready for his style of leadership.

The black urban guerrillas have already accepted Williams' challenge. The white power structure, when LBJ placed the black colonial problem under the tender mercies of the Department of Defense, also served warning that it would meet Williams' challenge blow for blow, in open military terms. Black urban guerrillas now dream of liberating black communities with the gun by eliminating America's police power over black people, i.e., by breaking the power of the mother country over the black colony.

The dream is to bring Robert Williams home. Black people know that they will not have achieved success in this goal until they can bring Robert Williams home and guarantee him safe conduct; until Williams can stand up in the center of Harlem and deliver a speech and the black people can prevent the troops of the occupying army from coming in and taking him prisoner; until Rap Brown and Stokely Carmichael can speak before any audience of assembled black people without fear of arrest by the gestapo of the mother country.

In order to bring this situation about, black men know that they must pick up the gun, they must arm black people to the teeth, they must organize an army and confront the mother country with a most drastic consequence if she attempts to assert police power over the colony. If the white mother country is to have victory over the black colony, it is the duty of black revolutionaries to insure that the Imperialists receive no more than a Pyrrhic victory, written in the blood of what America might have become.

Julius Lester

Julius Lester is a young writer, photographer, musician, and activist. His recent book, from which the title essay is printed here, is an example of contemporary radical black thinking. As the first sentence makes clear, Lester's posture is that of a revolutionary. In a sense, of course, every writer in this book would agree that "America as it now exists must be destroyed," but Lester's proposal for destruction seems to go deeper and further than most—although one can never be sure. Drawing on Malcolm X and Stokely Carmichael for many of his ideas, Lester anticipates a bloody race war (brought on by whites) in the name of —what? Perhaps the most difficult question to answer about Lester's essay, and about Black Power in general, is, What are its fundamental ends or governing principles? In Lester's case, one might say the end is some combination of retribution, black cultural integrity, and socialist equality—but this is a bare beginning,

193

and the reader should consider how much further it can be taken and refined on the basis Lester provides.

Additional Readings: Although the immediate source and inspiration of much of present-day black radical writing is Malcolm X (excluding the psychological side and, incidentally, the gutter language, for which Malcolm X had no patience), another prime source is to be found in the myriad writings of W. E. B. Du Bois. This applies not only to the theme of black culture but also to the Marxism, to which Du Bois finally turned and which is an element (if not always a well-digested one) in much present-day black

Look Out, Whitey!
Black Power's
Gon' Get Your Mama

It is clear that America as it now exists must be destroyed. There is no other way. It is impossible to live within this country and not become a thief or a murderer. Young blacks and young whites are beginning to say NO to thievery and murder. Black Power confronts White Power openly, and as the SNCC poet Worth Long cried: "We have found you out, false-faced America. We have found you out!"

Having "found you out," we will destroy you or die in the act of destroying. That much seems inevitable. To those who fearfully wonder if America has come to the point of a race war, the answer is not certain.

radical thought. Books and articles along the lines of Lester's work are available in ever-increasing abundance, although most of them fail to qualify as serious political thought. Another series of Lester's own essays has been published under the title, *Revolutionary Notes*. The best collection, as has been said, is Floyd B. Barbour's *The Black Power Revolt*. Some of the essays in Le Roi Jones' *Home* are interesting and important. Anticipating the flood of Black Power literature, and more penetrating than most of it, is John Killen's *Black Man's Burden*. H. Rap Brown's *Die Nigger Die!*, with its strenuous attempts to shock, is typical.

However, all signs would seem to say yes. Perhaps the only way that it might be avoided would be through the ability of young white radicals to convince blacks, through their actions, that they are ready to do whatever is necessary to change America.

The race war, if it comes, will come partly from the necessity for revenge. You can't do what has been done to blacks and not expect retribution. The very act of retribution is liberating, and perhaps it is no accident that the symbolism of Christianity speaks of being washed in Blood as an act of purification. Psychologically, blacks have always found an outlet for their revenge whenever planes have fallen, autos have collided, or just every day when white folks die. One old black woman in Atlanta, Georgia, calmly reads through her paper each day counting the number of white people killed the previous day in wrecks, storms, and by natural causes. When the three astronauts were killed in February, 1967, black people did not join the nation in mourning. They were white and were spending money that blacks needed. White folks trying to get to the moon, 'cause it's there. Poverty's here! Now get to that! Malcolm X spoke for all black people when a plane full of Georgians crashed in France: "Allah has blessed us. He has destroyed twenty-two of our enemies."

It is clearly written that the victim must become the executioner. The executioner preordains it when all attempts to stop the continual executions fail. To those who point to numbers and say that black people are only ten percent, it must be said as Brother Malcolm said: "It only takes a spark to light the fuse. We are that spark."

Black Power is not an isolated phenomenon. It is only another manifestation of what is transpiring in Latin America, Asia, and Africa. People are reclaiming their lives on those three continents and blacks in America are reclaiming theirs. These liberation movements are not saying give us a share; they are saying we want it all! The existence of the present system in the United States depends upon the United States taking all. This system is threatened more and more each day by the refusal of those in the Third World to be exploited. They are colonial people outside the United States; blacks are a colonial people within. Thus, we have a common enemy. As the Black Power movement becomes more politically conscious, the spiritual coalition that exists between blacks in America and the Third World will become more evident. The spiritual coalition is not new. When Italy invaded Ethiopia in 1938, blacks in Harlem held large demonstrations protesting this. During World War II, many blacks were rooting for the Japanese. Blacks cannot overlook the fact that it was the Japanese who were the guinea pigs for the atomic bomb, not the Germans. They know, too, that if the U.S. were fighting a European country, it would not use napalm, phosphorus and steel-pellet bombs, just as they know that if there had been over one hundred-thousand blacks massed before the Pentagon on October 21, 1967, they would not have been met by soldiers with unloaded guns. In fact, they know they would never have been allowed to even reach the Pentagon.

The struggle of blacks in America is inseparable from the struggle of the Third World. This is a natural coalition—a coalition of those who know that they are dispossessed. Whites in America are dispossessed also, but the difference is that they will not recognize the fact as yet. Until they do, it will not be possible to have coalitions with them, even the most radical. They must recognize the nature and character of their own oppression. At present, too many of them recognize only that they are white and identify with whites, not with the oppressed, the dispossessed. They react against being called "honky" and thereby establish the fact that they are. It is absolutely necessary for blacks to identify as blacks to win liberation. It is not necessary for whites. White radicals must learn to nonidentify as whites. White is not in the color of the skin. It is a condition of the mind: a condition that will be destroyed. It should be possible for any white radical to yell "honky" as loud as a black radical. "Honky" is a beautiful word that destroys the mystique surrounding whiteness. It is like throwing mud on a sheet. Whiteness has been used as an instrument of oppression; no white radical can identify himself by the color of his skin and expect to fight alongside blacks. Black Power liberates whites also, but they have refused to recognize this, preferring to defend their whiteness.

Black Power is not anti-white people, but is anti anything and everything that serves to oppress. If whites align themselves on the side of oppression, then Black Power must be antiwhite. That, however, is not the decision of Black Power.

For blacks, Black Power is the microscope and telescope through which they look at themselves and the world. It has enabled them to focus their energies while preparing for the day of reckoning. That day of reckoning is anticipated with eagerness by many, because it is on that day that they will truly come alive. The concept of the black man as a nation, which is only being talked about now, will become reality when violence comes. Out of the violence will come the new nation (if the violence is successful) and the new man. Frantz Fanon wrote that "For the colonised people this violence, because it constitutes their only work, invests their characters with positive and creative qualities. The practice of violence binds them together as a whole, since each individual forms a violent link in the great chain, a part of the great organism of violence which has surged upwards in reaction to the settler's violence in the beginning. The groups recognize each other and the future nation is already indivisible. The armed struggle mobilises the people; that is to say, it throws them in one way and in one direction."

It is obvious, of course, that White Power will not allow Black Power to evolve without trying to first subvert it. This is being attempted, as was mentioned in the previous chapter. This attempt will fail and White Power will have no choice but to attempt to physically crush Black Power. This is being prepared for, with intensive riot-control training for the National Guard, chemicals for the control of large crowds, and concentration camps. It is to be expected that eventually black communities across the country will be cordoned off and a South African passbook system introduced to control the comings and goings of blacks.

At the moment, though (but, oh, how short a moment is), the tactic is one of subversion. Particular attention and energy is being given toward the subversion of SNCC. An inordinate number of SNCC men have received draft notices since January of 1967. Another tactic has been the calling of court cases to trial that have lain dormant for two or three years, cases that in many instances had been forgotten by SNCC. The most sophisticated tactic has been the legal maneuvers the government has used to keep SNCC's chairman, H. Rap Brown, confined to Manhattan Island, thus preventing him from traveling around the country and speaking. Having accomplished that, the government now seems content to take its own good time about bringing Brown's cases up for trial.

Black Power, however, will not be denied. America's time is not long and the odds are on our side.

Black Power seeks to destroy what now is, but what does it offer in replacement? Black Power is a highly moral point of view, but its morality is one that sees that a way of life flows from the economic and political realities of life. It is these that must be changed. Mrs. Ida Mae Lawrence of Rosedale, Mississippi, put it beautifully when she said, "You know, we ain't dumb, even if we are poor. We need jobs. We need houses. But even with the poverty program we ain't got nothin' but needs. . . . We is ignored by the government. The thing about property upset them, but the things about poor people don't. So there's no way out, but to begin your own beginning, whatever way you can. So far as I'm concerned, that's all I got to say about the past. We're beginning a new future."

In his 1966 Berkeley speech, Stokely Carmichael put it another way. ". . . our vision is not merely of a society in which all black men have enough to buy the good things of life. When we urge that black money go into black pockets, we mean the communal pocket. We want to see money go back into the community and used to benefit it. We want to see the cooperative concept applied in business and banking. . . . The society we seek to build among black people is not a capitalistic one. It is a society in which the spirit of community and humanistic love prevail. The word love is suspect; black expectations of what it might produce have been betrayed too often. But those were expectations of a response from the white community, which failed us. The love we seek to encourage is within the black community, the only American community where men call each other 'brother' when they meet. We can build a community of love only where we have the ability and power to do so; among blacks."

Those whites who have a similar vision and want to be a part of this new world must cast down their bucket where they are. If this kind of a world is as important and as necessary for them as it is for us, they must evolve an approach to their own communities. We must organize around blackness, because it is with the fact of our blackness that we have been clubbed. We therefore turn our blackness into a club. When this new world is as totally necessary for whites as it is for blacks, then maybe we can come together and work on some things side by side. However, we will always want to preserve our ethnicity, our community. We are a distinct cultural group, proud of our culture and our institutions, and simply want to be left alone to lead our good, black lives. In the new world, as in this one, I want to be known, not as a man who happens to be black, but as a black man. With that knowledge I can visit the graves of my slave foreparents and say, "I didn't forget about you . . . those hot days you worked in the fields, those beatings, all that shit you took and just grew stronger on. I'm still singing those songs you sang and telling those tales and passing them on to the young ones so they will know you, also. We will never forget, for your lives were lived on a spider web stretched over the mouth of hell and yet, you walked that walk and talked that talk and told it like it t.i. is. You can rest easy now. Everything's up-tight."

The old order passes away. Like the black riderless horse, boots turned the wrong way in the stirrups, following the coffin down the boulevard, it passes away. But there are no crowds to watch as it passes. There are no crowds, to mourn, to weep. No eulogies to read and no eternal flame is lit over the grave. There is no time, for there are streets to be cleaned, houses painted, and clothes washed. Everything must be scoured clean. Trash has to be thrown out. Garbage dumped and everything unfit, burned.

The new order is coming, child.
The old is passing away.

Albert B. Cleage, Jr.

Pastor of the Shrine of the Black Madonna in Detroit, Michigan, Albert B. Cleage, Jr., stands in the tradition of the radical black preacher. The lessons he finds in the Bible, especially in the history of Israel, are not those of patience, long-suffering, and otherworldliness, but of vigorous action by the Black Nation to preserve itself and to grow in the face of its enemies. At the same time he argues that the Black Nation, like the Nation of Israel, needs the support that only God can provide. With a good deal of intelligence, rhetorical skill, and theological insight, Cleage explores and makes relevant to the streets of Detroit the radicalism of Christianity. While he can match heat and violence with any black radical, he sees, as many do not see, that Black Power and the Black Nation are good to the extent that they make black men "part of something" that is worthwhile. "If anything gives a black man a sense of pride and dignity, it is good. If it destroys his pride and dignity, it is bad."

Additional Readings: The other sermons in Cleage's *Black Messiah* are well worth pursuing for their politics, rhetoric, and theology. On all counts they might profitably be compared with those of the other Christian ministers represented here, Joseph H. Jack-

"We Are God's Chosen People"

"How long will you set upon a man to shatter
him, like a leaning wall, a tottering fence?
They only plan to tear him down from his
dignity" (*Psalms* 62:3).*

Speaking about the enemies of Israel, the Psalmist says: "How long will you set upon a man to shatter him, like a leaning wall, a tottering fence? They only plan to tear him down from his dignity" (Ps.62:3,4).

Forget for a moment that this is from the Bible and was written a long time ago. Just think about the simple words themselves. It is as if we were talking about the enemies of the Black Nation today. How long will they continue to oppress and to exploit and to do all the things they

*Many scholars translate "excellency" as "dignity."

son and Martin Luther King, Jr. Also interesting are the various writings of Joseph R. Washington, and J. H. Cone's *Black Theology and Black Power. Keep the Faith, Baby,* a collection of sermons by Adam Clayton Powell, Jr., is disappointingly thin.

have been doing? How long will they continue to use violence in an effort to destroy us? As we see the plight of black people in this white man's world, we echo the words of the Psalmist, "How long will you set upon a man to shatter him like a leaning wall?" That is a beautiful figure of speech because if a wall is leaning, it isn't going to stand long. Certainly we can say, "You only plan to tear us down from our dignity."

Often we don't think of our dignity as something of great value. We even laugh at it, as when someone is said to be putting on airs. But then we are only thinking of dignity in a superficial way. Take from you your dignity and you have nothing left. Take from you the right to hold up your head, to feel that you are a man, the right to think, to be — take away that dignity and there is nothing left but a groveling animal, a slave.

Let us look for a moment at the Psalm from which our text is taken. It begins with a statement of faith in God, "For God alone my soul waits in silence." The Psalmist is leading up to the description of what the enemy is trying to do, but he begins with this plaintive, and yet, heroic statement. "From him comes my salvation. He only is my rock and my salvation, my fortress. I shall not be moved." It may seem strange to us in the 20th Century that the Psalmist should move from this simple primitive statement of faith, through a description of what the enemies of Israel are trying to do, and then at the close of the Psalm, re-affirm his faith by repeating, "From him comes my salvation."

I think that it is well in this day for black militants, black nationalists, and those who believe that we must rebuild the Black Nation as
Jesus tried to rebuild it two thousand years ago, to remember the Psalmist's simple words. "From him comes my salvation." We have a great
tendency, as we become emancipated from slave religion, from slave
thinking and from a desire to identify with the enemy, to reject God
altogether. We begin to say to ourselves that we never did need God.
He was only a stumbling block to our people.

Young people find this an almost irresistible temptation as they become involved in the black revolution and committed to struggle and
sacrifice. The Movement exists today because black young people have
been willing to make tremendous sacrifices to bring it into being and to
maintain its momentum. I think of the young people at Texas Christian
University who fought to protect their campus from police invasion. But
more and more as they struggle they are beginning to say, "what do we
need God for? We can do it ourselves. All we really need is the courage
to get out there and fight."

You hear this everywhere and perhaps there are echoes in your own
mind. "If only we could have gotten together a long time ago and stopped
talking about God, we would be farther along." That is why in most cities
those who are actively engaged in the Freedom Struggle are not a part
of the Church. They look with contempt and scorn upon the Church
and in many instances, rightly so, because the Church has not lived up
to its obligations. It does not represent God. It does not fulfill the revelation of God which we have in Jesus Christ. It is important for us who have
come into the Black Nation as disciples of the Black Messiah to remember these simple words. "For God only is my rock, and my salvation,
my fortress, and I shall not be moved."

You may think that it is unnecessary, that we don't need this. Why
should we clutter up our thinking with a God who is off somewhere,
who may or may not have created the universe, who may or may not
have spoken through the prophets?

You need it for the same reason the Psalmist needed it, that Israel
needed it. Because a man cannot maintain dignity in a world of exploitation, suffering, and oppression all by himself. If you are going to believe
that you are somebody, that you have worth and value, then you must
know that that worth and value was built into you. You were created
with worth and value. You didn't make it by yourself. You were created
by God with certain inalienable rights.

This is why you need God. It is not enough to just look at the world
in which you live, to look at the people, to understand what suffering
and systematic exploitation have done to you, and say that despite all
of this, I am going to maintain my dignity. You can't do it by yourself.

The Psalmist was not talking about his little individual dignity. He wasn't sitting off some place talking about a God who was going to do something for him. The Psalmist was talking about a God who was concerned with the Nation Israel, a God who was concerned with the destiny and the problems of the Nation Israel. This we must remember today if we are to maintain our dignity. In the greatest adversity, Israel depended upon God.

We can say that in today's world, with our knowledge of science, atomic energy and many mysterious things which we do not understand even as we use them, we don't need God any more. But we do. In the greatest adversity, the Nation Israel depended upon God. No matter what the enemy did, the Gentiles, the white people, no matter what they did to Israel, Israel was still confident.

As we look back at the history of Israel, we can ask, "How did this little handful of people, at the crossroads of the world, hemmed in by great nations on every side, maintain its identity and its confidence, even as it was conquered by first one enemy and then another? How could this little handful of people still believe that somehow they would emerge triumphant? In every adversity they believed that God was concerned about them. They believed it. They believed that their strength was a strength that their enemies could neither conquer nor destroy because it came from their unique relationship with God.

During the Egyptian bondage, it would have been easy for Israel to have given up. The conditions of their slavery were very much like our own. But they continued to believe that somehow freedom would come, somehow conditions would be changed. The enemy found it impossible to destroy them because their dignity could not be affected by anything men could do to them. Men could not destroy a dignity which had been given to them by God. So, efforts to destroy their dignity failed. No matter what the enemy did, Israel knew that it was special. When they were taken into Babylon, it was not into a harsh kind of captivity. The Babylonians had no need to destroy them. They were not that important. Only the leaders were taken to Babylon. This seemed sufficient to destroy their institutions and their identity. The Babylonians didn't beat them or use cattle prods or fire hoses on them. They just took the cream of the nation to Babylon. The Psalmist says, "Our captors required of us mirth, saying, 'Sing us the songs of Zion.'" The Babylonians weren't vicious men. They weren't beating or whipping them. They just laughed at them. "They required of us mirth," just as today in the Gentile nightclubs they say, "You black people have such a talent for singing. Sing us your spirituals."

The other night I saw the Clara Ward Gospel Singers on TV, entertaining in a Las Vegas nightclub. They were singing the very songs which our people sang in their suffering and misery, while the white folks laughed. When the Babylonians said to the Jews in captivity (these biblical Jews were the Black Nation Israel), "Sing us the songs of Zion, laugh and make merry for us, we like your songs," what did the Jews reply? "How can we sing the Lord's songs in a strange land?" They said, "The Nation is shattered. We aren't going to sing the Lord's songs for these Gentiles." It wasn't a place that they remembered. It was a Nation, a people. They wept because they were God's people. They were not going to make light of God so white folks could laugh and make merry.

Do you know what the difference was? The ancient Jews had dignity. You may not think that dignity is important. But you know that when the Ward Singers jazzed up our spirituals, those white folks in Las Vegas had less respect for all of us. They knew that those songs were religious songs. They knew that when those songs were first sung, black women were being raped, their children were being snatched from them and sold into slavery, and their men were being whipped and killed. When they heard the Ward Singers singing those songs for entertainment, they said, "These people have no dignity"; and they thought less of all of us.

"How can we sing the Lord's songs in a strange land?" is a statement of dignity. Don't act a fool for white folks. You see it so often. Some black people think that they have emancipated themselves when they act a fool. You see it on the bus all the time. A black man without dignity will talk loud and act simple and think that somehow he is showing white folks that they don't frighten him any. A black man without dignity will do foolish things to make white people laugh. He'll talk to some imaginary friend at the other end of the bus. All the time he is talking for the man's entertainment, laughing for the man, performing for the man. The man sees him and thinks that we are all fools. It's no use my just sitting there and looking the other way because he is destroying me.

As black people, we don't have a lot of separate dignities. We have one dignity. If you mess it up, you mess it up for all of us. Or you see our black kids acting a fool out on the streets. They are messing up *our* dignity. You know why they are doing it? Because they don't understand. Because they are living in a world in which they have been shattered — leaning walls, tottering fences. So they are out there fighting back in their own little way, making a fool of themselves for the man.

We have got to find dignity somewhere because we will never be a Nation until we can first build a sense of dignity. That means that anywhere, on the job, on the bus, on the street, there are certain things that the man is not going to make you do. What can he give you if he takes your dignity? Nothing he has is worth it. You say, "I've got to eat." And I say, "Eating is not that important." You say, "I got a wife and children." I am not going to tell you that they are not that important. I am going to say that they *are* that important. They don't want a clown feeding them, and if you feed them, acting a clown, you are destroying them at the same time. "They only tear him down from his dignity." The Psalmist analyzed it all a long time ago, and he knew that it was possible to take a man and make a clown out of him.

John O. Killens means the same thing when he says the white folks took a black man and made a Nigger out of him. They robbed him of his dignity. The children of Israel remembered this one thing, and struggled to keep their dignity. They remembered that God had chosen Israel.

Don't laugh at that because *we* are God's chosen people. You don't fully recognize yet what that means. When we talk about the Black Nation, we have got to remember that the Black Nation, Israel, was chosen by God. Out of the whole world God chose Israel to covenant with, to say, "You will be my people and I will be your God." What else does a man need for dignity? He didn't go to the big nations with their big armies. He went to this little nation and said, "You are my chosen people." Perhaps if we could just remember that we are God's chosen people, that we have a covenant with God, then we would know that God will not forsake us. Even in the midst of violence and oppression, we would know that we are God's chosen people. We could look the white man straight in the eye and say, "There is nothing you can do to destroy us, and you cannot take from us our dignity."

The concept of the Nation must include the basic truth that the Nation consists of God's chosen people. Don't be afraid to say the word "God" because this is the 20th Century. You know what God means. It means that somebody is taking care of us. Don't try to make something selfish out of God. Don't try to use God to get something for *you* that *you* want. Understand that God is going to take care of *us*, the Black Nation, because we are God's chosen people. Because of this simple fact, the enemy is not going to destroy us. The time of our greatest strength (I am talking now about black people in this country) has not been in recent years, when we have had jobs and money and the illusion of being accepted. The time of our greatest strength was back in slavery when our slave forefathers believed that God was going to do something for them. They didn't just sit down because they believed this and wait for God to free them. The Underground Railroad was possible because black men and women were willing to take risks to get free. These black men and women were willing to go back into slave territory to bring out their people.

Nat Turner's faith in God did not stop his insurrection, nor thousands of slave insurrections all over the South. Every time a black man led an insurrection, he knew that he was doing the will of God. When you fight, you must believe that you are doing the will of God. Just being mad is not enough. That is the trouble with most of our rebellions. We get mad because somebody did something we didn't like, and we start throwing Molotov Cocktails and breaking out windows. This isn't enough. We must believe that our struggle is a revolutionary struggle designed to change the world and to establish us in our rightful position. We must have faith that we are doing the will of God who created us in his own image.

Anything that destroys a black man's dignity is bad. This is our yardstick. Just ask yourself, "Is this building a black man's dignity?" Then it is good. If it is destroying a black man's dignity, then it is bad. That is the only yardstick there is. It doesn't make any difference how much money is involved. Anything you do that makes black people proud, that is good. Anything that makes black people ashamed, that is bad. That is why so many black preachers in pulpits throughout this country are bad. They use the name of God but what they are doing is bad because they make black people ashamed. That is why Muhammad Ali is good, because what he did makes us proud. So he is good. What Muhammad Ali did and is doing is the will of God. You know how we know? Because it makes black people proud. That is God's will, but what preachers are doing in so many pulpits is bad. It doesn't make any difference how many times they say God on Sunday morning, or how big their Bible is, or how many songs they sing about what God is going to do in the great bye-and-bye. It is bad because they are destroying our dignity, and even the little children sitting in these churches are getting to the point where they are ashamed. It is bad, it is not the will of God.

Don't be afraid to try to figure it out in terms of the will of God. God wants us to be men. If he had wanted us to be something else, he would have made us something else. If he had wanted us to be snakes or bears, he would have made us snakes or bears. He made us men; he expects us to be men. We tend to forget. Back in slavery our people remembered. We look back and think that this is a time we would like to forget. But we must never forget it because back there we had men and women with dignity. In the midst of the most difficult conditions, they had dignity. There were men and women that Ole Massa couldn't break. That was what he was trying to do. The things he did were not only designed to make him money, but to break black men.

That is still what the white enemy is trying to do today, to break you. That is why he is happy to get Clara Ward and her singers to shuffle for him. That is why he is happy when he can get Roy Wilkins to issue ridiculous statements. He knows that he is making us ashamed. If he can take our little children and make them think that being a pimp is the greatest thing in the world, he is happy. He is breaking us, making us ashamed.

Everything he has done to us was intended to make us ashamed, to destroy our pride. Why do you think he gives black children second-class schools which teach white supremacy? Because he knows that this is one certain way to keep a people down, by robbing them of pride. It is a miracle that we have a Black Nation today, that so many black men and women and children believe that they are somebody, after the systematic effort that has gone into breaking us. But millions of us are bewildered and confused, not even understanding that the man is deliberately trying to break us by robbing us of our dignity.

I was talking to a friend of mine in the barber shop the other day. He means well. He bought a house out there where some of you are trying to buy or have already bought. He lived around the corner for a long time, but when he started making a little money he wanted something better for his children. He wanted good schools for them and a good neighborhood. So he took his children out of public school and put them into a Catholic school. He was getting the best for them. There were only a few black children in the school or in the neighborhood. Everything was so fine. He was telling me about his son.

I said, "You are destroying that child." He loves that boy more than anything in the world. He works 12 hours a day trying to do his best for the boy.

He said, "How am I destroying the child? Everything I do is for that boy. That's why I took him out there so he wouldn't be with these. . . ."

"That is the first wrong thing, telling him that you took him out there so that he wouldn't be with us."

"But I look out on 12th Street at night and see little children running up and down the street. I don't want that for my children." So I said, "If I had to choose, I'd choose one of those running up and down 12th Street, because if he comes out of it alive, he is going to have some sense of identity with his own people. Out there where your child is, you have destroyed that possibility. How is he going to get it in a white Catholic school, in a white neighborhood? What can you say to him?"

"I tell him to stay in school and he will get a better job. He won't be like. . . ."

"There you go again—won't be like *them.* That is what you are trying to say. You can get a better job, you can live in a white neighborhood, you can send your children to a white school, that is what you are trying to tell him. You are separating him from the Black Nation. Your whole way of life is designed to separate him from his own people."

He said, "Oh, no, he knows he's black, he has pride in being black."

"Does he know that white people are his enemy?"

"That isn't so, white people are not his enemy," he said. "Let me give you a little illustration. My little boy and another little boy play together, and there is a little white girl who lives across the street. So my little boy and the boy he plays with were talking to the little white girl, and they asked her which one she liked best. The little white girl said that she liked the other little boy best. She didn't like my boy best, yet the little boy she picked is darker than my little boy."

I said, "Now how about *that?* Do you think you have really proved your point? Don't you know that they were both little 'Niggers' to that little white girl, and don't you see what you have done? You've got your little black boy out there in a white neighborhood, begging a little white girl to say that she likes him. Now there's no hope for either one of you."

The important thing is that this black father doesn't see anything wrong with his little boy trying to get a little white girl across the street to say that she likes him.

I asked, "How many times have they called your little boy 'Nigger' in school?"

Now he was getting defensive, "Not much, just once or twice, that's all."

"Do you think that being called 'Nigger' once or twice a day is doing him a whole lot of good?" I asked. "And do you think that all these white folks teaching him all about white supremacy are really going to make him a better black man? Don't you think that all of this will ruin his mind?"

"No," he replied, "what he is learning is good. He's in the best school that I can afford."

I asked, "Don't you think that when he gets through the day with all those white teachers, priests, and nuns, he must hate you when he comes home because you are black and inferior?"

"Oh, no, you don't understand," he protested, "I am protecting him from all that. I will give you another illustration. You know all these slick-headed 'processes' that the boys wear in black neighborhoods? Well, out in our neighborhood, he never sees one. Well, the other day a teen-age black boy came to pick up a maid from across the street and he had a 'process.' He is nine years old and he had never seen a process, isn't that good?"

I said, "I'm on the verge of tears, go on with your story."

"Well, that night when I came home, he told me that he would like to have his hair fixed like that so it would be long and slick and shiny. He didn't know what to call it, but he wanted one."

I asked, "What did you think about that?"

He said, "I was glad that he won't see that kind of thing very often out where we live."

I said, "Aren't you worried about the fact that the very first time he saw a black boy with a 'process' he wanted one? Why do you think he wanted it? Can't you see that your little boy is ashamed of being black with kinky hair, and he wants to be white?"

He said, "Oh, no, it just shows what a little bad influence can do to a child."

There we have a poor little black boy being torn to pieces by white people—or as the Psalmist says, "being shattered." And his poor father, thinking that he is doing the best thing for his child, sacrificing, working himself to death, and his wife working herself to death, and this poor little black boy going straight to hell. By "hell" I mean the place where a man has no dignity and no respect for himself.

We have only one basis for judgment. If anything gives a black man a sense of pride and dignity, it is good. If it destroys his pride and dignity, it is bad. Remember this when you get ready to buy a house in a white neighborhood. Is it going to give your child a sense of pride to be out there in an all-white school where he is despised by teachers and students alike? The public schools are not good and the fight to improve them seems almost futile, so you are going to send him to some Lutheran or Catholic school and destroy him completely. Many black people see other black people only through the white man's eyes. The white man has completely destroyed their love of self. They have no sense of pride. They are actually afraid of us and of our influence upon their children.

We are not going to hurt their little children. From the front steps of the Church everyday, I see hundreds of little children who live in our neighborhood. They are all better off than this black child in his better white neighborhood. They look around and everybody is black. I may scream at them for throwing stones through the back windows, but I scream at them because I am concerned about them. I don't want them tearing up our Church building, but I don't hate them and I don't despise them. I can't call them "Nigger" because they are a part of me. And that is the way everybody else is, up and down the street. But out in my friend's better white neighborhood, his little boy isn't a part of anything, and he knows it. He can walk up and down the street and ask little white girls whether or not they like him, but every day his dignity is slipping away and self-hate is taking its place.

Those of us who are in the Black Nation realize that we are God's chosen people. No matter what the enemy does to us, we are God's chosen people and we must love each other. We fight together against a common enemy, confident of ultimate victory because we are God's chosen people. "How long will you set upon a man to shatter him, like a leaning wall, a tottering fence? They only plan to tear him down from his dignity."

James Baldwin

One of the first of the present generation of angry blacks to achieve popularity through his searing exposure of black pain and American injustice, James Baldwin helped to set a fashion. But unlike many of his imitators, Baldwin not only burns; he thinks. The essay here, taken from Baldwin's first book of essays, *Notes of a Native Son,* represents an impressive and unusual range and depth of thought about the black man's relation to the white Western world. Beginning with reflections on the gulf between him and the Swiss villagers among whom he lived for some time, Baldwin explores the relation of the black man and white civilization. "The idea of white supremacy rests simply on the fact that white men are the creators of civilization . . . and are therefore civilization's guardians and defenders. Thus it was impossible for Americans to accept the black man as one of themselves, for to do so was to jeopardize their status as white men. But not so to accept him was to deny his human reality, his human

weight and complexity, and the strain of denying the overwhelmingly undeniable forced Americans into rationalizations so fantastic that they approached the pathological."

Additional Readings: Baldwin's early reputation was established
by the essays in his two books, *Notes of a Native Son* and *Nobody*

Stranger in the Village

From all available evidence no black man had ever set foot in this
tiny Swiss village before I came. I was told before arriving that I would
probably be a "sight" for the village; I took this to mean that people of
my complexion were rarely seen in Switzerland, and also that city people
are always something of a "sight" outside of the city. It did not occur
to me — possibly because I am an American — that there could be people
anywhere who had never seen a Negro.

It is a fact that cannot be explained on the basis of the inaccessibility
of the village. The village is very high, but it is only four hours from Milan
and three hours from Lausanne. It is true that it is virtually unknown.
Few people making plans for a holiday would elect to come here. On
the other hand, the villagers are able, presumably, to come and go as
they please — which they do: to another town at the foot of the mountain,
with a population of approximately five thousand, the nearest place to
see a movie or go to the bank. In the village there is no movie house,

Knows My Name, which contain some of his finest writings, polit- ical and literary. His more emphatically political and polemical *The Fire Next Time,* although less comprehensive in theme and sometimes problematical in its argument, is a major contemporary statement and deserves to be read along with the essay here.

no bank, no library, no theater; very few radios, one jeep, one station wagon; and, at the moment, one typewriter, mine, an invention which the woman next door to me here had.never seen. There are about six hundred people living here, all Catholic—I conclude this from the fact that the Catholic church is open all year round, whereas the Protestant chapel, set off on a hill a little removed from the village, is open only in the summertime when the tourists arrive. There are four or five hotels, all closed now, and four or five *bistros,* of which, however, only two do any business during the winter. These two do not do a great deal, for life in the village seems to end around nine or ten o'clock. There are a few stores, butcher, baker, *épicerie,* a hardware store, and a money- changer—who cannot change travelers' checks, but must send them down to the bank, an operation which takes two or three days. There is something called the *Ballet Haus,* closed in the winter and used for God knows what, certainly not ballet, during the summer. There seems to be only one schoolhouse in the village, and this for the quite young children; I suppose this to mean that their older brothers and sisters at some point descend from these mountains in order to complete their education—possibly, again, to the town just below. The landscape is absolutely forbidding, mountains towering on all four sides, ice and snow as far as the eye can reach. In this white wilderness, men and women and children move all day, carrying washing, wood, buckets of milk or water, sometimes skiing on Sunday afternoons. All week long boys and young men are to be seen shoveling snow off the rooftops, or dragging wood down from the forest in sleds.

The village's only real attraction, which explains the tourist season, is the hot spring water. A disquietingly high proportion of these tourists are cripples, or semi-cripples, who come year after year — from other parts of Switzerland, usually — to take the waters. This lends the village, at the height of the season, a rather terrifying air of sanctity, as though it were a lesser Lourdes. There is often something beautiful, there is always something awful, in the spectacle of a person who has lost one of his faculties, a faculty he never questioned until it was gone, and who struggles to recover it. Yet people remain people, on crutches or indeed on deathbeds; and wherever I passed, the first summer I was here, among the native villagers or among the lame, a wind passed with me — of astonishment, curiosity, amusement, and outrage. That first summer I stayed two weeks and never intended to return. But I did return in the winter, to work; the village offers, obviously, no distractions whatever and has the further advantage of being extremely cheap. Now it is winter again, a year later, and I am here again. Everyone in the village knows my name, though they scarcely ever use it, knows that I come from America — though, this, apparently, they will never really believe: black men come from Africa — and everyone knows that I am the friend of the son of a woman who was born here, and that I am staying in their chalet. But I remain as much a stranger today as I was the first day I arrived, and the children shout *Neger! Neger!* as I walk along the streets.

It must be admitted that in the beginning I was far too shocked to have any real reaction. In so far as I reacted at all, I reacted by trying to be pleasant — it being a great part of the American Negro's education (long before he goes to school) that he must make people "like" him. This smile-and-the-world-smiles-with-you routine worked about as well in this situation as it had in the situation for which it was designed, which is to say that it did not work at all. No one, after all, can be liked whose human weight and complexity cannot be, or has not been, admitted. My smile was simply another unheard-of phenomenon which allowed them to see my teeth — they did not, really, see my smile and I began to think that, should I take to snarling, no one would notice any difference. All of the physical characteristics of the Negro which had caused me, in America, a very different and almost forgotten pain were nothing less than miraculous — or infernal — in the eyes of the village people. Some thought my hair was the color of tar, that it had the texture of wire, or the texture of cotton. It was jocularly suggested that I might let it all grow long and make myself a winter coat. If I sat in the sun for more than five minutes some daring creature was certain to come along and gingerly put his fingers on my hair, as though he were afraid of an electric shock, or put his hand on my hand, astonished that the color did not rub off. In all of this, in which it must be conceded there was the charm of genuine wonder and in which there was certainly no element of intentional unkindness, there was yet no suggestion that I was human: I was simply a living wonder.

I knew that they did not mean to be unkind, and I know it now; it is necessary, nevertheless, for me to repeat this to myself each time that I walk out of the chalet. The children who shout *Neger!* have no way of knowing the echoes this sound raises in me. They are brimming with good humor and the more daring swell with pride when I stop to speak with them. Just the same, there are days when I cannot pause and smile, when I have no heart to play with them; when, indeed, I mutter sourly to myself, exactly as I muttered on the streets of a city these children have never seen, when I was no bigger than these children are now: *Your* mother *was a nigger.* Joyce is right about history being a nightmare—but it may be the nightmare from which no one *can* awaken. People are trapped in history and history is trapped in them.

There is a custom in the village—I am told it is repeated in many villages—of "buying" African natives for the purpose of converting them to Christianity. There stands in the church all year round a small box with a slot for money, decorated with a black figurine, and into this box the villagers drop their francs. During the *carnaval* which precedes Lent, two village children have their faces blackened—out of which bloodless darkness their blue eyes shine like ice—and fantastic horsehair wigs are placed on their blond heads; thus disguised, they solicit among the villagers for money for the missionaries in Africa. Between the box in the church and the blackened children, the village "bought" last year six or eight African natives. This was reported to me with pride by the wife of one of the *bistro* owners and I was careful to express astonishment and pleasure at the solicitude shown by the village for the souls of black folk. The *bistro* owner's wife beamed with a pleasure far more genuine than my own and seemed to feel that I might now breathe more easily concerning the souls of at least six of my kinsmen.

I tried not to think of these so lately baptized kinsmen, of the price paid for them, or the peculiar price they themselves would pay, and said nothing about my father, who having taken his own conversion too literally never, at bottom, forgave the white world (which he described as heathen) for having saddled him with a Christ in whom, to judge at least from their treatment of him, they themselves no longer believed. I thought of white men arriving for the first time in an African village, strangers there, as I am a stranger here, and tried to imagine the astounded populace touching their hair and marveling at the color of their skin. But there is a great difference between being the first white man to be seen by Africans and being the first black man to be seen by whites. The white man takes the astonishment as tribute, for he arrives to conquer and to convert the natives, whose inferiority in relation to himself is not even to be questioned; whereas I, without a thought of conquest, find myself among a people whose culture controls me, has even, in a sense, created me, people who have cost me more in anguish and rage than they will ever know, who yet do not even know of my existence. The astonishment with which I might have greeted them, should they have stumbled into my African village a few hundred years ago, might have rejoiced their hearts. But the astonishment with which they greet me today can only poison mine.

And this is so despite everything I may do to feel differently, despite my friendly conversations with the *bistro* owner's wife, despite their three-year-old son who has at last become my friend, despite the *saluts* and *bonsoirs* which I exchange with people as I walk, despite the fact that I know that no individual can be taken to task for what history is doing, or has done. I say that the culture of these people controls me — but they can scarcely be held responsible for European culture. America comes out of Europe, but these people have never seen America, nor have most of them seen more of Europe than the hamlet at the foot of their mountain. Yet they move with an authority which I shall never have; and they regard me, quite rightly, not only as a stranger in their village but as a suspect latecomer, bearing no credentials, to everything they have — however unconsciously — inherited.

For this village, even were it incomparably more remote and incredibly more primitive, is the West, the West onto which I have been so strangely grafted. These people cannot be, from the point of view of power, strangers anywhere in the world; they have made the modern world, in effect, even if they do not know it. The most illiterate among them is related, in a way that I am not, to Dante, Shakespeare, Michelangelo, Aeschylus, Da Vinci, Rembrandt, and Racine; the cathedral at Chartres says something to them which it cannot say to me, as indeed would New York's Empire State Building, should anyone here ever see it. Out of their hymns and dances come Beethoven and Bach. Go back a few centuries and they are in their full glory — but I am in Africa, watching the conquerors arrive.

The rage of the disesteemed is personally fruitless, but it is also absolutely inevitable; this rage, so generally discounted, so little understood even among the people whose daily bread it is, is one of the things that makes history. Rage can only with difficulty, and never entirely, be brought under the domination of the intelligence and is therefore not susceptible to any arguments whatever. This is a fact which ordinary representatives of the *Herrenvolk,* having never felt this rage and being unable to imagine it, quite fail to understand. Also, rage cannot be hidden, it can only be dissembled. This dissembling deludes the thoughtless, and strengthens rage and adds, to rage, contempt. There are, no doubt, as many ways of coping with the resulting complex of tensions as there are black men in the world, but no black man can hope ever to be entirely liberated from this internal warfare—rage, dissembling, and contempt having inevitably accompanied his first realization of the power of white men. What is crucial here is that, since white men represent in the black man's world so heavy a weight, white men have for black men a reality which is far from being reciprocal; and hence all black men have toward all white men an attitude which is designed, really, either to rob the white man of the jewel of his naïveté, or else to make it cost him dear.

The black man insists, by whatever means he finds at his disposal, that the white man cease to regard him as an exotic rarity and recognize him as a human being. This is a very charged and difficult moment, for there is a great deal of will power involved in the white man's naïveté. Most people are not naturally reflective any more than they are naturally malicious, and the white man prefers to keep the black man at a certain human remove because it is easier for him thus to preserve his simplicity and avoid being called to account for crimes committed by his forefathers, or his neighbors. He is inescapably aware, nevertheless, that he is in a better position in the world than black men are, nor can he quite put to death the suspicion that he is hated by black men therefore. He does not wish to be hated, neither does he wish to change places, and at this point in his uneasiness he can scarcely avoid having recourse to those legends which white men have created about black men, the most usual effect of which is that the white man finds himself enmeshed, so to speak, in his own language which describes hell, as well as the attributes which lead one to hell, as being as black as night.

Every legend, moreover, contains its residuum of truth, and the root function of language is to control the universe by describing it. It is of quite considerable significance that black men remain, in the imagination, and in overwhelming numbers in fact, beyond the disciplines of salvation; and this despite the fact that the West has been "buying" African natives for centuries. There is, I should hazard, an instantaneous necessity to be divorced from this so visibly unsaved stranger, in whose heart, moreover, one cannot guess what dreams of vengeance are being nourished; and, at the same time, there are few things on earth more attractive than the idea of the unspeakable liberty which is allowed the unredeemed. When, beneath the black mask, a human being begins to make himself felt one cannot escape a certain awful wonder as to what kind of human being it is. What one's imagination makes of other people is dictated, of course, by the laws of one's own personality and it is one of the ironies of black-white relations that, by means of what the white man imagines the black man to be, the black man is enabled to know who the white man is.

I have said, for example, that I am as much a stranger in this village today as I was the first summer I arrived, but this is not quite true. The villagers wonder less about the texture of my hair than they did then, and wonder rather more about me. And the fact that their wonder now exists on another level is reflected in their attitudes and in their eyes. There are the children who make those delightful, hilarious, sometimes astonishingly grave overtures of friendship in the unpredictable fashion of children; other children, having been taught that the devil is a black man, scream in genuine anguish as I approach. Some of the older women never pass without a friendly greeting, never pass, indeed, if it seems that they will be able to engage me in conversation; other women look down or look away or rather contemptuously smirk. Some of the men drink with me and suggest that I learn how to ski—partly, I gather, because they cannot imagine what I would look like on skis—and want to know if I am married, and ask questions about my *métier*. But some of the men have accused *le sale nègre*—behind my back—of stealing wood and there is already in the eyes of some of them that peculiar, intent, paranoiac malevolence which one sometimes surprises in the eyes of American white men when, out walking with their Sunday girl, they see a Negro male approach.

There is a dreadful abyss between the streets of this village and the streets of the city in which I was born, between the children who shout *Neger!* today and those who shouted *Nigger!* yesterday—the abyss is experience, the American experience. The syllable hurled behind me today expresses, above all, wonder: I am a stranger here. But I am not a stranger in America and the same syllable riding on the American air expresses the war my presence has occasioned in the American soul.

For this village brings home to me this fact: that there was a day, and not really a very distant day, when Americans were scarcely Americans at all but discontented Europeans, facing a great unconquered continent and strolling, say, into a marketplace and seeing black men for the first time. The shock this spectacle afforded is suggested, surely, by the promptness with which they decided that these black men were not really men but cattle. It is true that the necessity on the part of the settlers of the New World of reconciling their moral assumptions with the fact—and the necessity—of slavery enhanced immensely the charm of this idea, and it is also true that this idea expresses, with a truly American bluntness, the attitude which to varying extents all masters have had toward all slaves.

But between all former slaves and slave-owners and the drama which begins for Americans over three hundred years ago at Jamestown, there are at least two differences to be observed. The American Negro slave could not suppose, for one thing, as slaves in past epochs had supposed and often done, that he would ever be able to wrest the power from his master's hands. This was a supposition which the modern era, which was to bring about such vast changes in the aims and dimensions of power, put to death; it only begins, in unprecedented fashion, and with dreadful implications, to be resurrected today. But even had this supposition persisted with undiminished force, the American Negro slave could not have used it to lend his condition dignity, for the reason that this supposition rests on another: that the slave in exile yet remains related to his past, has some means—if only in memory—of revering and sustaining the forms of his former life, is able, in short, to maintain his identity.

This was not the case with the American Negro slave. He is unique among the black men of the world in that his past was taken from him, almost literally, at one blow. One wonders what on earth the first slave found to say to the first dark child he bore. I am told that there are Haitians able to trace their ancestry back to African kings, but any American Negro wishing to go back so far will find his journey through time abruptly arrested by the signature on the bill of sale which served as the entrance paper for his ancestor. At the time—to say nothing of the circumstances—of the enslavement of the captive black man who was to become the American Negro, there was not the remotest possibility that he would ever take power from his master's hands. There was no reason to suppose that his situation would ever change, nor was there, shortly, anything to indicate that his situation had ever been different. It was his necessity, in the words of E. Franklin Frazier, to find a "motive for living under American culture or die." The identity of the American Negro comes out of this extreme situation, and the evolution of this identity was a source of the most intolerable anxiety in the minds and the lives of his masters.

For the history of the American Negro is unique also in this: that the question of his humanity, and of his rights therefore as a human being, became a burning one for several generations of Americans, so burning a question that it ultimately became one of those used to divide the nation. It is out of this argument that the venom of the epithet *Nigger!* is derived. It is an argument which Europe has never had, and hence Europe quite sincerely fails to understand how or why the argument arose in the first place, why its effects are so frequently disastrous and always so unpredictable, why it refuses until today to be entirely settled. Europe's black possessions remained — and do remain — in Europe's colonies, at which remove they represented no threat whatever to European identity. If they posed any problem at all for the European conscience, it was a problem which remained comfortingly abstract: in effect, the black man, *as a man*, did not exist for Europe. But in America, even as a slave, he was an inescapable part of the general social fabric and no American could escape having an attitude toward him. Americans attempt until today to make an abstraction of the Negro, but the very nature of these abstractions reveals the tremendous effects the presence of the Negro has had on the American character.

When one considers the history of the Negro in America it is of the greatest importance to recognize that the moral beliefs of a person, or a people, are never really as tenuous as life — which is not moral — very often causes them to appear; these create for them a frame of reference and a necessary hope, the hope being that when life has done its worst they will be enabled to rise above themselves and to triumph over life. Life would scarcely be bearable if this hope did not exist. Again, even when the worst has been said, to betray a belief is not by any means to have put oneself beyond its power; the betrayal of a belief is not the same thing as ceasing to believe. If this were not so there would be no moral standards in the world at all. Yet one must also recognize that morality is based on ideas and that all ideas are dangerous — dangerous because ideas can only lead to action and where the action leads no man can say. And dangerous in this respect: that confronted with the impossibility of remaining faithful to one's beliefs, and the equal impossibility of becoming free of them, one can be driven to the most inhuman excesses. The ideas on which American beliefs are based are not, though Americans often seem to think so, ideas which originated in America. They came out of Europe. And the establishment of democracy on the American continent was scarcely as radical a break with the past as was the necessity, which Americans faced, of broadening this concept to include black men.

This was, literally, a hard necessity. It was impossible, for one thing, for Americans to abandon their beliefs, not only because these beliefs alone seemed able to justify the sacrifices they had endured and the blood that they had spilled, but also because these beliefs afforded them their only bulwark against a moral chaos as absolute as the physical chaos of the continent it was their destiny to conquer. But in the situation in which Americans found themselves, these beliefs threatened an idea which, whether or not one likes to think so, is the very warp and woof of the heritage of the West, the idea of white supremacy.

Americans have made themselves notorious by the shrillness and the brutality with which they have insisted on this idea, but they did not invent it; and it has escaped the world's notice that those very excesses of which Americans have been guilty imply a certain, unprecedented uneasiness over the idea's life and power, if not, indeed, the idea's validity. The idea of white supremacy rests simply on the fact that white men are the creators of civilization (the present civilization, which is the only one that matters; all previous civilizations are simply "contributions" to our own) and are therefore civilization's guardians and defenders. Thus it was impossible for Americans to accept the black man as one of themselves, for to do so was to jeopardize their status as white men. But not so to accept him was to deny his human reality, his human weight and complexity, and the strain of denying the overwhelmingly undeniable forced Americans into rationalizations so fantastic that they approached the pathological.

At the root of the American Negro problem is the necessity of the American white man to find a way of living with the Negro in order to be able to live with himself. And the history of this problem can be reduced to the means used by Americans—lynch law and law, segregation and legal acceptance, terrorization and concession—either to come to terms with this necessity, or to find a way around it, or (most usually) to find a way of doing both these things at once. The resulting spectacle, at once foolish and dreadful, led someone to make the quite accurate observation that "the Negro-in-America is a form of insanity which overtakes white men."

In this long battle, a battle by no means finished, the unforeseeable effects of which will be felt by many future generations, the white man's motive was the protection of his identity; the black man was motivated by the need to establish an identity. And despite the terrorization which the Negro in America endured and endures sporadically until today, despite the cruel and totally inescapable ambivalence of his status in his country, the battle for his identity has long ago been won. He is not a visitor to the West, but a citizen there, an American; as American as the Americans who despise him, the Americans who fear him, the Americans who love him—the Americans who became less than themselves, or rose to be greater than themselves by virtue of the fact that the challenge he represented was inescapable. He is perhaps the only black man in the world whose relationship to white men is more terrible, more subtle, and more meaningful than the relationship of bitter possessed to uncertain possessor. His survival depended, and his development depends, on his ability to turn his peculiar status in the Western world to his own advantage and, it may be, to the very great advantage of that world. It remains for him to fashion out of his experience that which will give him sustenance, and a voice.

The cathedral at Chartres, I have said, says something to the people of this village which it cannot say to me; but it is important to understand that this cathedral says something to me which it cannot say to them. Perhaps they are struck by the power of the spires, the glory of the windows; but they have known God, after all, longer than I have known him, and in a different way, and I am terrified by the slippery bottomless well to be found in the crypt, down which heretics were hurled to death, and by the obscene, inescapable gargoyles jutting out of the stone and seeming to say that God and the devil can never be divorced. I doubt that the villagers think of the devil when they face a cathedral because they have never been identified with the devil. But I must accept the status which myth, if nothing else, gives me in the West before I can hope to change the myth.

Yet, if the American Negro has arrived at his identity by virtue of the absoluteness of his estrangement from his past, American white men still nourish the illusion that there is some means of recovering the European innocence, of returning to a state in which black men do not exist. This is one of the greatest errors Americans can make. The identity they fought so hard to protect has, by virtue of that battle, undergone a change: Americans are as unlike any other white people in the world as it is possible to be. I do not think, for example, that it is too much to suggest that the American vision of the world—which allows so little reality, generally speaking, for any of the darker forces in human life, which tends until today to paint moral issues in glaring black and white—owes a great deal to the battle waged by Americans to maintain between themselves and black men a human separation which could not be bridged. It is only now beginning to be borne in on us—very faintly, it must be admitted, very slowly, and very much against our will—that this vision of the world is dangerously inaccurate, and perfectly useless. For it protects our moral high-mindedness at the terrible expense of weakening our grasp of reality. People who shut their eyes to reality simply invite their own destruction, and anyone who insists on remaining in a state of innocence long after that innocence is dead turns himself into a monster.

The time has come to realize that the interracial drama acted out on the American continent has not only created a new black man, it has created a new white man, too. No road whatever will lead Americans back to the simplicity of this European village where white men still have the luxury of looking on me as a stranger. I am not, really, a stranger any longer for any American alive. One of the things that distinguishes Americans from other people is that no other people has ever been so deeply involved in the lives of black men, and vice versa. This fact faced, with all its implications, it can be seen that the history of the American Negro problem is not merely shameful, it is also something of an achievement.

For even when the worst has been said, it must also be added that the perpetual challenge posed by this problem was always, somehow, perpetually met. It is precisely this black-white experience which may prove of indispensable value to us in the world we face today. This world is white no longer, and it will never be white again.

NOTES

(Full publication data for all books referred to in notes and in the suggestions for additional reading will be found in the Bibliography on page 227.)

1. W. E. B. Du Bois, *The Souls of Black Folk.* (See page 87.)
2. "Of the Training of Black Men," *The Souls of Black Folk,* p. 109.
3. Philip Foner, *The Life and Writings of Frederick Douglass,* Vol. I, p. 236.
4. *The Autobiography of W. E. B. Du Bois,* p. 421.
5. H. Rap Brown, *Die Nigger Die!,* p. 128. A more clear-headed view is presented in Julius W. Hobson's essay, "Black Power: Right or Left?" in Floyd E. Barbour, *The Black Power Revolt.*
6. Robert Scheer, ed., *Eldridge Cleaver: Post-Prison Writings and Speeches,* p. 39.
7. Floyd McKissick, *Three-Fifths of a Man,* p. 101.
8. LeRoi Jones, *Home: Social Essays,* p. 244.
9. James Farmer, *Freedom—When?,* p. 85.
10. Stokely Carmichael and Charles V. Hamilton, *Black Power: The Politics of Liberation in America,* ch. 3, "The Myths of Coalition."
11. James Baldwin, *The Fire Next Time,* p. 95.
12. See LeRoi Jones, "The Need for a Cultural Base to Civil Rites and Bpower Mooments," in Floyd E. Brown, ed., *The Black Power Revolt,* and Harold Cruse, *The Crisis of the Negro Intellectual.* This was a major concern of the New Negro Movement or Harlem Renaissance of the 1920's. See Alain Locke, ed., *The New Negro,* recently reprinted as an Atheneum paperback.
13. Julius Lester, *Look Out, Whitey! Black Power's Gon' Get Your Mama,* p. 87.
14. Baldwin, *The Fire Next Time,* p. 95.
15. *Ibid.,* p. 54.
16. John Oliver Killens, *Black Man's Burden,* p. 20.
17. McKissick, *Three-Fifths of a Man,* p. 85.

BIBLIOGRAPHY

(Note: This is not a complete bibliography but is intended to provide publication data for the books referred to in the text. Paperback editions are noted in parentheses, although these are subject to rather frequent change.)

Aptheker, Herbert, *Documentary History of the Negro People in the United States.* New York: Citadel Press, 1951. (Citadel)

Baldwin, James, *The Fire Next Time.* New York: Dial Press, 1963. (Dell)

Baldwin, James, *Nobody Knows My Name.* New York: Dial Press, 1961. (Dell)

Baldwin, James, *Notes of a Native Son.* Boston: Beacon Press, 1955. (Beacon)

Barbour, Floyd, ed., *The Black Power Revolt.* Boston: Porter Sargent, 1968. (Macmillan, Collier; Porter Sargent)

Breitman, George, ed., *Malcolm X Speaks.* New York: Merit Publishers, 1965. (Grove)

Broderick, Francis and Meier, August, *Negro Protest Thought in the Twentieth Century.* Indianapolis: Bobbs-Merrill Co., 1965. (Bobbs-Merrill, American Heritage)

Brotz, Howard, *Negro Social and Political Thought.* New York: Basic Books, 1966. (Basic Books)

Brown, H. Rap, *Die Nigger Die!* New York: Dial Press, 1969.

Carmichael, Stokely and Hamilton, Charles V., *Black Power: The Politics of Liberation in America.* New York: Random House, 1967. (Random House, Vintage)

Clark, Kenneth, *Prejudice and Your Child.* Boston: Beacon Press, 2nd ed., 1963. (Beacon)

Cleage, Albert B., *The Black Messiah.* New York: Sheed and Ward, 1968. (Sheed and Ward)

Cleaver, Eldridge, *Soul on Ice.* New York: McGraw-Hill, 1968. (Dell)

Cone, J. H., *Black Theology and Black Power.* New York: Seabury Press, 1969. (Seabury)

Cruse, Harold, *The Crisis of the Negro Intellectual.* New York: William Morrow & Co., 1967. (Thomas Y. Crowell, Apollo)

Delany, Martin, *The Condition, Elevation, Emigration and Destiny of the Colored People of the United States.* Philadelphia, 1852 (Arno Press and New York Times)

Douglass, Frederick, *Life and Times of Frederick Douglass.* Hartford, Conn., 1881. (Collier)

Douglass, Frederick, *Narrative of the Life of Frederick Douglass.* Boston, 1845. (Doubleday, Dolphin; Harvard; New American Library, Signet)

Du Bois, W. E. B., *The Autobiography of W. E. B. Du Bois.* New York: International Publishers, 1968. (International Publishers)

Du Bois, W. E. B., *Black Reconstruction in America.* New York: Harcourt, Brace & Co., 1935. (World Publishing Co., Meredian)

Du Bois, W. E. B., *Darkwater.* New York: Harcourt, Brace & Howe, 1920. (Schocken)

Du Bois, W. E. B., *Dusk of Dawn.* New York: Harcourt, Brace & Co., 1940. (Schocken)

Du Bois, W. E. B., *The Philadelphia Negro.* Philadelphia: University of Pennsylvania Press, 1899. (Schocken)

Du Bois, W. E. B., *The Souls of Black Folk,* Chicago: A. C. McClurg & Co., 1903. (Fawcett, Premier Americana; New American Library, Signet)

Epps, Archie, ed., *The Speeches of Malcolm X at Harvard.* New York: William Morrow & Co., 1968.

Farmer, James, *Freedom — When?* New York: Random House, 1965.

Foner, Philip, ed., *The Life and Writings of Frederick Douglass.* New York: International Publishers, 1950. (International Publishers)

Franklin, John Hope, ed., *Three Negro Classics.* New York: Avon Books, 1965. (Avon)

Jackson, Joseph H., *The Eternal Flame.* Philadelphia: Christian Education Press, 1956.

Jackson, Joseph H., *Many But One.* New York: Sheed and Ward, 1964.

Jackson, Joseph H., *Unholy Shadows and Freedom's Holy Light.* Nashville, Tenn.: Townsend Press, 1967.

Jacques-Garvey, Amy, ed., *Philosophy and Opinions of Marcus Garvey.* New York: Universal Publishing House, 1923 & 1925, 2 vols. (Humanities Press; Atheneum)

Johnson, James Weldon, *Along This Way.* New York: Viking Press, 1933.

Johnson, James Weldon, *Negro Americans, What Now?* New York: Viking Press, 1935.

Jones, LeRoi, *Home: Social Essays.* New York: William Morrow & Co., 1966. (Morrow)

Killens, John Oliver, *Black Man's Burden.* New York: Trident Press, 1965. (Pocket Books)

King, Martin Luther, Jr., *Strength to Love.* New York: Harper & Row, 1963. (Pocket Books)

King, Martin Luther, Jr., *Stride Toward Freedom.* New York: Harper & Row, 1958. (Harper & Row, Perennial)

King, Martin Luther, Jr., *Where Do We Go From Here?* New York: Harper & Row, 1967. (Beacon; Bantam)

King, Martin Luther, Jr., *Why We Can't Wait.* New York: Harper & Row, 1963. (New American Library, Signet)

Lester, Julius, *Look Out, Whitey! Black Power's Goin' Get Your Mama.* New York: Dial Press, 1968. (Grove, Black Cat)

Lester, Julius, *Revolutionary Notes.* New York: Richard W. Baron, 1969.

Locke, Alain, ed., *The New Negro.* New York: Albert & Charles Boni, Inc., 1928. (Atheneum)

Lomax, Louis E., *When the Word is Given.* New York: New American Library, 1964. (New American Library, Signet)

McKissick, Floyd, *Three-Fifths of a Man.* New York: William Morrow & Co., 1969. (William Morrow)

Malcolm X, *The Autobiography of Malcolm X.* New York: Grove Press, 1965. (Grove, Evergreen)

Malcolm X, *Malcolm X on Afro-American History.* New York: Merit Publishers, 1967 (pamphlet)

Powell, Adam Clayton, Jr., *Keep the Faith Baby.* New York: Trident Press, 1967.

Scheer, Robert, ed., *Eldridge Cleaver: Post-Prison Writings and Speeches.* New York: Random House, 1969. (Random House, Vintage)

Washington, Booker T., *My Larger Education.* Garden City, N.Y.: Doubleday, Page & Co., 1911.

Washington, Booker T., *The Story of the Negro.* New York: Doubleday, Page & Co., 1909.

Washington, Booker T., *Up From Slavery.* New York: Doubleday, Page & Co., 1901. (Airmont; Thomas Bouregy; Dell, Laurel Leaf)

Washington, Booker T., *Working With the Hands.* Garden City, N.Y.: Doubleday, Page & Co., 1904.

Washington, Booker T., et al., *The Negro Problem.* New York: James Pott & Co., 1903.

Washington, E. Davidson, ed., *Selected Speeches of Booker T. Washington.* Garden City, N.Y.: Doubleday, Doran & Co., 1932.

Washington, Joseph R., *Black Religion.* Boston: Beacon Press, 1964. (Beacon)

Washington, Joseph R., *Black and White Power Subreption.* Boston: Beacon Press, 1969.

Washington, Joseph R., *The Politics of God.* Boston: Beacon Press, 1967. (Beacon)

White, Walter, *A Man Called White.* New York: Viking Press, 1948.

Woodson, Carter G., *The Mind of the Negro as Reflected in Letters Written During the Crisis 1800–1860.* Washington, D.C.: The Association for the Study of Negro Life and History, 1926.

Woodson, Carter G., *Negro Orators and Their Orations.* New York: Russell & Russell, 1925.

Wright, Nathan, Jr., *Black Power and Urban Unrest.* New York: Hawthorn Books, Inc., 1967. (Hawthorn)

Young, Whitney, *Beyond Racism.* New York: McGraw-Hill, 1969.

Young, Whitney, *To Be Equal.* New York: McGraw-Hill, 1964. (McGraw-Hill)

INDEX

126–129, 141, 179, 213 (*see
  also* Discrimination)
effects on Whites, 40, 73–74,
  115–116, 151
Innocence, of Europeans, 214–225
Integration, 4–6, 10–11, 57, 75, 93,
  105–109, 127, 130, 161,
  166–181, 185–187, 209–210
  (*see also* Assimilation *and*
  Amalgamation)
"new integration," 5–9, 11, 61,
  82–87, 166–181
Islam, 6, 13, 146, 148, 158
Isolation (*see* Segregation)
Israel, 189–190, 201–206

Justice, vi, 12, 29–33, 114–116,
  120–130, 137, 140, 155,
  176, 179

Labor (*see* Work)
Land, 3, 183–184, 187–188
Law, 12, 137–139, 179, 190
  and justice, 12, 121–123
  obedience to, 60–64, 111, 121
Leadership, 10, 16–17, 83, 92–102,
  102–104, 111, 125, 130, 133,
  140, 149, 172–179, 191 (*see
  also* Elite *and* Statesmanship)
Legal action, 4, 5, 120, 139–141,
  154–155
Liberty (*see* Freedom)
Love, 12, 23, 113–116, 122,
  125–126, 131, 177, 198

Manhood, 3, 14–17, 21–22, 27, 30,
  41, 54, 74, 84–87, 94–103,
  162, 197, 203, 208
Masses, black, 60, 77, 101–103, 124,
  172, 179
Materialism, American, 2, 6, 82,
  90–92, 97, 100–104,
  170–171, 198

Melting pot (*see* Pluralism)
Middle-class America, 170–171,
  176–180
Modernization, 171–172
Moral suasion, 19–20, 113–114, 139,
  142, 159, 222

National liberation, 3, 186–191, 196
Nationalism, 78–79, 101, 126,
  134, 205
Natural law, 77, 81, 121
"Negro," 79, 96, 156–157, 168
Negro problem, 92, 101, 223–225
New citizen, 64–65
"Nigger," 72, 170, 188, 207,
  210–211, 216–217, 220–221
Nonviolence, 5, 112–116, 118ff, 153,
  155, 161, 163, 173, 178–179

Open society (*see* Pluralism)
Opportunity, 62, 87, 92, 134–135,
  142–143, 152, 176 (*see also*
  Civil rights *and* Equality)
Order, 30, 129

Patience, 8, 60–64, 74, 98, 101,
  120–124, 130, 177–178
Patriotism, 30, 48, 50, 55, 100,
  133, 136
"People of color," 96
Pluralism, 5–6, 11–12, 76–86,
  169–178, 186
Political action, black, 5, 59, 74–76,
  92–102, 133, 138–139,
  146–163, 165–181, 188
Political society, nature of, 3, 11–12,
  30, 170–171
Political thought, iv–v, 1–2, 4–5,
  9–12, 76, 111
Poverty, 2, 65, 88, 90, 120, 171, 174,
  188–189, 195, 198
Power structure, 118, 128, 147,
  170–172, 185–188, 191, 197

Stokely Carmichael,
& Charles Hamilton